Edition KWV

Die „Edition KWV" beinhaltet hochwertige Werke aus dem Bereich der Wirtschaftswissenschaften. Alle Werke in der Reihe erschienen ursprünglich im Kölner Wissenschaftsverlag, dessen Programm Springer Gabler 2018 übernommen hat.

Weitere Bände in der Reihe http://www.springer.com/series/16033

Nadja Trhal

Experimental Studies on Partnership Dissolution, R&D Investment, and Gift Giving

Nadja Trhal
Wiesbaden, Germany

Bis 2018 erschien der Titel im Kölner Wissenschaftsverlag, Köln
Dissertation Universität zu Köln, 2009

Edition KWV
ISBN 978-3-658-24666-2   ISBN 978-3-658-24667-9 (eBook)
https://doi.org/10.1007/978-3-658-24667-9

Springer Gabler
© Springer Fachmedien Wiesbaden GmbH, part of Springer Nature 2009, Reprinted in 2019
Originally published by Kölner Wissenschaftsverlag, Köln, 2009
This work is subject to copyright. All rights are reserved by the Publisher, whether the whole or part of the material is concerned, specifically the rights of translation, reprinting, reuse of illustrations, recitation, broadcasting, reproduction on microfilms or in any other physical way, and transmission or information storage and retrieval, electronic adaptation, computer software, or by similar or dissimilar methodology now known or hereafter developed.
The use of general descriptive names, registered names, trademarks, service marks, etc. in this publication does not imply, even in the absence of a specific statement, that such names are exempt from the relevant protective laws and regulations and therefore free for general use.
The publisher, the authors and the editors are safe to assume that the advice and information in this book are believed to be true and accurate at the date of publication. Neither the publisher nor the authors or the editors give a warranty, expressed or implied, with respect to the material contained herein or for any errors or omissions that may have been made. The publisher remains neutral with regard to jurisdictional claims in published maps and institutional affiliations.

This Springer Gabler imprint is published by the registered company Springer Fachmedien Wiesbaden GmbH part of Springer Nature
The registered company address is: Abraham-Lincoln-Str. 46, 65189 Wiesbaden, Germany

Meinen Eltern

Acknowledgements

Financial support by the Deutsche Forschungsgemeinschaft DFG is gratefully acknowledged.

First of all, I am greatly indebted to my first supervisor, Axel Ockenfels, for his motivating support, encouragement and advice.

I am also very grateful to Matthias Sutter for making the efforts of being my second supervisor and for his valuable comments and suggestions.

I thank my co-authors Donja Darai, Jens Großer, Thomas Kittsteiner, Axel Ockenfels and Ralf Radermacher for fruitful discussions and common work.

I thank my colleagues for their support in various ways and for being such a good company. I benefitted a lot from the very friendly working environment and from discussions with all my former and current colleagues Michael Bartels, Jeannette Brosig, Ben Greiner, Veronika Grimm, Jens Großer, Burkhard Hehenkamp, Lyuba Ilieva, Felix Lamouroux, Felix Müsgens, Xavier del Pozo Somoza, Alexander Rajko and Peter Werner. I thank Imke Jungjohann for looking after all of us.

I thank the whole student staff for valuable assistance and help and especially Julian Conrads, René Cyranek, Christoph Feldhaus, Johannes Mans, Andreas Pollak, Karin Ruëtz and Thomas Wolfgarten for excellent research assistance in the lab. A great help was Felix Lamouroux who programmed two experiments for this thesis.

Many thanks are due to my friends and my family for sharing good and bad days with me and for keeping fingers crossed.

I especially thank Carsten for being there for me no matter what.

I am deeply indebted to my parents for their invaluable support and help in all possible ways.

Cologne, May 2009   Nadja Trhal

Table of Contents

I	**Introduction**		**1**
II	**Partnership Dissolution Mechanisms**		**5**
	II.1	General Introduction…………………………………………..	5
	II.2	Related Literature……………………………………………..	8
	II.3	Partnership Dissolution with Independent Private Values……............	11
		II.3.1 Introduction……………………………………………..	11
		II.3.2 The Model………………………………………………	14
		II.3.3 Experimental Design and Procedures……………………….	19
		II.3.4 Experimental Performance of the Dissolution Mechanisms…	20
		II.3.4.1 Efficiency………………………………………..	20
		II.3.4.2 Payoffs……………………………………………	23
		II.3.4.3 Individual Bidding/Proposing Behavior…………..	23
		II.3.5 Conclusions…………………………………………….	27
	II.4	Partnership Dissolution with Interdependent Valuations……………..	28
		II.4.1 Introduction…………………………………………….......	28
		II.4.2 Partnership Structure, Dissolution Mechanisms and Efficiency…………………………………………………..	32
		II.4.3 Experimental Design and Procedures……………………….	35
		II.4.4 Experimental Results……………………………………...	37
		II.4.4.1 Efficiency………………………………………..	37
		II.4.4.2 Payoffs…………………………..………………	43
		II.4.4.3 Individual Behavior……………………………..	49
		II.4.5 Conclusions……………………………………………..	53
	II.5	Appendix to Chapter II………………………………………....	58
III	**The Influence of Patents and Subsidies on R&D Investment Incentives**		**77**
	III.1	Introduction………………………………………………….	77

	III.2	The Model...	81
		III.2.1 Market Stage..	83
		III.2.2 R&D Investment Stage..	84
		III.2.3 Distributional Effects...	85
		III.2.4 Experimental Setup: Equilibrium Predictions and Hypotheses..	87
	III.3	Experimental Design and Procedures.....................................	89
	III.4	Experimental Results...	91
		III.4.1 R&D Investments...	91
		III.4.1.1 Investment Dynamics...........................	92
		III.4.1.2 Individual Investment Decisions...........	95
		III.4.2 Cost Structure, Prices and Profits......................	100
		III.4.2.1 Cost Structure......................................	100
		III.4.2.2 Prices and Mark-Ups...........................	101
		III.4.2.3 Profits..	105
		III.4.3 Welfare and Distributional Effects.....................	107
	III.5	Conclusions..	109
	III.6	Appendix to Chapter III..	112
IV	**The Impact of Responsibility on Gift Giving**		**129**
	IV.1	Introduction...	129
	IV.2	Experimental Design and Procedures.....................................	134
	IV.3	Results..	136
		IV.3.1 Gift Giving and Behavioral Types – Allocation Matters........	137
		IV.3.2 The Impact of Responsibility – Process Matters.................	139
		IV.3.3 The Impact of Responsibility on Safety Choosers and Risk Choosers..	141
		IV.3.4 Impact of Responsibility on Expectations of Actions...........	144
	IV.4	A Cross-Cultural Comparison – Evidence from Germany and India....	146
	IV.5	Discussion and Conclusions..	149
	IV.6	Appendix to Chapter IV..	152
V	**Conclusions**		**163**
Bibliography			**167**

List of Tables

II.1	Mean efficiency	21
II.2	Panel probit regression IPV	22
II.3	Mean payoffs	23
II.4	Proposals and bids	24
II.5	Categories of proposal setting/bidding behavior	26
II.6	Procedure in each round	37
II.7	Mean efficiency INT and IPV	38
II.8	Panel probit regression INT	41
II.9	Mean payoffs INT	43
II.10a	Gains from trade	46
II.10b	Gains from trade – Intermediate types	46
II.11	Categories of proposal setting/bidding behavior INT	52
II.12	Choosers' decision	53
II.A1	Panel probit regression IPV with CCM as base category	72
II.A2	Panel probit regression INT with CCM as base category	73
II.A3	Gains from trade – Different ranges of types	73
III.1	Treatment parameters	88
III.2	Experimental predictions	88
III.3	Average observed and predicted R&D investments	92
III.4	OLS regression results	94
III.5	Discrete symmetric and asymmetric Nash equilibrium investment levels	97
III.6	Observed (predicted) cost structure in the Bertrand markets	101
III.7	Average of lowest prices observed (predicted) in the Bertrand markets	103
III.8	Average mark-ups in the Bertrand markets	104
III.9	Average market profits per high and low cost firms	105
III.10	Average observed and predicted round profits	106
III.11	Average welfare effects	108
III.A1	Discrete symmetric and asymmetric Nash equilibrium investment levels	123

III.A2	OLS regression results with *CR*1 as base category	123
III.A3	OLS regression results with *SUB* as base category	124
IV.1	Means of gift giving	137
IV.2	Types of gift giving behavior	139
IV.3	Means of gift giving of *A*-players and *B*-players	141
IV.4	Means of gift giving and means of expected gifts in the ST	144
IV.5	Means of gift giving and of expected gifts in the RT of *A*-players	145
IV.6	Means of gift giving and of expected gifts in the RT of *B*-players	145
IV.7	Means of gift giving in India and Germany (in rupees)	147
IV.8	Means of gift giving of *A*-players and *B*-players in India	148
IV.A1	Means of gift giving and means of expected gifts in the ST (India)	159
IV.A2	Means of gift giving and of expected gifts in the RT (India)	159

List of Figures

II.1	Scatter plots – Valuations and bids/proposals................................	25
II.2	Mean efficiency per round..	42
II.3	Mean payoffs per round – proposer and chooser...........................	44
II.4	Scatter plots – Private signals and bids/proposals........................	49
II.A1	Average net-payoffs of bidders and proposers over rounds...........	74
II.A2	Average net-payoffs of bidders and proposers with intermediate types over rounds...	74
II.A3	Scatter plots – True valuations and bids/proposals.......................	75
III.1	Observed and predicted R&D investments over rounds.................	92
III.2	Investment frequencies...	95
III.3	Dynamic view on investment level choices – *NO*........................	98
III.4	Dynamic view on investment level choices – *SUB*.....................	98
III.5	Dynamic view on investment level choices – *PAT*.....................	99
III.6	Average market price...	102
III.A1	Individual investment behavior..	125
III.A2	Average lowest prices for each cost structure over rounds...........	126
IV.1	Directions of the means...	140
IV.A1	Options in the RT (Germany)	160
IV.A2	Options in the RT (India)	160

Chapter I

Introduction

In recent years, traditional economic theory has been enriched by behavioral components. There is huge and rapidly growing evidence from empirical and experimental studies that mere profit maximization is in many cases not a good proxy of real-life decision-making and interaction in economic situations. Yet, although the concept of homo oeconomicus has subsequently been dismissed by many authors, behavior is not random or arbitrary, but follows systematic patterns and rules that researchers in the field of behavioral economics aim at understanding (for an overview see e.g. Camerer (2003)).

This thesis adds to the understanding of actual economic decision-making by analyzing behavior in three different economic applications. The main research method is an experimental approach; insights from theoretical models are used to derive benchmarks against which actual behavior is evaluated. Hence, in addition to the conceptional insights of a theoretical analysis, experiments test the robustness of results and thereby help to discover relevant behavioral phenomena. This is an essential premise for a systematic prediction of behavior and thus for further policy implications.

The first application in Chapter II concerns experimental studies on the performance of partnership dissolution mechanisms. The dissolution mechanisms are basically judged according to two criteria: allocative efficiency and fairness in terms of equality of ex-ante payoff expectations. Chapter III is an application to investment in research and development (R&D). This chapter studies the effects of a policy instrument (subsidies or patents) on a firm's incentives to invest in R&D. Finally, the third application in Chapter IV takes a more fundamental research approach and tests the prerequisites for solidarity behavior of economic agents. More precisely, we investigate the impact of responsibility for being in a disadvantageous situation through deliberate risk-taking on voluntary gift giving.

© Springer Fachmedien Wiesbaden GmbH, part of Springer Nature 2009
N. Trhal, *Experimental Studies on Partnership Dissolution, R&D Investment, and Gift Giving*, Edition KWV, https://doi.org/10.1007/978-3-658-24667-9_1

The first two studies in Chapter II are standard mechanism design studies dealing with a bilateral bargaining situation: A two-parent partnership is to be dissolved and the agents negotiate who becomes sole owner of the object and which compensation is paid to the selling partner. As institutional arrangements to allocate the object we consider two dissolution mechanisms: the cake-cutting mechanism and the winner's bid auction. The performance of the two mechanisms is measured by two criteria: (1) ex-post allocative efficiency (i.e., the higher value bidder receives the object) and (2) ex-ante payoff expectations (i.e., ex-ante means before subjects know their value for the object). In an independent private values framework in which agents exhibit homogeneous risk preferences it has been shown theoretically that auctions are more efficient mechanisms than the cake-cutting mechanism and that the cake-cutting mechanism leads ex ante to unequal payoff expectations in case of risk neutrality (see e.g. McAfee (1992) and Cramton et al. (1987)). Yet, despite the clear theoretical superiority of auctions under these assumptions, the cake-cutting mechanism is the prevalent dissolution mechanism in practice. Thus, Chapter II provides experimental investigations of how actual behavior influences allocative efficiency and fairness of these competing mechanisms both in the simplest possible framework with independent private values as well as in a more complex framework with interdependent valuations.

The first part of Chapter II (based on joint work with Thomas Kittsteiner and Axel Ockenfels) starts with independent private values. The experimental data contradict standard theoretical predictions concerning efficiency results and rather support the mechanism selection we observe in reality. However, the theoretical predictions with respect to ex-ante payoff expectations could be corroborated by our data. To give a possible explanation for our findings we develop a theoretical model in which agents might exhibit heterogeneous risk preferences.

The second part of Chapter II provides an experimental robustness check of the ranking of the two mechanisms if we assume more complex preferences, namely if the valuations structure is characterized by interdependent valuations rather than independent private values. The robustness of results is an important question as in practice these mechanisms must operate in a variety of contexts. We rank the two mechanisms again with regard to efficiency and ex-ante payoff expectations. While the payoff expectations results remain robust, we observe the reverse ranking in terms of efficiency. Thus, the experiment provides evidence

INTRODUCTION

that preferences play a considerable role in how the dissolution mechanisms perform. The winner's bid auction turns out to be more robust independent of a specific valuation structure than the cake-cutting mechanism. Moreover, according to theory the interdependent valuations case gives rise to a new problem also in the laboratory: Due to adverse selection effects subjects who receive an intermediate signal for the valuation of the partnership would not participate voluntarily in the dissolution as they realize negative gains from trade.

Chapter III (which originated from joint work with Donja Darai and Jens Großer) examines two differing policy instruments, namely subsidies and patents, widely used to enhance firms' incentives to invest in R&D. The need for policy instruments arises since many empirical studies have found evidence that firms tend to underinvest in R&D compared to the socially optimal R&D investment level. We study the effects of both subsidies and patents on incentives to innovate in a simple theoretical model as well as in a controlled laboratory setting. The theoretical framework is a two-stage game consisting of an investment stage followed by a market stage. At the first stage, the firms can invest in a stochastic R&D project which might lead to a reduction of the marginal production costs and at the second stage, the firms face price competition. Parameters are chosen such that in equilibrium both patents and subsidies induce the same amount of R&D investment which is higher than the investment without governmental incentives. In the experiment subsidies as well as patents indeed increase investment levels of the firms substantially. However, contrary to the theoretical prediction, this has no significant positive effect on welfare. The reason for this result is that we observe overinvestment in all treatments which destroys the positive welfare effects to some extent. The observed overinvestment can be partly explained by discrete asymmetric equilibria. Considering distributional effects shows that firms would prefer patents whereas consumers benefit most if subsidies are introduced. This result illustrates that, although both instruments are consistent with the social goal (namely both set similar incentives to increase investment levels), the selection of a specific instrument determines which group is able to reap the benefits of it.

Chapter IV (based on joint work with Ralf Radermacher) tests the influence of self-inflicted neediness on the perceived fairness and thus on the solidarity behavior of subjects. This chapter is based on the solidarity game experiment of Selten and Ockenfels (1998) who found strong evidence for positive conditional gift giving in a situation in which the ex-ante probability of becoming needy is the same for all group members and in which all group members are potential donors and potential recipients at the time of their decision. Standard economic theory is not able to capture this empirical phenomenon that is at odds with pure payoff maximization. In this context, we extend the seminal study by Selten and Ockenfels (1998) and explore whether the willingness to transfer money depends on responsibility and self-inflicted neediness. In fact, the data provide evidence that, controlling for payoff distributions, subjects are less generous towards those whose bad outcome is a result of their own risk-taking actions compared to those who cannot be blamed for their bad outcome. Hence, the study on gift giving shows that there indeed exists solidarity as such, but that it is crowded out to a considerable amount if subjects are thought to be responsible for being in need. A cross-cultural comparison of Indian and German data indicates qualitatively robust results concerning the driving forces behind solidarity behavior in our experiment in spite of various cultural influences.

Chapter II

Partnership Dissolution Mechanisms

II.1 General Introduction

Partnerships like business entities are built to improve commercial performance by sharing property, expertise, effort as well as profits and losses. In case these initial benefits of building a partnership cease and partners do not take any longer advantages of their complementary skills, it might be of common interest for the partners to dissolve their partnership.[1] Partnership dissolution is defined as "trading co-ownership of an asset into single ownership, within a given group."[2] If a partnership falls prey to dissolution the question arises which is the 'best' mechanism to realize this. This chapter investigates the experimental performance of two simple dissolution mechanisms using a framework with two partners initially possessing an indivisible object in equal shares. Object of investigation are the cake-cutting mechanism (CCM)[3] and the winner's bid auction (WBA). The CCM is considered as one possible dissolution mechanism, because this mechanism is frequently used in reality.[4] However, as an alternative mechanism the WBA is examined since auctions have a long tradition (in economic theory) and proved to be easily implementable and efficient mechanisms in a variety of environments.

---

[1] Note that we consider situations in which it is in both partners' interest to dissolve the partnership (for instance, among other reasons one can think of increasing returns in the ownership share or disagreement about future strategy) and it is inefficient to sell the good on the market to a third party (due to e.g. specific capital or transaction costs).

[2] Wolfstetter (2002), p. 86. The sentence implies that there is no outside party involved in trade, but that rather one partner buys out the other. Thus, we consider a particular market in which seller and buyer are determined endogenously by market rules not knowing whether they will be sellers/buyers at the time the market opens (cf. Kittsteiner and Ockenfels (2006)).

[3] This mechanism is often referred to as buy-sell clause, divide-and-choose method, shotgun clause or Texas shoot out and has been object of research in fair division literature. For a survey of the literature on fair division see e.g. Young (1994), Brams and Taylor (1996) and Barbanel (2004).

[4] The CCM is the prevalent dissolution mechanism in Anglo-Saxon corporate law (Kittsteiner and Ockenfels 2006). See also Brams and Taylor (1999) for an overview of the extensive applications of the CCM throughout history. Moreover, at first glance the CCM might be the more 'natural' mechanism in practice as the partner who first wants to dissolve the partnership just starts the dissolution process by announcing a price. It seems easier to initiate dissolution that way than to start a simultaneous auction where all partners have to state their bids.

The CCM applies to two-parent partnerships and stipulates that one of the two partners (the proposer) has to offer a price (per share) to his partner. This receiving party (the chooser) can then decide to either sell his shares to his partner at the proposed price or to buy his partner's shares at the proposed price. Contrary to this sequential game structure the WBA is a simultaneous game: both partners propose a sealed bid simultaneously and the partner with the higher bid obtains the object and pays the other partner out. Note that the WBA follows a first price rule but differs from an ordinary first price auction with respect to two important aspects: There is no outside seller and consequentially, agents in the WBA have to face two roles at the same time. This is due to the particular market, whose rules determine endogenously who becomes buyer and who becomes seller.

The main focus of this chapter is on the experimental performance of the two dissolution mechanisms whereas performance is measured especially according to two criteria: allocative efficiency of the mechanism and fairness in terms of ex-ante equal payoff expectations.[5] The first is more of interest to a mechanism designer who wants to achieve socially optimal allocations; the latter is more of interest to the partners who are mainly interested in their own payoffs.

The simplest environment and thus a decisive starting point to study efficient partnership dissolution is to assume agents with independent private values for the object (for seminal theoretical papers see McAfee (1992) and Cramton et al. (1987)).[6] McAfee shows that the WBA always leads to efficient dissolution whereas the CCM might result in inefficiencies.[7] Efficiency means ex-post efficiency in the sense that the partner with the higher value receives the object. Assuming risk neutrality of the agents McAfee ranks expected payoffs of the agents comparing the two mechanisms: Choosers' payoffs are higher than bidders' payoffs in the CCM which are higher than proposers' payoffs. In Section II.3 we evaluate the experimental performance of the CCM and the WBA to test these theoretical predictions. Surprisingly, concerning the efficiency of both mechanisms our data contradict the theoretical results. Our experiment provides evidence that the CCM in general performs well, as measured by

---

[5] Morgan (2001) also emphasizes that efficiency should not be the sole goal. Transparency, effectiveness and perceived fairness are also important for the judgment of a mechanism. See also the study on fairness of dissolution mechanisms by Morgan (2004).
[6] The symmetric partnership model with independent private values and risk-neutral partners was introduced in Cramton et al. (1987).
[7] Note that if both partners have complete (rather than private) information about all partners' valuations the CCM also provides allocative efficiency (e.g. compare McAfee (1992) and Moldovanu (2002)).

efficiency of final allocations. In particular it turns out to be at least as efficient as the WBA which might provide an explanation for its extensive use in practice. The theoretical payoff ranking, however, could be corroborated. Average payoffs between all subjects do not differ significantly between the CCM and the WBA, but a chooser in the CCM fares better than a participant in the WBA who fares better than a proposer in the CCM. Hence, a comparison of both mechanisms reveals a trade-off between allocative efficiency and equality of expected payoffs. We present a model with heterogeneous partners that exhibit different degrees of risk aversion which can explain these findings.

In the context of partnership dissolution one might ask if the independent private values assumption is adequate. Independent private values are a realistic assumption for non-durable consumer goods (i.e., in settings in which the value of an object is derived from its consumption or use alone). In this case it is realistic that a bidder knows his own value for the object and that other bidders may value the object differently. However, if bidders assign values on the basis of how much the object will possibly fetch in the resale market (viewing it as an investment), then one should consider instead interdependent values (compare Krishna (2002)). The assumption of interdependent values seems to fit better the nature of most partnerships than the independent private values framework (which is nevertheless a valuable starting point for the analysis of partnership dissolution as it provides the simplest possible environment). For instance, imagine a partnership in which each partner is responsible for a particular project which are not (closely) related to each other. In this case each agent has private information that also determines his partner's valuation. A precise estimate of the value of the entire business depends on the information of all projects and is no longer easily available to the agents.[8] The purpose of Section II.4 is to examine the performance of the CCM and the WBA in the more realistic case of interdependent valuations in an explorative approach and thus to test the robustness of results obtained in Section II.3 in a controlled laboratory experiment. In terms of allocative efficiency the main findings are that assuming interdependent valuations we observe the reverse ranking of the two mechanisms (the WBA turns out to be at least as efficient as the CCM) and that the results for the WBA are more robust (the WBA is not as sensitive to asymmetric

---

[8] Kittsteiner (2003) also states: "A common situation is one where different partners are responsible for different parts or departments of their firm. It is natural to assume that they gain different information that helps them valuing their partnership", p. 54.

information[9] and increased complexity as the CCM). Moreover, we find that the WBA results again in more homogeneous payoff expectations. The relative standing of subjects remains the same as in the benchmark case with independent private values: The chooser fares better than an agent in the auction who fares better than a proposer. Further, with interdependent valuations a new problem arises. In line with theoretical predictions we observe that subjects with an intermediate signal for the value of the partnership realize negative gains from trade. This indicates that those types would not participate voluntarily, because dissolution makes them worse off than their initial share of the partnership.

The remainder of this chapter is structured as follows. In Section II.2 we briefly review the related literature. Section II.3 presents a study on partnership dissolution mechanisms under the assumption of independent private values, followed by an investigation of the mechanisms with interdependent valuations in Section II.4.

II.2 Related Literature

The question of efficient dissolution mechanisms is discussed in the theoretical mechanism design literature. The term efficient mechanism refers to the implementation of such a mechanism. In the mechanism design literature a mechanism is called efficient if the following conditions are fulfilled: individual rationality (IR), incentive compatibility (IC), value maximizing (VM) and budget balance (BB).[10] First, we briefly review the most important results for an independent private values environment; second, we introduce the findings for interdependent valuations.

For the independent private values setting with symmetric agents Cramton et al. (1987) show that in general there exist efficient mechanisms if initial shares are not too far from the equal-share partnership. Yet the efficient mechanism depends on distribution functions. However, Cramton et al. (1987) reveal that in case of equal partnerships a mechanism designer who does not know the distribution of types can implement a distribution-free k-double auction[11] which

---

[9] Note that following the related literature we employ the term asymmetric information (concerning information about the own valuation) with reference to the assumption of interdependent valuations.
[10] Value maximizing corresponds to ex-post efficiency. In this section the term 'efficiency' is referred to the fulfillment of all four conditions, not only to ex-post efficiency as in the remaining chapter.
[11] In the k-double auction bidders submit bids simultaneously. The bidder with the highest bid obtains the partnership and pays a combination of the highest (b_f) and the second highest bid (b_s) divided by the number of bidders n: $p(b_1, b_2, ..., b_n) = \frac{1}{n}[kb_s + (1-k)b_f]$ where $k \in [0,1]$. Note that the WBA in our two-

dissolves the partnership efficiently. This implies that an efficient dissolution is possible independent of the distribution of types if initial shares are equal.[12]

McAfee (1992) ranks the WBA and the CCM assuming independent private values and shows that if partners have constant absolute risk aversion (CARA) utility functions with the same degree of absolute risk aversion then the WBA is (ex-post) efficient whereas the CCM is not. In the CCM it is a dominant strategy for the chooser to buy if and only if his valuation exceeds the offered price. As the proposing partner does not know the precise valuation of his partner, he will offer a price above (below) his own valuation if that valuation is below (above) the median valuation, because in this case he faces a higher probability of becoming seller (buyer). Hence, in the CCM the partner with the lower valuation might end up with all shares (in case the chooser's valuation lies between the proposer's valuation and the proposal), which creates inefficiencies. Concerning the equality of payoff expectations McAfee (1992) shows that the expected payoff of a proposer is lower than that of a chooser with the same valuation if partners are risk neutral.

In case of interdependent valuations Fieseler et al. (2003) derive the existence condition for efficient mechanisms assuming separability of valuation functions and maintaining symmetric assumptions. Their main result is that in comparison to the independent private values benchmark setting of Cramton et al. (1987), the implementation of efficient mechanisms becomes even easier if the interdependence is negative.[13] Interdependence is negative if valuations are decreasing functions of the partner's signal. In this case information revealed ex post is always a blessing. However, if valuations are increasing functions of partner's signal, information revealed ex post is always 'bad news'. Therefore agents must be cautious to avoid winner's and loser's curses. For positively interdependent valuations it is not possible – independently of the distribution of types – to dissolve a partnership efficiently, even if initial shares are equal. This still holds for arbitrarily small common value components. More precisely, under interdependent valuations a designer is not able to say if efficient dissolution is possible without knowledge of precise specifications of valuation functions and distributions of types. Thus, in case of interdependent valuations there does not

---

parent partnership framework where the winning bidder pays half of his bid to his losing partner is a special case of the k-double auction.

[12] This contrasts the result of Myerson and Satterthwaite (1983) who show that for extreme ownership the existence condition cannot be satisfied.

[13] They show that it is 'easier' that the existence condition is fulfilled (i.e., the condition is fulfilled in more cases).

exist a mechanism whose rules do not depend on the distribution of types and that always lead to efficient trade. This is in stark contrast to the independent private values environment (Cramton et al. (1987)), where an efficient outcome could be assured if property rights are equally distributed by a distribution-free k-double auction.

Although the k-double auction is not a first-best mechanism with interdependent values, Kittsteiner (2003) investigates this mechanism in more detail.[14] It turns out that there might be a participation problem of agents receiving an intermediate private signal. If valuations are increasing in partner's private signals, bidders may be reluctant to participate as they do not know whether to buy or to sell (double curses). For intermediate types of agents the simultaneous winner's and loser's curse is most severe. In this case a bidder may be better off keeping his share in the partnership and may not voluntarily participate in the auction. However, if the own signal is either very high or very low voluntary participation is no problem. Kittsteiner notes that if participation of agents is forced, the k-double auction results in ex-post efficient allocations.[15] Forced participation is a quite realistic assumption especially for partnerships. E.g. existing law or previous contracts initially closed might force partners to participate in a dissolution process.

Chien (2007) looks for incentive efficient dissolution mechanisms (i.e., second-best mechanisms) in situations in which no efficient (first-best) mechanism exists.[16] Chien proposes a hybrid game to solve the participation problem of intermediate types. This hybrid game combines a double auction with posted prices and works as follows: At a first stage, prices p_H and p_L are posted by a mediator. At a second stage, agents indicate their intention to engage in a double auction. Each agent who wants to participate in the auction sets his bid. If both agents prefer the auction the partnership is dissolved by a k-double auction. If both want to stay out the status quo remains. However, if one agent prefers the auction, then the partnership is dissolved according to the posted prices in the following way: If an agent's bidding price is higher than a threshold, he receives

---

[14] The mechanism might not be implementable as IR might not be fulfilled for all distributions. However, note that the WBA always leads to VM, i.e., it is an ex-post efficient mechanism.

[15] Kittsteiner (2003) also investigates a modified mechanism if participation is voluntary: the k-double auction with veto where agents can refuse dissolution and choose a strategy which implements the status quo.

[16] Note that an incentive efficient mechanism is a second-best mechanism and thus better than the k-double auction. An IC, IR, and BB mechanism is (ex ante) incentive efficient (IE) if it maximizes the sum of expected payoffs, i.e., if there exists no other feasible and implementable mechanism that would Pareto dominate the mechanism.

the asset at the posted price p_H (specifically, he pays $p_H/2$ for acquisition). Otherwise, the other agent (who does not want to engage in an auction) receives the asset at p_L. This is a second-best mechanism which works in situations in which no first-best mechanism exists. Yet there is space for another problem as the mechanism designer needs information about agents' preferences in order to set the two prices.

For this reason we investigate the experimental performance of the CCM and the WBA, although both mechanisms are not first-best (and not even second-best) if valuations are interdependent. The great advantage of these mechanisms is that they are distribution-free and thus easy to implement for a mechanism designer. The mechanism designer (e.g. a court) does not need knowledge about distributions of valuations, utility functions of the agents and other characteristics of the environment. As lawyers and the courts for instance rarely know distributions of valuations, utility functions and other characteristics of the environment with the degree of precision required to implement a mechanism design solution, the sensitivity of the solution to the specification of the environment will deter people from employing the mechanism design solution. Furthermore, institutions must operate in a variety of contexts, so the specification of the institution should be as invariant as possible to the details of the environment (compare McAfee (1992), p. 267). Moreover, the rules of the mechanisms are simple (other mechanisms are so complex that one can suspect that agents do not understand these mechanisms). Thus, it is reasonable to investigate the CCM and the WBA as they are simple price-generating mechanisms that make use of partners' private information and they are therefore easily implementable and applicable.

II.3 Partnership Dissolution with Independent Private Values[17]

II.3.1 Introduction

Partners of a commonly owned business who find themselves trapped in a management deadlock can break the deadlock by dissolving their partnership and giving control to one of the partners. The details of the dissolution procedure might be laid out in the CCM which typically is part of the partnership contract. Even though restricted to partnerships with two shareholders the CCM is very popular and part of many modern partnership agreements (see e.g. de Frutos and

---

[17] This section is based on Kittsteiner, Ockenfels and Trhal (2009).

Kittsteiner (2008), and Brooks and Spier (2004)). Empirical studies suggest that the majority of partnerships has indeed only two shareholders (e.g., Veugelers and Kasteloot (1996)).

Given the broad use of the CCM it is surprising how little is known about its performance and in particular how it compares with potential alternative dissolution mechanisms like auctions[18] (and thus ultimately how little is known about why it is used so frequently). This section attempts to fill this gap in two ways: First, it analyzes the performance of the CCM in a controlled laboratory environment that reproduces the standard independent private values setup of the partnership models of Cramton et al. (1987) and McAfee (1992) and compares the CCM with a WBA. By doing so it provides to the best of our knowledge the first empirical study on its performance.[19] Second, it offers a new argument based on heterogeneity of partners that can help to explain the widespread use of the CCM in practice.

We evaluate the performance of the two mechanisms from a social planner's viewpoint as well as from the viewpoint of individual participants by applying two different measures: allocative efficiency and differences of individual partners' expected payoffs in the different roles in the CCM (i.e. proposer and chooser) and in the WBA. The main experimental findings are as follows:

1) The CCM performs very well, it achieves an efficient allocation of ownership in 89.69% of the observations. In particular it significantly outperforms the WBA (with 85.21% of efficient allocations), i.e., it more frequently results in an efficient allocation of shares.
2) A chooser prefers the CCM to the WBA and a proposer prefers the WBA to the CCM.

The first finding contrasts theoretical predictions of the standard independent private values model where partners are either risk neutral or exhibit the same degree of absolute risk aversion (see Cramton et al. (1987) and McAfee (1992)). McAfee argues that auctions should be preferred to the CCM as they are

---

[18] Auctions have been considered as alternative dissolution mechanisms by economists (e.g. see Cramton et al. (1987) and McAfee (1992)).
[19] To our knowledge there is no empirical study on the CCM (or other dissolution mechanisms) that uses field data. We suspect that this is because data on partnership dissolutions is difficult to obtain (the precise outcome of a CCM or auction is usually not made public) and to interpret (any performance measure is based on partners' estimates for the value of the dissolved firm, which, in general, is private information).

more efficient.[20] The theoretical part of this section shows that our experimental findings are consistent with equilibrium behavior in a model where partners are heterogeneous with respect to their degree of risk aversion.

In our model and the experimental design we make some simplifying assumptions. We assume that each partner knows his own valuation for the partnership, but only has an imperfect estimate about his partner's valuation. This assumption reflects the fact that partners have different abilities to run the company, which is their private information. It also implies that the value of assets that are not related to specific human capital is publicly known (e.g., because they can be valued at a market price). We also assume that the identities of proposer and chooser in the CCM are pre-determined (e.g. by a lottery). In practice CCMs do not have to be drafted this way (an example for a pre-specified proposer is the case of Parenting Magazine, discussed by Sahlman (1990)), they can instead rely on an endogenous selection of the proposer (see de Frutos and Kittsteiner (2008) for a discussion and examples).[21] Besides reflecting actual practice in (at least) some cases, the assumption of pre-determined specification of the proposer has two more advantages:

1) It simplifies the experimental setup and consequently reduces complexity and potential misunderstanding on the subjects' side and also allows for a clearer interpretation of experimental outcomes: It is the simplest possible starting point of allocating roles which enables us to test for the relevance of role assignment.

2) De Frutos and Kittsteiner (2008) have shown that endogenous determination of the proposer increases efficiency of the CCM. Hence, we expect our main finding concerning efficiency to become even stronger in a setup with endogenous proposer selection as our experimental design with a pre-determined proposer measures a 'lower bound'.

An important practical implication of the experimental finding that partners are better off choosing rather than proposing is that lawyers might want to put more attention on how they specify the rules according to which the proposer is selected. Non-specification can result in inefficient delay of the dissolution as both partners prefer not to name a price. This is what happened in

---
[20] This argument assumes (as we do) that the assignment of the roles (proposer or chooser) happens in a way that does not reveal any private information partners could have, see below for a discussion of this assumption.
[21] Often these clauses do not state who has the right/obligation to propose, leaving partners with a variety of options on how to determine the proposer.

the legal case Hotoyan v. Jansezian, in which two partners who had signed an agreement including a CCM-clause went to the Ontario Court as they could not agree on who had to propose (O.J. no. 4486, Court File no. 99-CL-3263, 1999, see also de Frutos and Kittsteiner (2008)). Our findings suggest that pre-specification of the proposer (at a time when valuations are still unknown) will not result in large efficiency losses but in large inequality. The partners might want to compensate the proposer for his (expected) disadvantage.

In this section we concentrate on a winner's bid auction but other auction formats (such as a loser's bid auction which follows a second price rule) could be analyzed as well. Our theoretical analysis (in Section II.3.2) extends to any auction where the price is some convex-combination of the two bids. Partnership dissolution with this kind of auction formats has been analyzed by Cramton et al. (1987) and McAfee (1992) for homogeneous partners who do not differ in their risk preferences. McAfee concludes that theoretically the WBA appears to be the best way to allocate a single item if partners are risk neutral. An experimental study by Güth et al. (2002) shows that the winner's bid auction is straightforward, easy to understand for the subjects and performs at least as efficient as the loser's bid auction.[22] Thus, we choose the WBA to compare the performance of the CCM with the best alternative mechanism.

The remaining sections of II.3 proceed as follows. In Section II.3.2 we present the basic framework and derive testable theoretical predictions and Section II.3.3 introduces the experimental design and procedures. Results are presented and discussed in Section II.3.4. Section II.3.5 concludes.

II.3.2 The Model

This section analyzes dissolution games, based on the CCM and the WBA rules. For simplicity we assume that both partners hold a 50% stake in the business partnership.[23] We denote partner i's valuation for the whole partnership by v_i and assume that v_i is privately known to partner i. The other partner knows that v_i is the realization of a uniformly distributed random variable on [0,100] and that v_1 and v_2 are stochastically independent.

---

[22] Güth et al. (2002, 2003) experimentally investigate auctions and fair division games with three players both under first- as well as under second-price rule collecting entire bid functions. (The fair division game under first-price rule is equivalent to the winner's bid auction in our experiment).

[23] Indeed, 50-50 partnerships are the most common form of partnerships (see Hauswald and Hege (2003)). Furthermore, management deadlocks (and the need for dissolution) are most likely to be relevant if control rights are shared equally, which again is more common for 50-50 partnerships.

The rules of the WBA resemble those of a standard first-price sealed bid auction with the modification that the winner pays the losing partner. To be more precise, in the WBA each partner submits a sealed bid b_i, $i = 1, 2$ for the whole partnership. In our setting with equal-share partnerships the price for half of the object equals half of the winning bid: The partner who submits the higher bid b_w receives all shares in the firm and pays a price of $p = \frac{1}{2} b_w$ to his partner.[24] The CCM, in contrast, is a sequential move game and works as follows: One partner (the proposer) offers a price P for the whole partnership. His partner (the chooser) can then decide to either buy his partner's share of the firm at a price of $p = \frac{P}{2}$ or sell his share at a price of $p = \frac{P}{2}$.[25] In both dissolution mechanisms the utility of the partner who eventually buys is given by $u_B = u_B(v_B - p)$ where $B \in \{1, 2\}$ denotes the identity of the buyer. The utility of the seller is $u_S = u_S(p)$ where $S \in \{1, 2\}$ denotes the identity of the seller. We assume that $u_B(\cdot)$ and $u_S(\cdot)$ are concave utility functions.

Efficiency, Expected Payoffs and Heterogeneity

A mechanism is called (ex-post) efficient if for any realization of valuations all shares end up in the hands of the partner with the higher valuation. We measure the performance of the mechanisms with two different measures of achieved efficiency (which both take a value of 1 if the mechanism is ex-post efficient):

1. the probability or frequency with which the allocation is efficient (i.e., with which the partner with the higher valuation obtains the object)
2. the efficiency rate, which is defined as[26]

$$\frac{1}{10000} \int_0^{100} \int_0^{100} \frac{v_B(v_1, v_2)}{\max(v_1, v_2)} dv_1 dv_2$$

where $v_B(v_1, v_2)$ denotes the valuation of the partner who purchases the partnership (given v_1 and v_2).

---

[24] If both partners submit the same bid, each partner wins with probability $\frac{1}{2}$.

[25] We here assume that the identities of the proposer (and chooser) are either pre-determined or that their determination does not reveal any information about their valuations. This is a strong assumption (see de Frutos and Kittsteiner (2008) for an extensive discussion). In practice there can be reasons unrelated to a partner's valuation that make him trigger the dissolution by proposing a price. It is also possible that the identity of the proposer is already agreed before the triggering event for the dissolution occurs.

[26] Alternatively, one could measure efficiency by expected welfare loss. We use the efficiency rate as it has been used in similar experiments (see Güth et al. (2002, 2003)). However, measuring efficiency by expected welfare loss does not change our findings.

First, we assume that both partners are either risk neutral or exhibit the same degree of constant absolute risk aversion with parameter $\lambda > 0$, i.e., their utility function has the form: $u^\lambda(x) \equiv \frac{1}{\lambda}(1 - e^{-\lambda x})$. The parameter x denotes the net monetary value, either v_i minus payment made if the agent i obtains the good or the payment received if the agent does not obtain the good. We will refer to this setup as the setup with homogeneous partners: Partners do not differ in their risk preferences (but they usually differ in their valuations for the partnership). The following proposition describes the equilibria for the setup with homogeneous partners.

Proposition II.1 *In the symmetric equilibrium of the model with homogeneous partners, the equilibrium strategies are as follows:*
1. *in the CCM a risk-neutral proposer with valuation v_p will offer $P(v_p) = 25 + \frac{1}{2}v_p$; the optimal proposal for a risk-averse proposer with utility function u^λ has the property that $P^\lambda(v_p) \in (v_p, 50)$ if $v_p < 50$, $P^\lambda(v_p) \in (50, v_p)$ if $v_p > 50$ and that $P^\lambda(v_p)$ is strictly increasing in v_p. A chooser with valuation v_c sells if and only if $v_c < P(v_p)$.*
2. *in the WBA if bidders are risk neutral they will bid according to $b(v) = \frac{2}{3}v$, if they are risk averse (with utility function u^λ) they will bid according to a strictly increasing function $b^\lambda(v)$.*

Proof of Proposition II.1. See McAfee (1997). ∎

An immediate consequence of Proposition II.1 is that the WBA is ex-post efficient whereas the CCM is not. As we will see in Section II.3.4 this prediction is not confirmed in our experiments. We thus provide another setup where partners are heterogeneous with respect to risk attitudes. We assume that a partner is either risk neutral or 'extremely' risk averse, i.e., his Arrow-Pratt measure of absolute risk aversion converges to infinity ($\lambda \to \infty$).[27] To simplify the exposition in this section we will refer to 'extremely' risk averse as risk

---
[27] Note that such a partner's preferences cannot be represented any more by a continuous utility function. We will get the behavior of such a type by assuming that he has a CARA utility function and taking the limit $\lambda \to \infty$ in his utility function. Essentially, such a partner only cares about payoffs that are certain. We can also interpret this 'extreme' risk aversion as 'extreme' loss aversion. Clearly, the assumption of extreme risk aversion is restrictive and unrealistic but necessary to obtain a tractable multi-dimensional screening problem which at the same time provides insights in how the mechanisms perform if partners are heterogeneous.

averse. We assume that a partner's risk attitude is private information and that he is risk neutral with a probability of α (and risk averse with the remaining probability $(1-\alpha)$).[28] We will refer to this setup as the setup (or model) with heterogeneous partners.

In the WBA as well as in the CCM bidding/proposing a price equal to the own valuation is the optimal strategy for a risk-averse type, regardless of whether his partner is also risk averse or not. The intuition behind this is simple:[29] In the CCM a deviation to a price above his valuation v_p increases the risk that the proposer might end up with less than $\frac{v_p}{2}$ as he could be buying at this price. A deviation to a price below his valuation increases the risk that he might end up with less than $\frac{v_p}{2}$ as well as he could be selling at this price. Both would be avoided by an extremely risk-averse proposer. The following proposition characterizes the equilibrium strategies:

Proposition II.2 *In the symmetric equilibrium of the model with heterogeneous partners, the equilibrium strategies are as follows:*

1. *in the CCM a risk-averse proposer with valuation v_p will offer $P(v_p) = v_p$ and a risk-neutral proposer $P(v_p) = 25 + \frac{1}{2} v_p$; the chooser with valuation v_c sells if and only if $v_c < P(v_p)$.*

2. *in the WBA a risk-averse partner (with valuation v) will bid $b(v) = v$ and a risk-neutral partner $b(v) = \frac{2}{3} v$.*

The WBA can only be inefficient if partners exhibit different degrees of risk aversion. For example, if partner 1 is risk neutral and partner 2 is risk averse (which happens with probability $(1-\alpha)\alpha$) the WBA will result in an inefficient allocation if and only if $v_2 \in (\frac{2}{3} v_1, v_1)$ which happens with probability $\frac{1}{3} v_1$ (and then the allocation is inefficient with probability $\int_0^{100} \frac{1}{3} v_1 \frac{1}{100} dv_1 = \frac{1}{6}$). Thus, the overall probability that the WBA is inefficient is $2\alpha(1-\alpha)\frac{1}{6}$. In contrast, the CCM can only be inefficient if the proposer is risk neutral, which happens with probability α. In that case the CCM is inefficient if and only if $v_p < 50$ and

---

[28] We therefore have a model where partners' types are two-dimensional, which in general is not tractable. The assumption that one component of the type can only take two different values will allow us to analyze the model analytically.

[29] And as it is similar for the WBA we here provide it for the CCM only. A formal proof of these statements is given in the Mathematical Appendix.

$v_c \in (v_p, P(v_p))$ or if $v_p > 50$ and $v_c \in (P(v_p), v_p)$. This happens with probability $\frac{1}{8}$. Thus, we have that the CCM is more likely to produce an efficient outcome if and only if $\frac{1}{8}\alpha < 2\alpha(1-\alpha)\frac{1}{6}$ or equivalently if and only if $\alpha < \frac{5}{8}$, i.e., if the proportion of risk-averse partners is sufficiently high (but not 1).[30] We summarize our observations on efficiency in the following corollary:

Corollary II.1 *Concerning the efficiency of the dissolution mechanisms we have*

1. *that in the setup with homogeneous partners the CCM performs worse than the WBA, i.e., the latter results in an efficient allocation with a higher probability (see McAfee (1992)).*
2. *that in the setup with heterogeneous partners the CCM might outperform the WBA depending on the distribution of types, i.e., there exist parameters α such that the CCM results in an efficient allocation with a higher probability.*

Whereas a designer of dissolution rules may be concerned with efficiency, partners who dissolve their partnership might also be interested in their own individual payoffs and their relative standing as compared to their partner. Thus, it is a natural question to ask which mechanism yields a higher expected payoff. As the CCM (other than the WBA) is asymmetric with respect to the different roles (proposer and chooser) we are also interested in which role is more profitable.

If partners are risk neutral McAfee shows that in the CCM the expected payoff of a proposer is lower than that of a chooser with the same valuation.[31] The same ranking is valid for a risk-neutral partner in the setup with heterogeneous partners:[32] If a risk-neutral chooser faces a risk-averse partner (rather than a risk-neutral partner) proposed prices are even further away from the median valuation (i.e., from 50) as those set by a risk-neutral proposer. Thus, the chooser receives a higher price when he is likely to be seller and a lower price otherwise. Hence a risk-neutral chooser is even better off as compared to the situation where he faces a risk-neutral proposer. On the other hand the payoff

---

[30] If we use the efficiency rate as performance measure, similar calculations show that the CCM outperforms the WBA if the fraction of risk-neutral bidders is sufficiently small.
[31] See Theorem 9 in McAfee (1992). For an intuition of this result see de Frutos and Kittsteiner (2008).
[32] For a formal proof, see the Mathematical Appendix, Proposition II.A1. The preference for chooser to proposer does not require the distribution to be uniform (this can be shown along the lines of the proof of Theorem 9 in McAfee (1992)).

for a risk-neutral proposer is independent of whether he faces a risk-averse or a risk-neutral chooser. Furthermore, for both models, a risk-neutral proposer's payoff is smaller than what he would get in the WBA, which again is smaller than what he gets as chooser.[33] From the viewpoint of a risk-averse partner it does not matter which role he has or which mechanism is played (he always guarantees himself a sure payoff of $\frac{v}{2}$ and does not care about the insecure component of his payoff).[34]

Corollary II.2 *Independently of his valuation, the expected payoff of a risk-neutral partner is higher as chooser than as proposer. His expected payoff in the WBA is smaller than in the CCM if he is chooser and higher than in the CCM if he is proposer. This ranking is valid for the setup with homogeneous and heterogeneous partners.*

An important conclusion from the theoretical considerations in this section is that a clear ranking based on efficiency cannot be obtained as it depends on the degree and kind of heterogeneity. In the next section we will therefore investigate how the dissolution rules compare in a controlled laboratory experiment.

II.3.3 Experimental Design and Procedures

The computerized experiment was conducted at the Cologne Laboratory for Economic Research in June 2006 using the programming software z-Tree (Fischbacher (2007)). Subjects were undergraduate students from the University of Cologne mostly belonging to the faculty of economics and business administration and they were recruited with ORSEE (Greiner (2004)).

We ran three sessions comprising two different treatments – the CCM and the WBA. Each session was run with 32 subjects using stranger matching. The subjects were divided into 8 matching groups consisting of 4 subjects. Subjects knew that their partner changed in each round. They were told the rules of the game (either the CCM or the WBA) and that they together with their partner possess a 'fictitious' indivisible object. In the CCM treatments subjects were also told whether they are proposer or chooser, a subject kept this role throughout the

---

[33] It should be noted that this result hinges on the uniformity assumption of the distribution, see McAfee (1992). The calculations behind this observation are given in the Mathematical Appendix (Proposition II.A2).

[34] This ranking obviously depends on the assumption of extreme risk aversion and only holds if the degree of absolute risk aversion is infinite. For partners who exhibit smaller degrees of risk aversion the WBA is at least as good as being proposer in the CCM.

session. Roles were allocated randomly; subjects knew that they will maintain their role during the whole experiment, such that (as in the WBA) they face the same decision situation in all 30 rounds.

In the WBA both partners submit their bid and in the CCM only one partner (the proposer) submits a price. We had two sessions with the CCM to get the same number of submitted prices as compared to the WBA session. Each session consisted of 30 rounds and lasted about one hour. In session 1 (CCM) subjects received average earnings of 12.81 € (with a minimum of 9 € and a maximum of 17.10 €), in session 2 (WBA) average earnings amount to 12.60 € (with a minimum of 8.90 € and a maximum of 15.10 €) and in session 3 (CCM) subjects earn on average 12.64 € (with a minimum of 8.70 € and a maximum of 16.60 €). These payments include a show-up fee of 2.50 €.

During the whole experiment an independent private values framework is used: each subject gets to know his own valuation for the object in each round, but not the valuation of his respective partner.[35] For each subject a random number is drawn (independently) from the uniformly distributed interval [0, 100] (2 decimal spaces). This number represents the subjects' own valuation for the object and also determines what the partner who acquired the partnership gets paid by the experimenter (e.g. if a partner has a valuation of 60 and paid 30 to the other partner, both partners will get the same monetary payoffs). In case two bidders in the WBA treatment submit the same bid, each is selected as winner with equal probability and the payoffs of buyer and seller arise afterwards as described above. In both treatments bids (proposals respectively) were restricted to 200 to avoid obvious type errors.

II.3.4 Experimental Performance of the Dissolution Mechanisms
II.3.4.1 Efficiency

First, we investigate the efficiency of both mechanisms. As explained in Section II.3.2 we apply two different measures for efficiency: the frequency (percentage) of partnerships dissolved efficiently and the efficiency rate which is defined as $\frac{v_B}{\max\{v_1, v_2\}}$, where v_B denotes the valuation of the buyer.

The percentage of efficient allocations and the mean efficiency rate over all rounds for our two treatments are given in Table II.1. It shows that both the

---

[35] Instructions are given in the Appendix.

mean percentage of efficient allocations as well as the mean efficiency rate is higher in the CCM than in the WBA treatment. However, pair-wise two-tailed Mann-Whitney-U tests reveal only weakly significant differences between the treatments for the former measure at the 10% significance level ($p=0.092$), but not for the efficiency rate ($p=0.264$).[36] The CCM seems to generate at least as efficient allocations as the WBA – as predicted in the setup with heterogeneous partners. Note that the homogeneous model with risk-neutral agents fails to provide a good explanation of our observations: In only about 50% of the cases in which theory predicts inefficient dissolution in the CCM, given the distribution of valuations in the experiment, inefficiencies actually take place.

In general one would expect an endogenous determination of the proposer to enhance efficiency (see de Frutos and Kittsteiner (2008)). As our main experimental findings show that the performance of the CCM already exceeds that of the WBA even for pre-determined proposers we would expect it to perform even better if we allowed for an endogenous selection of proposer.

Table II.1: Mean efficiency

	Percentage of efficient allocations	Efficiency rate
CCM	89.69%	97.29%
WBA	85.21%	96.43%

We examine which factors have an influence on efficient dissolution with panel probit regressions in which the binary variable 'efficient allocation' is regressed on a number of independent variables: Dummy variables for each treatment (WBA and CCM), the round number (1-30) and the absolute value of the distance of partners' private valuations ($|v_i-v_j|$). Moreover, we create dummy variables for both partners' private valuation being below the median (both $v_i<50$ and $v_j<50$), for both partners' private valuation being above the median (both $v_i>50$ and $v_j>50$), and for one partner's valuation being below and one partner's valuation being above ($v_i<50$ and $v_j>50$). We consider valuations below and above the median valuation separately as in the former case a subject becomes seller with a higher probability and in the latter case buyer. Theoretically, this has a different effect on proposal setting strategy in the CCM for both risk-neutral as well as risk-averse proposers (a higher probability of being seller provides

---

[36] The tests use matching group averages as independent observations (CCM: 16 matching groups; WBA: 8 matching groups). Additionally we also compare the average welfare loss (where welfare is measured as the sum of individuals' monetary payoff). Although the average welfare loss is lower in the CCM treatment, this difference is not significant (p-value is 0.238).

Table II.2: Panel probit regression IPV

Efficient allocation	(1) Coefficient	(Std. Errors)	(2) Coefficient	(Std. Errors)
WBA	0.1819812	(0.3025306)	0.2967402	(0.3716076)
CCM	0.7729401***	(0.2334461)	1.209842***	(0.303396)
Round*WBA	-0.0082324	(0.0090868)	-0.0078058	(0.0091201)
Round*CCM	0.0188885***	(0.0070533)	0.0182075***	(0.0070915)
Dist*WBA	0.0396143***	(0.0066109)	0.0358146***	(0.0091991)
Dist*CCM	0.0212942***	(0.0045556)	0.0106706*	(0.0060886)
Below*WBA	0.2601203	(0.2462205)	0.2850368	(0.4123102)
Below*CCM	-0.2550035	(0.2034501)	-0.8588613**	(0.3480503)
Above*WBA	0.0014486	(0.2246702)	-0.337495	(0.3984705)
Above*CCM	-0.6138709***	(0.1872445)	-1.190707***	(0.3209465)
Dist*below*WBA			-0.0066443	(0.0160483)
Dist*below*CCM			0.0236143*	(0.0134372)
Dist*above*WBA			0.0193444	(0.0160737)
Dist*above*CCM			0.0212048**	(0.0101901)
N	1440		1440	
$\chi^2(dF)$	130.44(9)		150.26(13)	

Standard errors are given in parentheses. *** denotes significance on the 1%-level, ** denotes significance on the 5%-level, * denotes significance on the 10%-level. Matching groups ($N=24$) are used as group variable. As we drop the constant in the estimated models (1) and (2), the reported $\chi^2(dF)$ is taken from the (analogous) model with a constant as presented in Table II.A1.

incentives to increase the price, a higher probability of being buyer to decrease the price as long as the proposer is not 'extremely' risk averse). Following this strategy results in inefficiencies if the chooser's valuation is between the proposer's valuation and the proposal; however, if the chooser's valuation is on the other side of the median valuation, allocations should never be inefficient.

The estimated models in Table II.2 – which measure the effects of the tested parameters in each treatment separately – indicate that the farther away partners' valuations are the more probable is an efficient allocation. This positive effect on efficient allocations is highly significant in both mechanisms and it is even stronger in the WBA (for a comparison of effects between treatments see

Table II.A1). In the CCM treatment both partners' valuations being above the median valuation has a strong and highly significant negative impact on the efficiency of allocations. This observation is driven by the fact that a higher percentage of proposers behaves according to theoretical predictions if their valuation is above the median (see also Section II.3.4.3). Moreover, in the CCM learning effects seem to play a role since higher rounds have a significantly positive influence on the probability of efficient allocations. This might indicate that the CCM is the more complex mechanism which subjects have to get used to.

II.3.4.2 Payoffs

The theoretical analysis in Section II.3.2 suggests that a partner's expected payoff is largest as chooser in the CCM and lowest as proposer whereas the payoff in the WBA lies between these two. This ordering is what we also find for the average payoffs obtained in our experiment. The first column of Table II.3 reports the average payoff for different mechanisms and roles respectively. Whereas participation in the CCM turns out to be almost as attractive (on average) as in the WBA[37], on average proposers in the CCM obtain a significantly lower payoff than participants in the WBA whose payoffs are significantly lower than choosers' payoffs.[38] Thus our experimental findings are consistent with both models in Section II.3.2.

Table II.3: Mean payoffs

	Mean payoff	Mean valuation	Relative payoff
CCM	33.91	52.45	64.65%
	26.42 (proposer)	52.74 (proposer)	50.09% (proposer)
	41.40 (chooser)	52.17 (chooser)	79.36% (chooser)
WBA	33.48	52.50	63.77%

Relative payoffs are characterized by mean payoff/mean valuation.

II.3.4.3 Individual Bidding/Proposing Behavior

Theory predicts that in the CCM risk-averse (and risk-neutral) proposers set prices between their own valuation and 50 (the median valuation) whereas

---

[37] Note that average prices for the partnerships (for each matching group) do not differ significantly between the CCM (49.72) and the WBA treatment (48.63).
[38] Two-tailed Mann-Whitney-U tests for matching group payoffs reveal $p<0.001$ for both cases. Column 2 shows that mean valuations were roughly the same over treatments and roles.

bidders in the WBA bid below their own valuation.[39] In both mechanisms the vast majority of proposals/bids is in line with these theoretical predictions (see Table II.4): In the CCM 78.85% of proposals lie between v and v_m and in the WBA 96.35% of bids are set below v. Surprisingly, proposers with a valuation below 50 more frequently propose prices that are inconsistent with these predictions than proposers with a valuation above 50 (a Chi-square goodness-of-fit test yields a significant difference on the 1% significance level). In this regard we observe more inefficient allocations in the CCM if $v_p>50$ (compare also the results of the panel probit regression given in Table II.2).

Not only is proposal setting in the CCM in line with theory in most cases (assuming risk-neutral or risk-averse agents) but also choosers' decision between buying and selling. For choosers it is a dominant strategy to never buy the object if the valuation is smaller than the proposal nor sell the object if the valuation is higher than the proposal. We find evidence for this prediction: In only 14 cases a chooser does a mistake (1.46% of dissolutions). Most mistakes are made in early rounds.

Table II.4: Proposals and bids

CCM	P between v and 50	N
All	78.85%	960
v>50	83.43%	507
v<50	73.73%	453
WBA	b below valuation	N
All	96.35%	960

We rounded P between v and 50 and b below valuation up to at most +-1.

Figure II.1 shows scatter plots of the valuations and the corresponding proposals (respectively bids) for the CCM (WBA) treatment. The black line determines the risk-neutral theoretical equilibrium bidding function as a benchmark. According to Propositions II.1 and II.2 the equilibrium function for a risk-neutral proposer in the CCM is given by $P^*=25+1/2v$ and for a risk-neutral bidder by $b^*=2/3v$. Note that these functions hold for the homogeneous as well as for the heterogeneous setup of Section II.3.2. A simple linear OLS regression with robust standard errors yields for the WBA a constant of 1.241 which does not differ significantly from 0 and a coefficient of 0.651 ($p<0.001$).[40] At first

---

[39] In the WBA bidding above the own valuation is clearly dominated by bidding the own valuation; for a formal proof of the statement concerning the CCM see McAfee (1992), Lemma 7.

[40] The bid function is estimated by $b_i = \alpha + \beta v_i$ in the WBA treatment and by $P_i = \alpha + \beta v_i$ in the CCM treatment respectively. Note that the calculated standard errors are robust concerning heteroscedasticity.

sight this would be in line with the risk-neutral equilibrium. However, a closer look indicates a lot of variation in the data. In the CCM the constant amounts to 14.839 and the coefficient is 0.661 (both are highly significant). The significantly steeper slope and the smaller intercept than the risk-neutral prediction suggest that proposals are set closer to the valuation and thus behavior might be driven by risk aversion. In the following we discuss actual behavior of subjects in more detail.

Figure II.1: Scatter plots – Valuations and bids/proposals

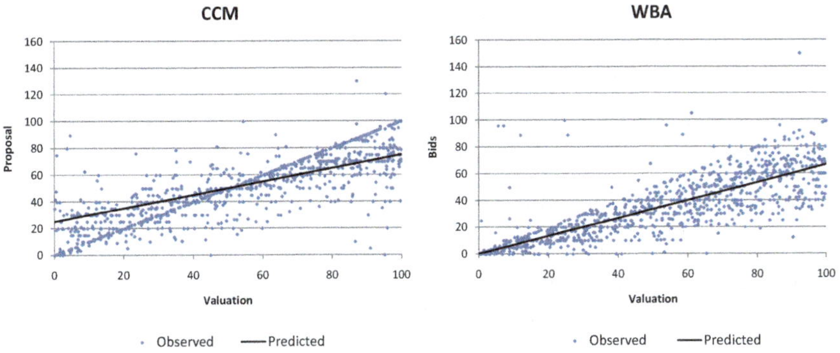

One extreme data point in the CCM is excluded in the figure (proposal of 200)

Behavioral Types

Our analysis in Section II.3.2 (concentrating only on two different types, namely risk-neutral and extremely risk-averse types) shows that inefficiencies are more likely to occur a) in the CCM if the proposer is risk-neutral and b) in the WBA if bidders are heterogeneous in their bidding behavior. This is consistent with the observed bidding behavior described in Table II.5 and the performance of the rules: In the CCM only few proposals are set according to the risk-neutral prediction but a lot of proposals equal the own valuation, whereas the fraction of risk-neutral and extremely risk-averse bidders in the WBA is nearly identical.[41]

Besides the two behavioral types our model is based on, the different categories given in Table II.5 indicate furthermore substantial heterogeneity in proposal and bid setting. In the CCM as well as in the WBA a subject's risk aversion can be inferred from how close he sets proposals or bids to his valuation. Very risk-averse subjects will bid/propose very close (or equal) to the own valuation; setting a proposal equal to or bidding the own valuation

---

[41] Note that heterogeneity of partners has no influence on efficiency in the CCM (the only relevant aspect is whether a proposer is risk neutral or not), whereas in the WBA heterogeneity is pivotal for inefficiency.

guarantees a payoff of at least half of the valuation whereas any other strategy results in a lower payoff with some positive probability.[42] Of course there can be other reasons for why a partner might bid/propose (closer to) the own valuation, such as, e.g., loss aversion. The driving force leading to a better performance of the CCM is heterogeneity in bidding behavior and therefore the underlying reasons for why different subjects bid/propose according to different strategies is not really essential for the points made in this section.

The experimental data provided by Table II.5 is more consistent with risk-averse behavior than with risk-neutral behavior:[43] In the CCM 64.06% of proposals is set equal to the own valuation or between own valuation and the risk-neutral proposal which is consistent with various degrees of risk aversion. Likewise in the WBA the percentage of risk-averse bids amounts to 55.62%. Of this a substantial fraction of proposals/bids is set equal to the own valuation (which is consistent with 'extreme' risk aversion as in the heterogeneous setup in Section II.3.2). In addition a smaller fraction of proposals/bids corresponds to the risk-neutral equilibrium strategy. This suggests that partners are heterogeneous with respect to their degrees of risk aversion.

We categorize proposals and bidding behavior respectively as follows: Proposals/bids corresponding to 'risk-neutral' behavior are given by $P=P^*$ in the CCM ($b=b^*$ in the WBA). 'Extremely risk-averse' subjects are those setting their proposals equal to their valuation (CCM: $P=v$ and WBA: $b=v$). All other degrees

Table II.5: Categories of proposal setting/bidding behavior

CCM	Risk neutral	Extremely risk averse	Too hesitant	Excessive	Dominated strategy
All (N=960)	6.67%	30.10%	33.96%	16.77%	18.23%
v_p>50 (N=507)	7.1%	28.01%	39.84%	19.53%	7.89%
v_p<50 (N=453)	6.18%	32.45%	27.37%	13.69%	29.8%
WBA	Risk neutral	Extremely risk averse	Too hesitant	Excessive	Dominated strategy
All (N=960)	10.1%	11.56%	44.06%	48.13%	4.38%

We rounded P (b) in cases $P=P^*$ ($b=b^*$) and $P=v$ ($b=v$) up to at most +-1. Note that the sum of percentages might exceed 100% due to the fact that rounded data fall into two categories. E.g. a bid of $b=b^*$+0.3 is counted both as risk neutral (rounded) and as too hesitant as we do not really know the 'true' risk attitude in these cases.

---

[42] Note that setting $P=v$ is the envy-free proposal, at which the proposer is indifferent between buying and selling as the proposer achieves the same utility independent of the chooser's decision: The proposer can divide in such a way that he is indifferent to his opponent's choice and the chooser only needs to choose his most preferred bundle. Therefore the players can insure that the outcome of the game is fair (see Crawford (1977)). This holds also for the auction: $b=v$ is the envy-free bid.

[43] Combining the two categories 'extremely risk-averse' behavior $P=P^*$ ($b=b^*$) and 'too hesitant' behavior from Table II.5 yields the total percentage of risk-averse behavior. Note that the CCM becomes more efficient the closer the proposal is set to the proposer's valuation.

of risk-averse behavior are grasped by the category '*too hesitant*' behavior. '*Too hesitant*' behavior indicates proposals and bids lying between the risk-neutral equilibrium and the valuation of the subjects (CCM: $v_p>P>P^*$ if $v_p>50$ and $v_p<P<P^*$ if $v_p<50$; WBA: $v>b>b^*$, note that in the WBA this behavior corresponds to overbidding).[44] However, we also observe behavior which is not in line with risk aversion: '*Excessive*' proposal setting in the CCM treatment is defined by setting $50<P<P^*<v_p$ in case $v_p>50$ and setting $50>P>P^*>v_p$ in case $v_p<50$ and corresponds to underbidding behavior in the WBA ($v>b^*>b$). '*Dominated strategy*' classifies a strictly dominated strategy for risk-averse or risk-neutral subjects: in this category P lies on the other side of the valuation than P^* (CCM: $P>v_p>P^*$ if $v_p>50$ and $P<v_p<P^*$ if $v_p<50$; WBA: $b>v>b^*$).

The proportion of proposals that equals the proposer's valuation in the CCM is larger than the proportion of bids that equals the bidder's valuation in the WBA (30.10% vs. 11.56%). This and the observation that over the rounds some individuals sometimes bid/propose their valuation and sometimes deviate from that strategy, suggests that the degree of heterogeneity differs between rounds and mechanisms. Whereas we do not have an explanation for this, it should be noticed that heterogeneity in partners' behavior is an explanation for the experimental performance of the two mechanisms.

II.3.5 Conclusions

In an independent private values setting, this section has investigated the performance of the predominant termination rule for partnerships: the CCM. In an experiment we compare its performance with that of an auction. Our main findings are that whereas both, the CCM and the WBA perform well, the former even outperforms the WBA as measured by frequency of resulting in an efficient allocation. Thus, our experiment provides a first empirical support for the use of what is a standard clause in modern partnership agreements. In addition the experiment provides evidence that the CCM can lead to very unequal payoffs: a proposer expects a significantly lower payoff as compared to a chooser. Ex ante, before the subjects are assigned their roles in the CCM sessions, the payoff expectations for all subjects are quite similar in the CCM and in the WBA treatment. But after the assignment of being proposer or chooser the payoffs differ significantly: Choosers in the CCM achieve significantly higher payoffs

---

[44] Note that $P=v$ and $b=v$ are not included in the category '*too hesitant*' behavior, but are itemized as a special category ('*extremely risk averse*').

than bidders in the WBA whose payoffs are significantly higher than those of proposers in the CCM.

Whereas the efficiency result cannot be obtained in a standard symmetric valuations model (as in Cramton et al. (1987), and McAfee (1992)), we show that the good performance of the CCM can be due to partners having idiosyncratic attitudes towards risk. It should be noted that other types of heterogeneity between partners can yield the same result, such as differences in loss aversion or ex-post rationality.[45] Rather than identifying the individual causes for heterogeneity, we observe that bidding in the WBA and proposing in the CCM display a high degree of heterogeneity, as is consistent with our model and explanation.

One limitation of our analysis is that in the CCM we assign the roles of proposer and chooser randomly, whereas in real life this is often determined by the partners themselves. In reality the rules according to which this allocation of roles work is often unspecified and can involve more complicated sub-games such as negotiations, which are difficult to implement and control in a laboratory environment. Furthermore, our approach allows us to test the hypothesis that partners are indeed not indifferent between different roles (and confirms the prediction that partners prefer to choose rather than propose, which also has important consequences for practitioners and corporate lawyers). De Frutos and Kittsteiner (2008) show that in a model with endogenized proposer selection, the CCM performs as good as the WBA, so that we would expect our results to become even more positive with respect to the CCM.

II.4 Partnership Dissolution with Interdependent Valuations[46]

II.4.1 Introduction

In Section II.3 we have analyzed the performance of the CCM and the WBA in an independent private values framework. The purpose of Section II.4 is to examine both mechanisms in the more realistic case of interdependent valuations. The main focus of the experimental investigation of two-parent equal-share

---

[45] Ex-post rationality refers to learning direction theory (see Neugebauer and Selten (2006); Ockenfels and Selten (2005)) which assumes that subjects change their behavior with regard to their experience. Subjects might react to feelings like winner's and loser's regret and qualitatively adjust their bids/proposals: The most often observed behavior in the experiment is that bids and proposals increase if the partner obtained the object in the previous round and that bids and proposals decrease if a subject himself received the object in the previous round.
[46] This section is based on Trhal (2009).

partnerships is aimed again at the two criteria: allocative efficiency and ex-ante payoff equality. The experimental results of Section II.3 serve as a benchmark: The robustness of results is tested with respect to the independent private values environment.

By providing an experimental robustness check, this study is based on an explorative approach due to three main reasons: First, the analytical complexity of the interdependent valuations case considerably hinders a theoretical analysis and in consequence we may assume that also agents rather adhere to simple heuristics (rules of thumb) than to an extensive equilibrium analysis.

Second, the standard assumption of risk neutrality (or homogeneous risk attitudes) in fact seems to fail to yield correct predictions even in the independent private values case and should be therefore questioned in this context. As Section II.3 has already shown theoretically assuming independent private values, the efficiency of the mechanisms strongly depends on the concrete assumptions of the model: Contrary to a homogeneous setup in which agents adhere to homogeneous risk attitudes (i.e., both partners are either risk neutral or have CARA utility functions with the same degree of absolute risk aversion), we have derived that one cannot predict which mechanism is more efficient in a heterogeneous setup. If agents' risk attitudes differ, the CCM might even outperform the WBA. The data of our experiment with independent private values support the assumption that subjects indeed differ in their risk attitudes[47] and provide evidence that the CCM performs at least as efficient as the WBA. An experimental approach helps to evaluate relevant patterns of actual behavior.

Third, "[g]iven the large range of settings where a first-best mechanism does not exist two important tasks remain: (1) the construction of incentive-efficient mechanisms; (2) the identification of well-performing mechanisms whose rules do not depend on features of the problem (e.g. valuation and distribution functions) that are unlikely to be known to a third party (e.g. a court)." (Moldovanu 2002, p. 79). Our applied approach to study the performance of two distribution-free and simple mechanisms is meant to contribute to point (2). Testing them in a controlled laboratory experiment (although they are neither first-best nor second-best (incentive-efficient) mechanisms, compare Section II.2) provides one complementary method which facilitates to identify 'well-performing' dissolution mechanisms.

---

[47] Note that heterogeneity in bidding behavior is the crucial assumption in our model, which can also be explained by other motives than risk aversion (like e.g. loss aversion, ex-post rationality or regret).

The interdependence of values is shaped in the following way: each agent's valuation consists of an independent private value component and a common value component. The common value component depends on the partner's private value signal. In contrast to a pure common value setting in which the object has a true value which is the same for all agents (agents just receive different signals), in the interdependent value setting each agent might have a different value for the partnership.[48] In the following it is assumed that agent i receives a private signal s_i and that his valuation function for the entire partnership is generally given by $v_i(s_1,...,s_n) = g(s_i) + \sum_{j \neq i} h(s_j)$, where g, h are continuously differentiable functions, g and h are strictly increasing[49] and $g' > h'$ (following e.g. Fieseler et al. (2003)).

Naturally, the assumption of interdependent values complicates the decision problem a lot. As an agent's value now depends also on other agents' signals the main problem is that the value of the entire object is *unknown* to the agent himself at the time of dissolution. The influence of the partner's private signal on the own value implies that an a priori estimate of the value may need to be revised each time new information about signals of other agents is available (e.g. like the announcement who has won the auction). In the independent private values case agents could always bid their 'true' valuation. This strategy entails positive net-payoffs for sure (i.e., an agent earns at least the amount which his share of the object is worth). With interdependent valuations however, this strategy is no longer available (this implies that if he wins (loses) he might pay more (get less) than his valuation for the object). Thus, the interdependent value setting gives rise to adverse selection effects.

Kittsteiner (2003) highlights these winner's and loser's curses.[50] If valuations are increasing functions of other agents' signals (as it is assumed in this section), information revealed ex post is always 'bad news' and agents must be cautious in order to avoid the respective winner's or loser's curses, which hinder efficient trade and further compound strategic manipulation of information (compare Moldovanu (2002)).

---

[48] In the pure common value setting there are no efficiency issues as all agents place equal value on the item.
[49] The assumption that h is strictly increasing implies a positive influence of the partner's private signal on an agent's valuation for the object. Fieseler et al. (2003) also consider a negative influence. However, as it seems to be the more realistic assumption for partnerships we concentrate in this section solely on a positive influence.
[50] Winner's and loser's curses are most apparent in a pure common value model and decrease with the interdependent component of the valuation function.

The winner's curse occurs, because if a partner wins this is 'bad news' since his partner's signal and therefore his own v are low. Hence, a buyer might pay more than his value if his value for the object is smaller than expected: He would prefer to be seller. Accordingly, the loser's curse arises, because if he loses this is 'bad news' since his partner's signal and therefore his own v are high. In this case, a seller might get less than his value (his value for the object is higher than expected): He would like to be buyer.

Note that winner's and loser's curses are most severe if a partner's private signal is intermediate, because these types face almost identical chances of becoming buyer or seller. If a partner's private signal is low, he will become seller with a higher probability; if a partner's private signal is high, he will become buyer with a higher probability. This makes it easier for these 'extreme' types to correct for the winner's curse (by decreasing their bid) or the loser's curse (by increasing their bid). An intermediate type, though, does not know whether to buy or sell and thus faces both curses at the same time with similar magnitudes. As the effect of both winner's and loser's curse is strongest for those intermediate types uncertainty about how to bid is highest. For them winning as well as losing is 'bad news': A partner is not able to correct for both curses at the same time (by raising and lowering the bid).[51] Thus, in contrast to the independent private values setting intermediate types might not want to participate in an auction to dissolve the partnership[52] assuming interdependent valuations (i.e., an agent might be better off keeping his share in the partnership), which is corroborated by the experimental data of this study.

Our data provide evidence that an interdependent valuations setting gives rise to negative net-payoffs especially for intermediate types. Hence, contrary to the assumption of independent private values, the interdependent values setting involves a novel 'risk of negative gains from trade' for agents as there does not exist any longer a secure strategy with which negative net-payoffs (i.e., losses compared to their status quo) could be avoided.

The main findings concerning the robustness are that assuming interdependent valuations the WBA turns out to be at least as efficient as the CCM (contrary to the ranking with independent private values) and that the WBA is not as sensitive to asymmetric information and complexity as the CCM

---

[51] For a more detailed discussion see Kittsteiner (2003), p. 55.
[52] Interestingly, Jehiel and Pauzner (2006) also find that no trade takes place for signals in the middle of the types' interval in an asymmetric setting where valuations only depend on private information of one of the two partners.

in terms of allocative efficiency. This result is mainly driven by a more homogeneous bidding behavior in the WBA and especially a substantial fraction of subjects setting their bid equal to their private signal. In the CCM however, proposing the own signal has no positive effect per se on allocative efficiency as the chooser also faces uncertainty concerning his true valuation. Moreover, the WBA still results in more homogeneous payoff expectations. The relative standing remains the same as in the benchmark case with independent private values: The chooser fares better than an agent in the auction who fares better than a proposer.

The remaining chapter is structured as follows. Section II.4.2 provides a brief description of the decision situation and summarizes some considerations on the efficient performance of the two mechanisms. Section II.4.3 introduces the experimental design and procedures. The results are presented in Section II.4.4, which is followed by discussion and conclusions in Section II.4.5.

II.4.2 Partnership Structure, Dissolution Mechanisms and Efficiency

In a symmetric framework with symmetric partners[53] two risk-neutral agents possess a partnership in equal shares. The valuation for the partnership depends on an agent's own and his partner's private signal. An agent's valuation for the entire partnership is an additive function $v_i(s_i, s_j) = s_i + \alpha s_j$ where s_i denotes the private signal of agent i and s_j his partner's private signal. The private signals of the agents are stochastically independent and drawn from the same commonly known uniform distribution function $s_i \in (0,...,100)$. The parameter α measures the degree of interdependence. Note that this kind of interdependent valuation function also covers the two extreme cases of independent private values ($\alpha = 0$) as well as common values ($\alpha = 1$) for two agents.

The rules of the two mechanisms are the same as in Section II.3. In the WBA each partner simultaneously submits a sealed bid b_i, $i=1, 2$. The partner with the higher bid buys his partner's share of the object (thus receiving the whole object) and pays a price of $p = \frac{1}{2}b_w$ to his losing partner. In the CCM the proposing partner offers a proposal P for the whole partnership. The choosing partner can then decide to either buy his partner's share of the firm at a price of $p = \frac{P}{2}$ or sell his share at a price of $p = \frac{P}{2}$. Bids and proposals are divided by 2 as a partner pays/gets half of the price for the whole object for his half of the object

---

[53] This means that partners are ex-ante indistinguishable.

he buys/sells (50% share). Again in both dissolution mechanisms the utility of the buying partner is given by $u_B = u_B(v_B - p)$ where $B \in \{1,2\}$ denotes the identity of the buyer. A seller's utility is given by $u_S = u_S(p)$ where $S \in \{1,2\}$ denotes the identity of the seller.

We are interested in the ex-post efficiency of the two mechanisms starting with the WBA. Kittsteiner (2003) derives for two risk-neutral partners the equilibrium bid function which is increasing in an agent's own private signal.[54] As long as the single crossing condition is fulfilled – that is keeping all other signals fixed v_i as a function of s_i is steeper than v_j (they cross at most once) – the own private signal has more influence on the value for the entire object than the partner's private signal: $\frac{\partial v_i}{\partial s_i} \geq \frac{\partial v_j}{\partial s_i}$. Thus, ex-post values of different bidders are ordered in the same way as their private signals. This leads to ex-post efficient allocations. As mentioned in Section II.2 the WBA leads to efficient dissolution if participation is forced which is the case in our experiment.

In contrast, as we discuss in the following, there does not exist a certain strategy in the CCM which guarantees efficient dissolution in the interdependent valuations case. In the CCM it is not sufficient for ex-post efficiency that P is increasing in the proposer's private signal as the CCM is a sequential game and asymmetric in its structure.[55] The farther away the proposal is from the proposer's 'true' valuation, the higher the probability is that inefficient allocations result. The only proposal which always leads to an efficient dissolution if both partners know their true valuation is proposing $P=v_p$.[56] Throughout the independent private values case this strategy is feasible. However, if valuations are interdependent proposers only know their private signals, but not their 'true' valuation for the partnership. Proposing the own private signal $P=s_p$, which is observable, does not guarantee efficiency either. For

---

[54] See Theorem 1 in Kittsteiner (2003).
[55] In the CCM first the proposer takes his decision which the chooser observes before he acts. This makes the design asymmetric. The simultaneous game in the WBA provides a symmetric structure, because both agents face the same strategy space.
[56] The intuition behind this is straightforward and most easily explained on the basis of the independent private values case: A proposer with a low valuation has a higher probability of being seller which provides incentives to increase the price, and vice versa a proposer with a high valuation has a higher probability of being buyer which provides incentives to decrease the price (assuming risk neutrality). This kind of proposal setting results in inefficiencies if a chooser's valuation lies in between the proposer's valuation and the proposal. However, the more risk averse a proposer becomes, the closer he sets his proposal to his valuation which gradually reduces the scope of allocative inefficiencies. In conclusion setting $P=v_p$, which is in line with the extremely risk-averse Nash equilibrium, always results in efficient dissolution. Thus, inefficiencies can be always prevented if the proposal equals the proposer's valuation and both partners know their valuations (see Mathematical Appendix Proposition II.A3).

certain parameter constellations inefficiencies might even occur under the very strong assumption that the chooser knows this strategy and thus could infer his own 'true' valuation.[57] If this assumption is relaxed inefficiencies occur even more often.

Moreover, the interdependent setting additionally gives rise to 'mistakes' of choosers as they face uncertainty with regards to their 'true' valuation as well. Accordingly, the chooser's decision also becomes more complex due to the interdependent valuations structure. With independent private values a chooser's decision is simple: it is payoff maximizing to buy the object if $v_c>P$, otherwise the own share should be sold regardless of a chooser's risk attitudes. Not knowing the 'true' valuation causes additional scope for inefficiencies at the second stage of the game where the chooser decides between buying and selling. Thus, even if the proposer happens to set P equal to his 'true' valuation of the entire partnership, ex-post efficiency is not guaranteed as the chooser neither knows his own true valuation nor consequently his payoff-maximizing strategy (i.e., a chooser can no longer assure to always buy (sell) if it is payoff maximizing to buy (sell)). Hence, efficient allocations are only assured for all possible parameter values in the CCM if the proposer's price equals his 'true' valuation, that is if $P=v_p$, and if the chooser also knows his own valuation. Both partners not knowing their 'true' value implies that there does not exist any strategy guaranteeing an ex-post efficient allocation with interdependent values in the CCM.

Thus, if partners are forced to participate and if we assume risk neutrality, the WBA is theoretically ex-post efficient, whereas the CCM is supposed to result in more inefficient allocations. However, these considerations apply to a risk-neutral, i.e., a homogeneous setup. As has been shown in Section II.3 heterogeneity of agents' bidding behavior can lead to a reverse ranking of the dissolution mechanisms in terms of ex-post efficiency. In the independent private values case heterogeneity enhances inefficiencies in the WBA but might reduce inefficiencies in the CCM.[58] If subjects adhere to different bidding strategies

---

[57] Under the assumption that the chooser anticipates the proposer's strategy to always set $P=s_p$, allocations are inefficient as long as $s_p > s_c > (1-\alpha)s_p$ (see Mathematical Appendix Proposition II.A4).

[58] As we have seen in Section II.3, in the independent private values case the assumption of heterogeneous types of partners gives rise to inefficiencies in the WBA contrary to the assumption of risk-neutral or equally risk-averse partners. However, in the CCM heterogeneous types in terms of proposers setting prices closer to their valuation (due to e.g. risk aversion) leads to less inefficiencies than under risk-neutral types.

there does not exist a clear ranking of the mechanisms if the valuation structure is characterized by independent private values.

The interdependent valuations setting might trigger heterogeneous bidding behavior in so far as subjects do not know their true valuation, i.e., it might be more difficult for them to follow a certain strategy. Note that the theoretically predicted ex-post efficiency in the WBA is driven by the fact that both bidders are bidding according to the *same* bidding strategy if they are risk neutral. Consequentially, heterogeneous bidding behavior gives rise to inefficiencies in the WBA with interdependent valuations as well. As the data presented in Section II.3 provide more evidence for heterogeneous than for homogeneous bidding behavior even in the independent private values case, this seems to be quite a realistic assumption also for the more complex interdependent valuations setting.

In the CCM inefficiencies should occur more often with interdependent valuations than in the independent private values case as subjects are not informed about their true valuations implying that the strategy $P=v_p$ is no longer available. Contrary to the independent private values case in the interdependent setting not only proposals are pivotal for an efficient allocation in the CCM, but now additionally choosers cannot simply make their payoff-maximizing decision, which might hinder efficient dissolution as well. Thus, we suppose both mechanisms being less efficient in the interdependent setting.

II.4.3 Experimental Design and Procedures

The computerized experiment was conducted at the Cologne Laboratory for Economic Research in January 2008 using the programming software z-tree (Fischbacher (2007)). Subjects were undergraduate students at the University of Cologne mostly belonging to the faculty of economics and business administration and they were recruited with ORSEE (Greiner (2004)).

The design is based on the former experiment in Section II.3. We run three sessions – twice the CCM and once the WBA[59] – each with 32 subjects using a stranger matching with 8 matching groups consisting of 4 subjects. In each treatment a single indivisible object has to be allocated among two partners. The valuation for the entire object for an agent i $i,j \in (1,2)$, $i \neq j$ is composed of

---

[59] The CCM is run twice and the WBA only once to get an equal number of observations concerning proposals and bids. In the CCM only one partner – the proposer – sets a proposal whereas in the WBA both partners submit their bids.

$v_i(s_i, s_j) = s_i + \frac{1}{2}s_j$. Thus, we test in our experiment an intermediate degree of interdependence of $\alpha = \frac{1}{2}$. The private signals of the agents are stochastically independent and drawn from the same commonly known uniform distribution function $s_i \in (0,...,100)$ with two decimal spaces. To run the experiment as similar as possible compared to Section II.3, we reuse the valuations drawn in our independent private values experiment as private signals and our matching of partners throughout the interdependent valuations experiment.[60] Note that the interdependent valuations structure leads to true valuations of partners lying closer together than in the IPV: As partners' private signals in INT equal partners' valuations in IPV, the distance of partners' signals (in INT) and the distance of valuations (in IPV) are exactly the same. Thus, the distance of 'given information' for each partnership is the same, but the distance of partners' actually true valuations for the object differs – the distance of true valuations in the INT experiment is half of the distance of valuations in the IPV experiment.[61]

Each session consists of 30 rounds and a short questionnaire. The CCM sessions last about one and a half hours, the WBA about one hour. Subjects receive in session 1 (CCM) average earnings of 15.29 € (with a minimum of 7.90 € and a maximum of 21.10 €), in session 2 (WBA) average earnings amount to 15.37 € (with a minimum of 11.30 € and a maximum of 18.30 €) and in session 3 (CCM) (with a minimum of 9.70 € and a maximum of 20.00 €) subjects earn on average 15.17 € (including a show-up fee of 2.50 €).

The procedure is as follows: In the CCM subjects are randomly assigned their role (proposer or chooser) with equal probability before the experiment starts. They keep their role during the whole experiment in order to conduct the two treatments WBA and CCM as parallel as possible. Table II.6 shows the procedure which is repeated in each of the 30 rounds.[62] In both treatments bids (proposals respectively) are restricted to 300 to avoid obvious type errors.

After the experiment subjects receive a short questionnaire. The first question of the questionnaire is formulated very generally. Each subject is asked which criteria he followed while making his decision. The second question is

---

[60] In the following we use IPV as an abbreviation for independent private values and INT for interdependent valuations.

[61] Given $v_i(IPV)=s_i(INT)$ in the IPV partners' absolute distance of true valuations is equal to $|s_i - s_j|$, whereas in the INT case the distance amounts to $|s_i + \frac{1}{2}s_j - s_j - \frac{1}{2}s_i| = \frac{1}{2}|s_i - s_j|$. Certainly, this has an influence on the measurement of efficiency. In the efficiency analysis in Section II.4.4.1 we control for this distance effect.

[62] Instructions are given in the Appendix.

Table II.6: Procedure in each round

	CCM	WBA
Signals	Signal $s_i \in (0,...,100)$ is drawn for each subject	Signal $s_i \in (0,...,100)$ is drawn for each subject
Prices/bids	*Proposer*: offers a price P	Both partners submit their bids b simultaneously
Allocation	*Chooser*: decides whether to buy or to sell at $p = P/2$	Higher bidder receives the object and pays half of his winning bid to the loser $p = b_w/2$
Payoffs	*Buyer*: $\pi_b = s_b + \alpha s_s - P/2$ *Seller*: $\pi_s = P/2$	*Winner*: $\pi_b = s_w + \alpha s_l - b_w/2$ *Loser*: $\pi_s = b_w/2$

The indices denote the following: buyer (*b*), seller (*s*), winning bidder (*w*) and losing bidder (*l*).

more concrete: subjects are asked which role their own signal and the unknown signal of their partner played (for their decision). Subjects do not get the second question before they answered the first one. The questionnaire after the experiment should help to categorize individual behavior[63] and to learn more about the actual decision-making process in such complex environments: Presumably subjects do not adhere to a certain optimized strategy, but rather behave according to rules of thumb and more simple heuristics.

II.4.4 Experimental Results

In the following section we discuss our experimental findings concerning allocative efficiency and fairness in terms of ex-ante equal payoff expectations. We focus especially on the robustness of these results, i.e., we investigate how sensitive these results are to the more complex setting.

II.4.4.1 Efficiency

Efficiency in the INT Setting

In this subsection we consider the efficiency of the mechanisms. To compare the allocative efficiency of the two mechanisms we use the percentage of efficient allocations (which gives the frequency of overall efficiency of the different

---

[63] For instance, the questionnaire might help to discover whether subjects' decisions are influenced both by their own private signal and an expected value of the partner's signal or just their own private signal.

treatments) as well as an efficiency rate (which measures the degree of inefficiency) over all partnerships. The efficiency rate is defined as $\frac{v_i(buyer)}{\max\{v_1, v_2\}}$. First of all, Table II.7 shows that both mechanisms perform quite well – even in the more complex setting. Although subjects do not know their true valuation for the object, they achieve efficient allocations at least in three quarters of the cases. Moreover, the degree of inefficiency is quite low as the efficiency rate amounts to over 96 percent. Table II.7 suggests that the WBA performs better in terms of total occurrence of efficient allocations (percentage) as well as in terms of the efficiency rate (smaller degree of inefficiency). However, using matching group averages[64] as independent observations a two-tailed Mann-Whitney-U test reveals only significant differences between the treatments for the efficiency rate ($p=0.011$),[65] but not for percentage of efficient allocations ($p=0.13$). Remarkably, as soon as the 'safe' strategy[66] $P=v$ falls apart with interdependent valuations, the CCM is no longer the more efficient mechanism. In Section II.3 we have shown

Table II.7: Mean efficiency INT and IPV

Mean	Percentage of efficient allocations	Efficiency rate
CCM_INT (N=960)	75.63%	96.43%
1st half of rounds	72.50%	95.93%
2nd half of rounds	78.75%	96.93%
WBA_INT (N=480)	80.21%	98.01%
1st half of rounds	72.08%	96.86%
2nd half of rounds	88.33%	99.16%
CCM_IPV (N=960)	89.69%	97.29%
WBA_IPV (N=480)	85.21%	96.43%

Note that percentage of efficient allocations and efficiency rate for the first (round 1 to 15) and the second half (round 16 to 30) of rounds is given separately.

---

[64] In the CCM (WBA) we have 16 (8) matching groups as two sessions (one session) are (is) run.

[65] As a higher efficiency rate might be simply driven by a higher percentage of efficient allocations we also calculate the efficiency rates considering only inefficient allocations (thereby measuring the degree of welfare loss in case inefficiency has already occurred). The efficiency rates concentrating solely on the inefficient allocations amount to 85.35% in the CCM and 89.97% in the WBA, which also differ significantly (two-tailed Mann-Whitney-U test $p=0.013$). Thus, the order of the efficiency rates between the treatments is robust.

[66] This strategy is a 'safe' strategy in the CCM in so far as the proposer knows his payoff for sure at the time of his proposal and there is no risk or uncertainty dependent on the chooser's decision. As discussed in Section II.4.1, this strategy guarantees non-negative net-payoffs (independent of whether he sells or buys in the CCM the proposer gains exactly half of his valuation, whereas in the WBA an agent obtains at least half of his valuation).

that the good experimental performance of the CCM with IPV is due to a high percentage of proposals set closer and especially equal to the true valuation.

Efficiency in the IPV and INT Setting – a Robustness Check

Table II.7 also depicts the efficiency results of Section II.3 in the IPV case for the two mechanisms. The total occurrence of efficient allocations is higher for both mechanisms in the IPV case. Comparing the mechanisms with regard to the different assumptions about valuation structures yields for the CCM treatments (CCM_INT vs. CCM_IPV) significant differences both between percentage of efficient allocations as well as between efficiency rates (percentage of efficient allocations $p<0.001$; efficiency rate $p=0.067$, two-tailed Mann-Whitney-U tests for matching groups). However, in the WBA treatments (WBA_IPV vs. WBA_INT) we find no significant difference for the percentage of efficient allocations, but rather significantly higher efficiency rates in INT than in IPV at the 10% significance level ($p=0.065$).

Note that the mean signal in the INT setting equals the mean valuation in the IPV setting as the experiment was designed in such a way that partners' private signals equal partners' benchmark valuations under independent private values in Section II.3. Therefore, as was already mentioned in Section II.4.3, the distance of partners' valuations for the partnership differs between IPV and INT (distance of true valuations is half the size with interdependent valuations than in the IPV benchmark case). This has no effect on the percentage of efficient allocations (the percentage remains the same, because the partner with the higher valuation is also the partner with the higher signal), but it affects the efficiency rate. To disentangle the information asymmetries effect from a simple distance effect the efficiency rate is calculated depending solely on partners' private signals and not on their true valuations (i.e., we use $\frac{s_i(buyer)}{\max\{s_1,s_2\}}$). This leads to efficiency rates measured by partners' private signals of 91.32% in the CCM_INT and of 94.88% in the WBA_INT. In the CCM a two-tailed Mann-Whitney-U test reveals efficiency rates being significantly smaller in the INT case than in the benchmark case IPV ($p<0.001$). However, in the WBA a two-tailed Mann-Whitney-U test yields no significant difference in efficiency rates between the two different valuation settings. Thus, under information asymmetries the CCM performs significantly worse than in the simple IPV case, whereas there is no evidence that the WBA becomes less efficient. The WBA seems to be more 'robust' concerning different settings.[67] Moreover, subjects with no experience seem to intuitively perform better in the WBA. In the first round the auction performs better than the CCM (percentage of efficient allocations: WBA=68.75% vs. CCM =53.13%; efficiency rate: WBA=93.30% vs. CCM=92.86%). This result holds also for the IPV case.

Which Factors Drive Efficiency? A First Approach

In the following we consider which parameters have an influence on the efficient dissolution of partnerships in each specific treatment. In panel probit regressions the binary variable 'efficient allocation' is regressed on a number of independent variables: dummy variables for each treatment (WBA and CCM), the round number (1-30) and the absolute value of the distance of partners' private signals ($|s_i - s_j|$). Moreover, we create dummy variables for both partners' private signals being below the median (both $s_i < 50$ and $s_j < 50$), for both partners' private signals being above the median (both $s_i > 50$ and $s_j > 50$), and for one partner's signal being below and one partner's signal being above ($s_i < 50$ and $s_j > 50$) as the base category.

It was already shown in the IPV setting that both partners' valuations being above the median valuation has a highly significant negative impact on the probability of efficient allocations in the CCM (for a discussion of this result and of the proposal setting behavior compare Section II.3). We test whether the fact that both partners receive signals below or above the median signal respectively has also an effect on allocative efficiency in the INT case. In the CCM a subject with a higher probability of becoming seller (buyer) has an incentive to increase (decrease) the price which results in inefficiencies if the chooser's valuation lies between the proposal and the proposer's valuation. Note however, that in the WBA there should be no effect of these dummies as risk-neutral equilibrium bids are increasing in own signals.

Likewise, the panel probit regression[68] (see Table II.8) indeed shows very similar results as in the IPV case. If both partners' private signals are above the median signal, this has a strong and significant negative impact on the probability of allocative efficiency in the CCM treatment also with interdependent

---

[67] Note that in the WBA there are only 5% less efficient allocations in the INT than in the IPV case whereas the CCM loses about 15%.

[68] This panel probit regression measures the effects of the tested parameters in each treatment (i.e., whether a parameter has an influence on the probability of efficient allocation for each mechanism *separately*). For a comparison of effects between the two treatments (i.e., whether a parameter has a stronger influence in one treatment than in the other) see Table II.A2 in the Appendix.

Table II.8: Panel probit regression INT

Efficient allocation	(1) Coefficient	(Std. Errors)	(2) Coefficient	(Std. Errors)
WBA	-0.4488733	(0.2830119)	-0.3824843	(0.351134)
CCM	0.0972714	(0.1668465)	0.0938984	(0.1699159)
Round*WBA	0.042757***	(0.0088485)	0.0430538***	(0.0089585)
Round*CCM	0.0179002***	(0.0054029)	0.0178872***	(0.0054097)
Dist*WBA	0.032973***	(0.0057659)	0.0309781***	(0.0080781)
Dist*CCM	0.0163097***	(0.003075)	0.016321***	(0.0030751)
Below*WBA	-0.0269552	(0.2343723)	-0.5103718	(0.4018579)
Below*CCM	-0.191487	(0.1473251)	-0.1903355	(0.1473726)
Above*WBA	-0.3284576	(0.2123328)	-0.1953723	(0.3750335)
Above*CCM	-0.3586391***	(0.1373193)	-0.3583654***	(0.1375611)
Dist*below*WBA			0.0338569*	(0.0181242)
Dist*below*CCM			0.0016571	(0.0053253)
Dist*above*WBA			-0.0104572	(0.0127172)
Dist*above*CCM			-0.0006483	(0.0046182)
N	1440		1440	
$\chi^2(dF)$	170.79(9)		173.67(13)	

Standard errors are given in parentheses. *** denotes significance on the 1%-level, ** denotes significance on the 5%-level, * denotes significance on the 10%-level. Matching groups (N=24) are used as group variable. As we drop the constant in the estimated models, the reported $\chi^2(dF)$ is taken over from the (analogous) model with a constant (as presented in Table II.A2).

valuations. However, both partners' signals being below the median signal has no significant effect.[69] Moreover, the positive coefficients for absolute value of distance of the partners' signals are again highly significant in both treatments: The farther away signals of partners are located from each other, the higher the probability is of achieving efficient dissolution. Table II.A2 in the Appendix

---

[69] In the WBA both partners' signals being below or above the median signal has no significant influence. As both partners' signals being located on the same side of the median might imply smaller distances of their signals we control for possible interaction effects (e.g. dist*below) in the second estimated model. Note that the Wald statistic for the variables below*WBA and dist*below*WBA of the estimated model (2) shows that these variables are jointly insignificant (p=0.1716) indicating that there is no significant total effect of both partners' signals being below the median signal in the WBA.

(allowing for comparisons of the effects of certain parameters *between* the two treatments as the treatment dummy CCM is dropped) shows that the positive effect of partners' distance of signals on the probability of efficient allocation is even significantly stronger in the WBA than in the CCM just as in the IPV setting.

In both treatments the coefficient for round is positive and highly significant, which indicates that learning plays a role. This is in contrast to the IPV experiment in which the round effect has a positive significant influence solely in the CCM. Efficiency over rounds is given in Figure II.2 which also depicts that the percentage of efficient allocations increases over time. Comparing the efficiency of the two mechanisms in the first half of rounds vs. the second half of rounds shows that both average percentage of efficiency as well as the efficiency rate increase in both treatments (see Table II.7). These results are highly significant in the WBA (one-tailed Wilcoxon Signed Rank test using matching group averages of the first half of rounds vs. second half of rounds yields $p=0.004$ for percentage of efficient allocations as well as for the efficiency rates). In the CCM one-tailed Wilcoxon Signed Rank test results in $p=0.027$ for percentage of efficient allocations, whereas the efficiency rates between first half of rounds and second half of rounds differ only weakly at the 10% significance level ($p=0.08$). Concerning the occurrence of efficient allocations learning seems to have an important influence on both mechanisms, however, learning effects in general seem to be stronger in the WBA than in the CCM (compare Figure II.2). The panel probit regression in Table II.A2 in the Appendix also yields a significantly stronger influence of round effects on the probability of efficient allocations in the WBA than in the CCM. Note also that

Figure II.2: Mean efficiency per round

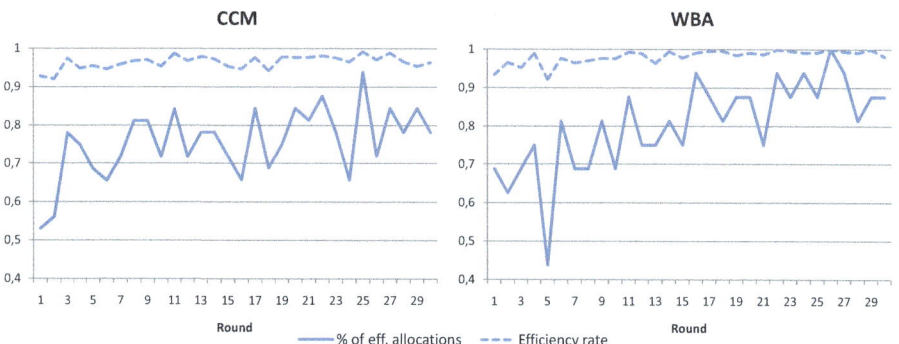

the percentage of efficient allocations is nearly the same in both mechanisms in the first half of rounds, but it is 10% higher in the WBA in the second half of rounds (see Table II.7).

II.4.4.2 Payoffs

This subsection first investigates the payoffs of the subjects dependent on the chosen mechanism. Second, it is asked whether dissolving the partnership provides gains from trade, i.e., whether subjects are better off after dissolution compared to their status quo, namely their share of the object. Specifically, we consider 'fairness' aspects of outcomes in both analyses by investigating whether particular subjects (depending e.g. on their role in a mechanism) are ex-ante systematically worse off than others.

Payoffs

In the following payoffs between the two mechanisms are compared as well as payoffs between the two roles in the CCM. Table II.9 presents the payoffs and the relative payoffs for all cases.

Table II.9: Mean payoffs INT

Mean	N	Payoff	Relative Payoff
CCM_INT			
All	1920	42.24	53.69%
Proposer	960	32.24	40.90%
Chooser	960	52.25	66.53%
WBA_INT	960	42.72	54.25%

Relative payoffs are given by mean payoff divided by mean true valuation.

Two-tailed Mann-Whitney-U tests using matching group averages show that in general payoffs obtained in the CCM and in the WBA do not differ significantly (p=0.383), but payoffs of proposers as well as payoffs of choosers in the CCM differ highly significantly from payoffs in the WBA (both p<0.001). Hence, just as in the IPV case the choosing partner in the CCM is still better off than an agent in the auction who is better off than the proposing partner in the CCM. Thus, ex ante proposers and choosers have different payoff expectations. Note that relative payoffs are smaller under INT than under IPV: Whereas subjects achieve on average about 54% relative payoffs in INT, relative payoffs for all subjects amount to about 64% in the IPV case. The relative payoffs of proposers and choosers are also about 10% higher in the IPV case (Table II.3 indicates the payoffs and relative payoffs for the IPV case). Strikingly, the relative standing of the proposer under INT does not change compared to the IPV case – in the IPV case a proposer's average payoff is 63.82% of a chooser's average payoff; similarly, in the INT case a proposer's average payoff amounts to 61.70% of that of a chooser. Figure II.3 visualizes payoffs over rounds distinguished between proposer (solid line) and chooser (dotted line) showing the ample differences between their payoffs.

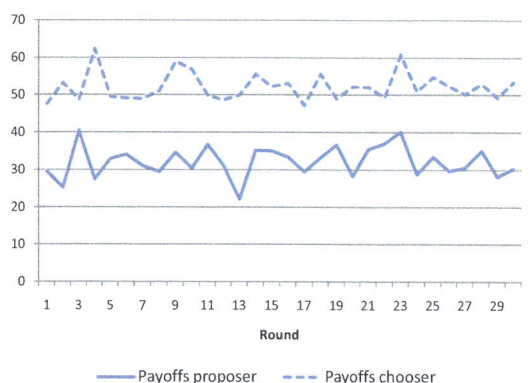

Figure II.3: Mean payoffs per round – proposer and chooser

Gains from Trade

In the following, we consider subjects' gains from trade to investigate whether dissolution of the partnership makes them better off than before dissolution. Gains from trade are measured by net-payoffs which consist of the subjects' payoffs after dissolution subtracted by their initial endowment (i.e., their share of the object which equals half of their true valuation for the object). Thus, gains from trade provide a measure for voluntary participation if subjects have the choice. Note that in our experiment participation is forced. Nevertheless, it is essential to understand if subjects suffer from losses and having the choice would reject participation, and which particular subjects systematically incur losses (i.e., whether negative net-payoffs are typical of a specific role or of a specific range of signals).

Table II.10a depicts average net-payoffs of all subjects. Table II.10a shows that on average subjects realize positive gains from trade in the CCM_INT as well as in the WBA_INT. However, proposers' average net-payoffs are negative. Proposers do not only achieve significantly lower payoffs than agents in the WBA and than choosers, but moreover participation in the dissolution makes them worse off than before (their 'endowment' before dissolution is higher than their payoff after dissolution).[70] Proposers would therefore not agree to participate voluntarily as trade on average generates losses compared to the situation before dissolution.

In contrast, we observe positive average net-payoffs for all subjects regardless of their role in the IPV case (even proposers' average net-payoff is non-negative). The finding of positive net-payoffs is in line with Kittsteiner (2003) who highlights that under IPV assumptions there always exists a certain strategy ensuring non-negative net-payoffs (i.e., an agent earns at least the amount which his share of the object is worth). Subjects can always set $b=v$ ($P=v$, respectively), because subjects know their true valuation. This holds no longer for interdependent valuations: If no partner knows the true value there is no secure strategy that prevents subjects from losses.

Note that if agents have independent private values for the partnership, gains from trade do not differ between the treatments (a two-tailed Mann-Whitney-U test taking average net-payoffs per matching group yields $p=0.350$). However, if information asymmetries are on hand, this results in a better performance of the WBA at the 10% significance level: We observe significantly higher gains from trade in the WBA than in the CCM if agents' valuations are interdependent ($p=0.070$).

We now examine the question if the IPV benchmark provides higher gains from trade than the INT setting. More precisely, we investigate for each mechanism separately whether information asymmetries destroy gains from trade and decrease subjects' net-payoffs. Given the parameter values and the fact that s_i in INT was chosen equal to v_i in IPV, expected gains from trade should be twice as high in IPV as in INT (see Mathematical Appendix Proposition II.A5). Thus, for a comparison of gains from trade between INT and IPV each data point of the INT case is multiplied by 2.[71] A two-tailed Mann-Whitney-U test taking matching group averages reveals no significant differences in the WBA (scaled data WBA_INT with an average net-payoff of 6.70 and WBA_IPV with an

---

[70] A net-payoff comparison of chooser vs. agent in the auction and of agent in the auction vs. proposer yields highly significant differences for all pair-wise comparisons in both the INT as well as in the IPV case ($p<0.001$; two-tailed Mann-Whitney-U tests). Therefore results for the relative standing are very robust. Not only do proposers earn lower payoffs but they are also worse off compared to their status quo than all other subjects.

[71] Note that this proceeding corresponds to measuring payoffs and net-payoffs with INT solely by signals instead of valuations (i.e., a buyer i's net-payoff consists of $\frac{1}{2}s_i-p$ and a seller j's payoff of $p-\frac{1}{2}s_j$, whereby $p=b_w/2$ and $p=P/2$ respectively).

average net-payoff of 7.23 do not differ significantly $p=0.328$). However, in the CCM settings differ significantly (a two-tailed Mann-Whitney-U test comparing scaled data CCM_INT (mean net-payoff of 5.80) vs. CCM_IPV (mean net-payoff of 7.68) yields $p<0.001$). Hence, if information asymmetries are assumed, gains from trade do not change significantly in the WBA, whereas in the CCM gains from trade decrease substantially. This result provides further evidence for the robustness of the WBA between settings characterized by different valuation structures.

Table II.10a: Gains from trade

Mean net-payoffs	N	INT	IPV
CCM			
All	1920	2.90	7.68
Proposer	960	-7.17	0.05
Chooser	960	12.98	15.31
WBA	960	3.35	7.23

Table II.10b: Gains from trade – Intermediate types

Mean net-payoffs	N	Intermediate types	N	All other types
CCM_INT				
All	372	-0.58	1548	3.74
Proposer	177	-9.11	783	-6.74
Chooser	195	7.15	765	14.46
WBA_INT	183	-0.74	777	4.31

Intermediate types: $40<s_i<60$, $\forall i \in \{1,2\}$

Gains from Trade – Intermediate Types

Kittsteiner (2003) alludes to the problem that intermediate types might not want to participate in an auction to dissolve the partnership. Uncertainty about how to bid (respectively propose) is highest for those intermediate types as the effect of both winner's and loser's curse is strongest which might result in negative net-payoffs.

Table II.10b indicates that intermediate types are indeed worse off, whereby intermediate types are classified as subjects with private signals between 40 and 60.[72] A one-tailed Wilcoxon Signed Rank test using matching groups reveals significant differences in the WBA as well as in the CCM between intermediate types and all other types at the 1% significance level.

---

[72] This range is chosen arbitrarily. However, taking for instance a range between 45 and 55 does not change results substantially.

As a robustness check we split the category 'all other types' and control for 'low types' with signals between 0 and 40 and 'high types' between 60 and 100 separately (mean net-payoffs for each of the three ranges are given in Table II.A3 in the Appendix). Note that, on average, in both mechanisms intermediate types are again the only ones that get negative gains from trade, both other ranges yield positive gains. Pair-wise one-tailed Wilcoxon Signed Rank tests using matching groups yield in the WBA only weakly significant differences between low and high signal types at the 10% significance level, but significant differences between low signal and intermediate types ($p=0.012$) as well as between intermediate and high signal types ($p=0.004$). Thus, intermediate types in the WBA are significantly worse off than low as well as high signal types (and high types are the best-off types). Similar results are provided in the CCM where intermediate types' net-payoffs are also lower than those of other types: We observe highly significant differences between intermediate types and high signal types and between low signal and high signal types at the 1% significance level, but only weakly significant difference between intermediate and low signal types ($p=0.08$).[73]

That intermediate types are worse off than low and high types is also shown by the fact that 62.5% (54.69%) of subjects in the WBA (in the CCM) always achieve higher mean net-payoffs both in the low as well as in the high range than in the intermediate one. For this comparison we calculate for *each* subject his mean net-payoff separately for each of the three ranges: low types (0-40), intermediate types (40-60) and high types (60-100).

Our data reveal that intermediate types indeed realize much smaller gains from trade. In the WBA as well as in the CCM (all subjects) mean net-payoffs become even negative for intermediate types. Choosers are the only subjects with intermediate types still having positive net-payoffs – all other subjects expect to incur losses. Thus, all subjects (except for choosers) with intermediate types

---

[73] However, note that the data in the above analyses are not completely independent, because the composition of groups changes. For further illustration we run Wilcoxon Signed Rank tests with observations on the subject level although these are not independent either: A two-tailed Wilcoxon Signed Rank test taking each subject as an observation yields for the WBA that intermediate types differ significantly both from high as well as from low types ($p<0.001$), whereas low and high types do not differ significantly ($p=0.270$). In the CCM all types differ highly at the 1% significance level: High types obtain higher net-payoffs than low types, who get higher net-payoffs than intermediate types. Taking only proposers in the CCM a two-tailed Wilcoxon Signed Rank test yields significantly smaller net-payoffs if signals are in the intermediate range than if signals are either low or high ($p=0.019$). The low and high types' net-payoffs do not differ significantly ($p=0.512$). This is also in line with our results above.

would be reluctant to participate if they had the choice. These results indicate a possible effect of winner's and loser's curses.[74]

We further analyze whether these adverse selection effects diminish over time. There exists experimental evidence that the winner's curse in standard common value auctions is sensitive to experience (see e.g. Kagel and Richard (2001), Kagel and Levin (1986, 1999), or Kagel et al. (1989) who state that bidders perform better in later rounds or after a series of auctions). Studies with other valuation settings and auction formats provide similar results, see e.g. Goeree and Offermann (2002) who find that experienced bidders with values depending on private and common value information perform better and Dyer et al. (1989) who conclude that winner's curse is likely to be strongest in the start-up phase of a market comparing naïve bidders and experienced business executives in common value offer auctions. Thus, we test experience effects by investigating whether in the last half of rounds winner's and loser's curses decrease. Surprisingly, intermediate types do no achieve significantly different net-payoffs in either treatment in the second half of rounds (two-tailed Wilcoxon Signed Rank test $p>0.1$). This indicates that learning does not diminish adverse selection effects considerably for intermediate types (for whom adverse selection effects should be strongest). In the CCM proposers' average net-payoffs are given by -9.28 (1st half of rounds) and -8.92 (2nd half of rounds), in the WBA average net-payoffs amount to 0.35 (1st half of rounds) and -1.80 (2nd half of rounds).[75] See also Figure II.A2 in the Appendix, which depicts net-payoffs over rounds.

All in all, the above analyses have shown that a subject would prefer being chooser in the CCM to being a participant in the auction both in terms of total payoffs as well as in terms of gains from trade. Moreover, choosers are the only subjects who would never refuse participation regardless of their type (i.e., the size of their signal) as they always achieve positive net-payoffs on average. In stark contrast, mean net-payoffs of proposers are always negative regardless of

---

[74] To test whether this result is really driven by information asymmetries and therefore due to winner's and loser's curses we check if subjects with intermediate valuations in the IPV experiment incur also losses compared to their status quo. Isolating intermediate types (agents with a valuation between 40 and 60) in the IPV setting without information asymmetries shows a lower average gain from trade for these types (WBA_IPV: 4.49 vs. 7.87; CCM_IPV: 5.44 vs. 8.22), but the gains from trade do not become negative as under information asymmetries (INT).

[75] Results are less clear-cut if we take not only intermediate types but all types of signals. In the CCM proposers' net-payoffs still become less negative (-7.75 (1st half of rounds); -6.60 (2nd half of rounds)), but do not differ significantly either, whereas in the WBA experience increases net-payoffs significantly (2.76; 3.94) (two-tailed Wilcoxon Signed Rank test for matching groups, $p<0.01$). See also Figure II.A1.

their type (see Table II.A3 in the Appendix), thus they would prefer not to participate in dissolution.[76] Clearly, intermediate types are worse off and neither proposers in the CCM nor subjects in the WBA of this type would voluntarily participate.

II.4.4.3 Individual Behavior

As we do not have a theoretical benchmark of equilibrium behavior to test, this subsection summarizes individual behavior providing some explorative and descriptive insights in 1) how subjects actually bid and propose and 2) after observing the proposal, whether choosers decide for selling or buying depending on their private signal.

Behavioral Patterns of Proposers and Bidders

Signals and corresponding proposals (bids) are depicted in the scatter plots given in Figure II.4. The scatter plots indicate a higher variation in proposals in the CCM_INT than in the WBA_INT. Obviously, in the WBA subjects bid closer to their private signal.[77]

Figure II.4: Scatter plots – Private signals and bids/proposals

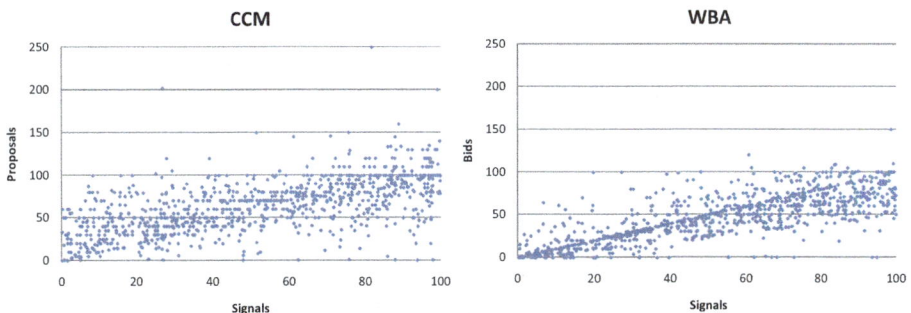

One extreme data point in the CCM ($P=300$, $s=64.23$) is omitted.

---

[76] Note that in our experiment the role of being proposer or chooser is randomly drawn. The above results, however, imply that agents will be reluctant to propose a price in a partnership if roles are not given exogenously. Thus, the CCM gives rise to management deadlocks.

[77] This observation is sustained by both the given scatter plots as well as a simple linear OLS regression with robust standard errors. Bid function and proposal function are estimated by $b_i = \alpha + \beta s_i$ and by $P_i = \alpha + \beta s_i$ respectively. The OLS regression estimates in the CCM a constant of 30.41 and a coefficient of 0.65, whereas in the WBA the constant amounts to 6.48 and the coefficient is 0.77. All coefficients are highly significant ($p<0.001$). Moreover, deviation from the private signal is measured by $\sum_{i=1}^{n}\frac{1}{n}(b_i - s_i)^2, n = 960$. Deviation from the signal in CCM amounts to 909.88, in the WBA deviation is given by only 391.37.

In the IPV setting of Section II.3 we find that a substantial fraction of proposals (bids respectively) is set equal to the own observable valuation.[78] However, this behavior differs across treatments: In the CCM_IPV this fraction amounts to 30.10% whereas in the WBA_IPV only 11.56% of bids equal the valuations. Surprisingly, we observe the reverse effect under information asymmetry: only 8.02% of proposals in the CCM_INT are set equal to the observable private signal of the subjects (rounded up to at most +/-1), but 21.15% of bids in the WBA_INT are set equal to the private signal.[79] A possible explanation might be that due to the interdependent valuation structure proposers in the CCM are reluctant to 'signal' their true type by setting $P=s$.

However, choosing $P=s$ ($b=s$) in the INT case reduces uncertainty about future payoffs: This strategy ensures a certain minimum payoff of $\frac{s_p}{2}$ which implies that following this strategy no loss (i.e., negative payoff) is possible.[80] Setting $P=s_p$ in the CCM_INT guarantees the proposer a payoff of exactly $\pi_p = \frac{s_p}{2}$ if the chooser buys the object. In case a chooser sells, the payoff of the proposer amounts to at least $\frac{s_p}{2}$ as half of the chooser's signal is added ($\pi_p = s_p + \frac{1}{2}s_c - \frac{s_p}{2} = \frac{1}{2}s_p + \frac{1}{2}s_c$). In the WBA bidding $b_i=s_i$ guarantees payoffs of at least $\pi_i \geq \frac{s_i}{2}$ no matter whether the agent becomes buyer or seller (if he becomes buyer half of his partner's private signal s_j is added; if he becomes seller his partner's winning bid b_j must have been at least marginal above his own bid).

In the following we consider different categories of proposal (bidding) behavior depending on the subjects' private signals. Table II.11 below gives the percentage of proposals (bids) that are set equal to the own private signal (rounded up to at most +/-1) and the remaining proposals (bids) that are set below or above the own private signal. The proposal setting behavior in the CCM is separately examined between subjects with signals below and above the median signal. This is done because in the former case subjects will become seller with a higher probability and in the latter case buyer. As discussed before, this might have different effects on their proposal setting.

---

[78] Note that the efficiency results of this section are mainly driven by this behavior. Heterogeneous types reduce efficiency in the WBA, whereas in the CCM efficiency is increased the closer proposals are set to the own valuation.
[79] We observe this behavior even less often taking only the worst-informed intermediate types (40<s_i<60) who do not know whether to buy or sell: CCM = 4.52%, WBA = 20.22%.
[80] Note that we mean in the following 'gross' payoffs (i.e., actual total payoffs from dissolution) if participation is forced, not net-payoffs (i.e., 'gross' payoffs minus what the share of the object is worth) as in the previous subsection.

The majority of proposals is set above the own signal (no matter whether private signal is below or above the median signal). In the auction we observe the reverse: the majority of bids is smaller than the own signal.[81] We subdivide the bids (proposals) that are set above the own signal into two categories: $2s$ is taken as a range due to the consideration that setting in the CCM a proposal of $2s$ guarantees a minimum payoff of zero (in case the proposer becomes seller he gets a zero payoff, in case he becomes buyer he gets at least zero depending on his partner's signal). Similar considerations are valid for the WBA: bidding $2s$ yields at least zero payoffs (in case the bidder becomes buyer and his partner's private signal is zero). Following this strategy, losses are avoided in either case. $1.5s$ is taken as another range, because subjects might use their own signal multiplied by 1.5 as a 'naïve benchmark valuation' (e.g. $1.5s$ is the expected true value for the object if an agent assumes his partner to have the same signal). In order to have categories of the same sizes $0.5s$ appears to be a 'natural' range (as the other categories are also given in 0.5 intervals).

Interestingly, the post-experimental questionnaire reveals that the expected value $E[v_i]=s_i+25$ does not seem to play a role in the decision process of most proposers and bidders respectively. Only few subjects (12.5% of both proposers in the CCM as well as of bidders in the WBA) mention in the questionnaire that they take the expected valuation into their consideration. This is also shown in the actual behavior. The strategy to propose (bid) the expected true value of the object was chosen very seldom. Bidding b (and setting P) equal to $E[v_i]=s_i+50\alpha$ occurs in the WBA (in the CCM) only in 1.98% (in 2.5%) of all cases (rounded up to at most +/-1).

Although the categories are set arbitrarily Table II.11 nevertheless indicates that subjects' behavior is heterogeneous. However, the scatter plots given in Figure II.4 and the categories of individual behavior show more variation and heterogeneity in the CCM than in the WBA. For instance, the majority of bids (63.5% of bids) in the WBA falls into one specific category, namely the range between $0.5s$ and s (including the bids which equal the private signal), whereas in the CCM this percentage amounts to only 26.56% and proposals are more uniformly distributed over the categories in general. As we have derived in the previous section in an IPV model, heterogeneity in bidding behavior leads to inefficiencies in the WBA. The same is valid under

---

[81] In the CCM 23.44% of proposals are set below and 68.54% above the own signal, whereas in the WBA 55.31% of bids are submitted below and 23.53% of bids above s_i.

interdependent valuations: the WBA is more efficient the more bidders adhere to the same strategy; the CCM is more efficient the closer proposals are set to the true valuation. The data indicate that there is less heterogeneity in the WBA than in the CCM.[82] This result might explain the higher efficiency in the WBA.

Table II.11: Categories of proposal setting/bidding behavior INT

CCM	$P \leq 0.5s$	$0.5s<P<s$	$P=s$	$s<P \leq 1.5s$	$1.5s<P \leq 2s$	$P>2s$
All (N=960)	4.90%	18.54%	8.02%	37.08%	12.29%	19.17%
$s_p>50$ (N=507)	5.92%	28.01%	7.69%	51.28%	5.92%	1.18%
$s_p<50$ (N=453)	3.75%	7.95%	8.39%	21.19%	19.43%	39.29%
WBA	$b \leq 0.5s$	$0.5s<b<s$	$b=s$	$s<b \leq 1.5s$	$1.5s<b \leq 2s$	$b>2s$
All (N=960)	12.81%	42.5%	21.15%	15.83%	3.85%	3.85%

The category $P=s$ ($b=s$) is rounded up to at most +/-1.

Behavioral Patterns of Choosers

As mentioned in Section II.4.2 a chooser's decision becomes more complex under interdependent valuations than in the IPV case. Table II.12 presents choosers' decisions for buying or selling dependent on the proposal proportional to their own private signal. Choosers' behavior is categorized with respect to these two parameters as these are the observable variables. We distinguish between three different categories: 1) the proposal is smaller than a chooser's private signal; 2) the proposal is located between the own signal and the expected mean value of the partnership ($E[v_c] = s_c + \alpha E[s_p] = s_c + 25$); and 3) the proposal is higher than the expected mean value of the partnership. Table II.12 gives the total percentage of decisions falling into a category both for all choosers and for choosers with private signals being located below and above the median signal of 50 separately. In general, in 57.5% of partnerships a chooser buys the object (in the remaining 42.5% he sells). Table II.12 implies that if a chooser's signal is higher than the proposal in 92.61% (92.45% if $s<50$; 92.64% if $s>50$) of the cases he buys the object (in this case selling is a dominated strategy). If the proposal lies between his own private signal and the expected value of the object he buys in 68.53% (57.47% if $s<50$; 77.27% if $s>50$) of the cases. However, if the proposal exceeds the expected value of the object, a chooser sells in 82.81% (87.79% if $s<50$; 64.20% if $s>50$) of the cases.

---

[82] This holds also for behavior compared to the true valuation. Scatter plots visualizing bids (proposals) and the corresponding true valuation are given in Figure II.A3 in the Appendix. Taking true valuations there is also more variation in the CCM than in the WBA.

Interestingly, the questionnaire after the experiment reveals that a substantial majority of choosers (62.5%) only take the proposal and their own private signal into consideration for their decision to buy or sell.[83] Thus, the inefficient allocations in the CCM might be driven by the fact that the majority of proposals are set above the own signal as the data show (see Table II.11 and footnote 81), but the majority of choosers' decisions is based solely on their own signal as the questionnaire reveals.

Table II.12: Choosers' decision

Chooser		$P \leq s_c$	$s_c < P \leq s_c+25$	$P > s_c+25$	Total
Buys	(N=552)	36.56%	14.06%	6.88%	57.50%
Buys $s<50$	(N=136)	11.06%	11.29%	8.35%	30.70%
Buys $s>50$	(N=416)	58.41%	16.44%	5.61%	80.46%
Sells	(N=408)	2.92%	6.46%	33.13%	42.50%
Sells $s<50$	(N=307)	0.90%	8.35%	60.05%	69.30%
Sells $s>50$	(N=101)	4.64%	4.84%	10.06%	19.54%
Total	(N=960)	39.48%	20.52%	40.00%	100.00%
Total $s<50$	(N=443)	11.96%	19.64%	68.40%	100.00%
Total $s>50$	(N=517)	63.06%	21.28%	15.67%	100.00%

II.4.5 Conclusions

In the second part of this chapter, we have provided a first experimental investigation of two prominent partnership dissolution mechanisms if valuations are assumed to be interdependent, whereby we have generalized the experimental framework of the study in the first part of this chapter. The main findings are that in general both mechanisms perform well in terms of efficiency, but that in the CCM ex-ante payoff expectations highly depend on the role of the subject – on principal a proposer is essentially worse off than a chooser. In these terms, the CCM is the more 'unfair' mechanism.

The main purpose of this section has been to shed further light on the applicability of both mechanisms with the help of a robustness check. Specifically, the experiment gives insight into how robust the performance of the mechanisms is assuming either an independent private values framework or a more complex interdependent valuations setting. Our data provide evidence that efficiency in the CCM depends on how precise the information about the 'true' valuation of the object is – under interdependent valuations the percentage of

---

[83] Answers of choosers (N=32) in the post-experimental questionnaire fall into four categories: 1) Choosers' decision depend only on their own signal (62.5%); 2) Choosers take the expected value of $s_p=25$ into account (9.375%); 3) Choosers expect P and s_p to be positively correlated and include this in their decision (15.625%); and 4) no category (12.5%).

efficient allocations as well as the efficiency rate (for comparability reasons measured by signals instead of true valuations) significantly decrease compared to the independent private values case. In the WBA treatment both the percentage of efficient allocations as well as the efficiency rate decrease, albeit not significantly. This result suggests that the WBA is more 'robust' concerning these different settings. Note that the ranking of mechanisms in terms of efficiency changes into its complete opposite if values are interdependent: In the IPV setting the CCM performs at least as good as the WBA, but assuming INT we observe the reverse. The relative decline of the CCM compared to the WBA might be partly driven by the fact that in the interdependent case the complexity not only of the proposer's but also of the chooser's decision situation increases. This causes additional scope for inefficiencies at the second stage of the game, because by now also the chooser faces uncertainty concerning his payoff-maximizing strategy. In contrast, in the IPV benchmark case only proposals are pivotal for efficiency, because a chooser's decision is simply restricted to choosing the higher (known) payoff. The experimental data show that the CCM seems to respond more sensitively to the more complex valuation structure than the WBA in terms of efficiency.[84] Moreover, the main drawbacks of the CCM turn out to be that 1) ex-ante payoff expectations vary considerably depending on the role (in both valuation settings), and 2) furthermore, with interdependent valuations no agent would voluntarily start proposing a price as was shown by proposers achieving negative net-payoffs regardless of their signal type (i.e., a proposer is worse off compared to his status quo independent of the size of his signal). Thereby management deadlocks are very likely to occur in the CCM if participation is not forced and roles are not given exogenously.

The relative standing of the subjects in both mechanisms is a very robust result regardless of the specific valuation structure: We find strong evidence that a proposer's payoff is still smaller than that of an agent in the auction who in turn has a lower expected payoff than a chooser in the CCM. Just as in the IPV case a proposer's payoff is only about 60% of that of a chooser. However, information asymmetries lead in general to lower payoff levels (according to the lower efficiency level): Relative payoffs compared to one's own valuation of the object

---

[84] Besides the more 'robust' performance if complexity increases another advantage of the WBA for practical purposes might be that subjects seem to be more familiar with this mechanism if played the first time (it provides a better 'spontaneous' performance in INT as well as in the IPV benchmark case in the first round) and that it might be 'easier' due to its symmetric structure.

are 10% less under an interdependent valuations structure than compared to the IPV benchmark case in both treatments.

Moreover, gains from trade also decrease or become even negative for specific types. In line with theoretical predictions (see e.g. Kittsteiner (2003), or Moldovanu (2002)) our data reveal that intermediate types are the 'worst-off' types. They expect to be buyer or seller with similar probabilities contrary to types at the lower or upper boundary of types, who are better informed (i.e., expect with higher probabilities whether they become buyer or seller). We find net-payoffs of intermediate types being lower than those of types at the boundaries regardless of the treatment and the specific role. In particular bidders in the WBA (as well as all subjects on average in the CCM) with intermediate types actually achieve negative net-payoffs on average in contrast to both low and high types with positive net-payoffs. Thus, agents in the CCM (before knowing their specific role) as well as all agents in the WBA would not voluntarily participate in dissolution if they received an intermediate signal for the partnership. Hence, the crucial question how to process dissolution if participation is not forced e.g. by previous contracts and if subjects prefer to refrain from dissolution (which turns out to be critical for all types of proposers in the CCM as well as for intermediate types in the WBA) should be subject to future research.

The emergence of negative gains from trade might be triggered by winner's and loser's curses. In general with interdependent valuations a new force of inefficiency[85] comes into play: A bidder (a proposer respectively) may simply lack relevant information in making an appropriate bid. Bidding one's true valuation is impossible due to uncertainties about just what a bidder's value exactly is. This gives rise to winner's and loser's curses.

In the experimental auction literature (see e.g. for literature on common value auctions Kagel and Levin (2001) for an experimental survey on the winner's curse, Kagel and Levin (1986) or Laffont (1997) for a theoretical and empirical overview and for an experimental study with asymmetric interdependent valuations Kirchkamp and Moldovanu (2004)) winner's curse is

---

[85] More uncertainty about the object's value leads to a higher level of inefficiency compared to the IPV benchmark case. Inefficiencies should be expected when both private and common value elements play a role, because a bidder with an inferior private signal but an overly optimistic conjecture about his partner's private signal may outbid his partner with a superior private signal. The issue that interdependent valuations might give rise to inefficiencies (contrary to the 'extreme' cases of independent private or pure common values) has comprehensively been discussed in the theoretical and experimental auction literature (see e.g. Goeree and Offerman (2003) or Jehiel and Moldovanu (2001) for the former and Goeree and Offerman (2002) for the latter).

measured so far by overbidding (i.e., bidding above the expected value of the item conditional on having the high signal) and negative payoffs or lower payoffs than theoretically predicted. In a common value auction the winner's curse emerges if a partner overestimates the true value of an object and bids too high thus winning the object but paying 'too much' (this is also called 'overpaying').

Note however, that there are two main differences between our setting and a standard common value auction. First, compared to the common value framework the valuation structure in this experiment differs as partners do not have the same true valuation for the object. In a 'pure' common value experiment agents achieve different signals about the value, but the value is the same for everybody. This implies that in the end the agent with the highest signal has nevertheless the same valuation as all other agents. On the contrary, in our interdependent valuations setting a bidder with the highest signal has also in total the highest valuation for the object. Second, in this chapter partnerships are studied which adhere to a different market structure than standard auctions where a good is sold. Partners have limited liability in the sense that they also achieve a positive payoff in case they lose the auction (they become seller in this case).[86] The losing partner also achieves a payoff as he is paid off for his former share of the object (contrary to a classical common value auction in which only the winner gets his valuation for the object minus the price he has to pay).

In our experimental setting the magnitude of winner's and loser's curses is difficult to identify and quantify. We interpret negative (and decreasing) net-payoffs as an indication of adverse selection effects. It would be interesting to learn more under which conditions and which mechanisms these effects are more likely to appear theoretically and empirically, since they are expected to have an essential influence on the applicability of a dissolution mechanism as they can even cause non-participation. Thus, the concrete coherences should be further tested in future research.

This experimental investigation of the WBA and the CCM in a more complex environment contributes to a broader research agenda on partnership dissolution mechanisms from an applied perspective. Due to the practical relevance of dissolution mechanisms an empirical investigation is essential in order to test their robustness and to identify a 'well-performing' mechanism. An accurate design of dissolution mechanisms is pivotal as a bad design might not

---

[86] For a discussion of the impact of bidders' limited liability for losses on the winner's curse refer to Kagel and Levin (2001).

only result in either deadlocks (if no partner starts proposing a price) or in inefficient and unfair allocations, but might even prevent people ex-ante from building a partnership. Our data suggest the WBA being the less setting-sensitive mechanism, which provides higher gains from trade and eliminates unequal ex-ante payoff expectations (before subjects learn their valuation or their signal respectively).

II.5 Appendix to Chapter II

Instructions

Written instructions IPV experiment (II.3) (translation from German)

Welcome and thank you very much for participating in this experiment. Please read the instructions carefully. The instructions are identical for each participant. If you have any questions please raise your hand; we will come at your place. You receive 2.50 € for your participation irrespective of your decisions during the experiment. Additionally, you can earn money in this experiment. How much you earn depends on both your decisions and the decisions of other participants. All decisions and payoffs remain anonymously. During the whole experiment, starting now, communication with other participants is strictly forbidden. In case of non-compliance, we must exclude you from the experiment and all payoffs.

General Information

You and another participant possess together a 'fictitious' *object* in equal shares. This object is indivisible. You have to negotiate who obtains the object and which compensation the other participant receives.

Payoffs

The participant obtaining the object is paid out after the negotiation a resale value for the object. Before the negotiation starts each participant gets to know his resale value for the object which can be different for both participants. The participant not obtaining the object receives from his negotiating partner a compensation having to be bargained.

Negotiation

[TREATMENT WBA] The negotiation proceeds as follows. You and the other participant take part in an auction in which the shared object is auctioned off between you and the other participant. You and the other bidder each submit a (freely selectable) bid for the whole object. The bidder with the higher bid wins the auction and *buys* **for half of his bid** the losing bidder's share of the object from the losing bidder. The losing bidder *sells* his share of the object and receives in return **half of the highest bid**. This means:

- The losing bidder *sells* his half of the object and receives instead half of the winning bid from the other bidder:

$$\text{Payoff losing bidder} = \frac{\text{highest bid}}{2}$$

- The winning bidder *buys* half of the object, pays the losing bidder half of his bid and receives in return his own resale value:

$$\text{Payoff winning bidder} = \text{resale value of the bidder} - \frac{\text{highest bid}}{2}$$

- In case you and the other bidder submit the *same* bid, then a winner (=buyer) is randomly chosen and the payoffs of buyer and seller arise afterwards as described above.

[Negotiation
[TREATMENT CCM] The negotiation proceeds as follows. One of you will become *proposer* and the other participant will become *chooser*. The proposer has to submit a (freely selectable) *proposal* for the whole object. Then the chooser decides whether he wants to sell **for half of this proposal** his share of the object or whether he wants to buy the proposer's share of the object:

- If the chooser decides to *sell*, he receives instead half of the proposal from the proposer (and the proposer receives his value for the object):

$$\text{Payoff proposer} = \text{proposer's resale value for the object} - \frac{\text{proposal}}{2}$$

$$\text{Payoff chooser} = \frac{\text{proposal}}{2}$$

- If the chooser decides to *buy*, he pays the proposer half of the proposal and receives in return his own resale value for the object:

$$\text{Payoff proposer} = \frac{\text{proposal}}{2}$$

$$\text{Payoff chooser} = \text{chooser's value for the object} - \frac{\text{proposal}}{2} \text{]}$$

Procedure
[TREATMENT WBA]
1) At the beginning of each round you are informed about your resale value for the object. Participants might typically have unequal resale values; these are drawn randomly and independently of each other from a distribution of 0 to 100 Eurocents (2 decimal places) in which each amount is equiprobable.
2) Then each negotiating partner chooses his bid for the whole object (2 decimal places are possible).

3) Afterwards it is ascertained who has the higher bid and therefore buys the other half of the object for half of his bid and who submits the lower bid and therefore sells his half of the object for half of the highest bid.

[Procedure
[TREATMENT CCM]
1) At the beginning of the experiment it will be randomly drawn with equal probability if you become proposer or chooser. You will maintain the chosen role during the *whole* experiment.
2) At the beginning of each round you are informed about your resale value for the object. Participants might typically have unequal resale values; these are drawn randomly and independently of each other from a distribution of 0 to 100 Eurocents (2 decimal places) in which each amount is equiprobable.
3) Then the proposer chooses a proposal for the whole object (2 decimal places are possible).
4) Afterwards the chooser will be informed about the proposal and has to decide whether he wants to sell his half of the object or whether he wants to buy the half of the proposer for half of the proposal.]

This negotiation situation is repeated altogether 30 times. Your negotiating partner as well as your resale value is again randomly drawn anew in each of the 30 rounds. At the end of the experiment you are disbursed your overall earnings over all rounds including your 2.50 €.

Are there any questions?

Written instructions INT experiment (II.4) (translation from German)

Welcome and thank you very much for participating in this experiment. Please read the instructions carefully. The instructions are identical for each participant. If you have any questions please raise your hand; we will come at your place. You receive 2.50 € for your participation irrespective of your decisions during the experiment. Additionally, you can earn money in this experiment. How much you earn depends on both your decisions and the decisions of other participants. All decisions and payoffs remain anonymously. During the whole experiment, starting now, communication with other participants is strictly forbidden. In case of non-compliance, we must exclude you from the experiment and all payoffs.

General Information

You and another participant possess together a 'fictitious' *object* in equal shares. This object is indivisible. You have to negotiate who obtains the object and which compensation the other participant receives.

Payoffs

The participant obtaining the object is paid out after the negotiation a resale value for the object. The resale value depends on one's own private signal and the signal of your negotiation partner. The private signals can be different for both participants. Before the negotiation starts each participant gets to know his private signal for the object, but not his partner's signal. The participant not obtaining the object receives from his negotiating partner a compensation having to be bargained.

Negotiation

[TREATMENT AUCTION] The negotiation proceeds as follows. You and the other participant take part in an auction in which the shared object is auctioned off between you and the other participant. You and the other bidder each submit a (freely selectable) bid for the whole object. The bidder with the higher bid wins the auction and *buys* **for half of his bid** the losing bidder's share of the object from the losing bidder. The losing bidder *sells* his share of the object and receives in return **half of the highest bid**. This means:

- The losing bidder *sells* his half of the object and receives instead half of the winning bid from the other bidder:

$$\text{Payoff losing bidder} = \frac{\text{highest bid}}{2}$$

- The winning bidder *buys* half of the object, pays the losing bidder half of his bid and receives in return his own resale value:

$$\text{Payoff winning bidder} = \text{resale value of the bidder} - \frac{\text{highest bid}}{2}$$

- In case you and the other bidder submit the *same* bid, then a winner (=buyer) is randomly chosen and the payoffs of buyer and seller arise afterwards as described above.

[Negotiation
[TREATMENT CCM] The negotiation proceeds as follows. One of you will become *proposer* and the other participant will become *chooser*. The proposer has to submit a (freely selectable) *proposal* for the whole object. Then the chooser decides whether he wants to sell **for half of this proposal** his share of the object or whether he wants to buy the proposer's share of the object:

- If the chooser decides to *sell*, he receives instead half of the proposal from the proposer (and the proposer receives his value for the object):

$$\text{Payoff proposer} = \text{proposer's resale value for the object} - \frac{\text{proposal}}{2}$$

$$\text{Payoff chooser} = \frac{\text{proposal}}{2}$$

- If the chooser decides to *buy*, he pays the proposer half of the proposal and receives in return his own resale value for the object:

$$\text{Payoff proposer} = \frac{\text{proposal}}{2}$$

$$\text{Payoff chooser} = \text{chooser's value for the object} - \frac{\text{proposal}}{2} \text{]}$$

Resale value for the object
The resale value of each negotiation partner consists of the own known private signal and half of the unknown signal of the negotiation partner. Your resale value for the whole object adds up to:

$$\text{Resale value} = \text{Your private signal} + 0.5 \times \text{signal of your negotiation partner}$$

Procedure

[TREATMENT Auction]

1) At the beginning of each round you are informed about your private signal for the object. Participants might typically have unequal private signals; these are drawn randomly and independently of each other from a distribution of 0 to 100 Eurocents (2 decimal places) in which each amount is equiprobable. Before negotiation starts each participant learns only his own private signal.
2) Then each negotiating partner chooses his bid for the whole object (2 decimal places are possible).
3) Afterwards it is ascertained who has the higher bid and therefore buys the other half of the object for half of his bid and who submits the lower bid and therefore sells his half of the object for half of the highest bid.

[Procedure

[TREATMENT CCM]

1) At the beginning of the experiment it will be randomly drawn with equal probability if you become proposer or chooser. You will maintain the chosen role during the *whole* experiment.
2) At the beginning of each round you are informed about your private signal for the object. Participants might typically have unequal private signals; these are drawn randomly and independently of each other from a distribution of 0 to 100 Eurocents (2 decimal places) in which each amount is equiprobable. Before negotiation starts each participant learns only his own private signal.
3) Then the proposer chooses a proposal for the whole object (2 decimal places are possible).
4) Afterwards the chooser will be informed about the proposal and has to decide whether he wants to sell his half of the object or whether he wants to buy the half of the proposer for half of the proposal.]

This negotiation situation is repeated altogether 30 times. Your negotiating partner as well as your private signal is again randomly drawn anew in each of the 30 rounds. At the end of the experiment there will be a short questionnaire. After the experiment you are disbursed your overall earnings over all rounds including your 2.50 €.

Are there any questions?

Questionnaire INT

First screen:

Please describe shortly what basic criteria determined your decision.

[Input box]

Second screen:

[TREATMENT WBA]

How did you set your bids? Which role did your private signal play in doing so? Which role did the unknown signal of your negotiation partner play?

[[TREATMENT CCM]

If you were proposer, how did you set your proposals? Which role did your private signal play in doing so? Which role did the unknown signal of your negotiation partner play?

If you were chooser, how did you make your decisions with regard to buying or selling? Which role did your private signal play in doing so? Which role did the unknown signal of your negotiation partner play?]

Mathematical Appendix

Mathematical Appendix to II.3

We prove, for CARA utility functions, that the difference between a bidder's bid and his valuation in the WBA and the proposer's offer and his valuation in the CCM becomes small as the Arrow-Pratt measure of absolute risk aversion becomes large. This justifies our assumption that 'very risk-averse' bidders (proposers) bid their valuation (propose a price equal to their valuation). In the following we consider the utility functions used in McAfee (1992):

$$u(x) = \frac{1}{\lambda}\left(1 - e^{-\lambda x}\right)$$

$$u'(x) = e^{\lambda x}$$

Lemma II.A1 *Consider the WBA and assume that the bids of bidder 2 are distributed according to a continuous distribution function G with density g>0. Denote the optimal bidding function of bidder 1 (with respect to bidder 2's bids) by $b_1^\lambda(v_1)$. Then we have that for all types v_1 of bidder 1 that:* $\lim_{\lambda \to \infty} b_1^\lambda(v_1) = v_1$.

Proof. The expected utility of bidder 1 with valuation v_1 and bid b_1 is given by

$$U(v_1, b_1) = \frac{1}{\lambda}\left(1 - e^{-\lambda\left(v_1 - \frac{b_1}{2}\right)}\right) G(b_1) + \int_{b_1}^{1} \frac{1}{\lambda}\left(1 - e^{-\lambda\frac{b_2}{2}}\right) g(b_2) db_2 .$$

The first order condition for optimum gives

$$\frac{\partial U(v_1, b_1)}{\partial b_1} = -\frac{1}{2} e^{-\lambda\left(v_1 - \frac{b_1}{2}\right)} G(b_1) + \frac{1}{\lambda}\left(1 - e^{-\lambda\left(v_1 - \frac{b_1}{2}\right)}\right) g(b_1) - \frac{1}{\lambda}\left(1 - e^{-\lambda\frac{b_1}{2}}\right) g(b_1)$$

$$= \frac{1}{\lambda} g(b_1) e^{-\lambda\frac{b_1}{2}} \left[-\frac{1}{2} \lambda e^{-\lambda(v_1 - b_1)} \frac{G(b_1)}{g(b_1)} - e^{-\lambda(v_1 - b_1)} + 1 \right] = 0.$$

From this follows that we must have $1 - e^{-\lambda(v_1 - b_1)}\left(\frac{1}{2}\lambda \frac{G(b_1)}{g(b_1)} + 1\right) = 0$ or equivalently

$$v_1 - b_1 = \frac{1}{\lambda} \ln\left(\frac{1}{2}\lambda \frac{G(b_1)}{g(b_1)} + 1\right)$$

which proves the lemma. ∎

For the model above, bidder 2 either bids his valuation or bids according to $b_2(v_2) = \frac{2}{3}v_2$, such that the distribution of v_2 satisfies the assumptions of the Lemma.

As the CCM can be seen as a WBA where the chooser bids his own valuation and the price equals the winning bid if the proposer wins and the losing bid if the chooser wins, the following lemma is shown in a similar way:

Lemma II.A2 *Consider the CCM. Denote the optimal proposed price by $P^\lambda(v_p)$. Then we have that for all types v_p of the proposer that:*
$\lim_{\lambda \to \infty} P^\lambda(v_p) = v_p.$

Proof. The expected utility of a proposer with valuation v_p and offer P is given by

$$U(v_p, P) = \frac{1}{\lambda}\left(1 - e^{-\lambda\left(v_p - \frac{P}{2}\right)}\right)P + \frac{1}{\lambda}\left(1 - e^{-\lambda\frac{P}{2}}\right)(1 - P).$$

The first order condition for optimum gives

$$\frac{\partial U(v_p, P)}{\partial P} = -\frac{1}{2}e^{-\lambda\left(v_p - \frac{P}{2}\right)}P + \frac{1}{\lambda}\left(1 - e^{-\lambda\left(v_p - \frac{P}{2}\right)}\right) - \frac{1}{2}e^{-\lambda\frac{P}{2}}(1-P) - \frac{1}{\lambda}\left(1 - e^{-\lambda\frac{P}{2}}\right)$$

$$= \frac{1}{\lambda}e^{-\lambda\frac{P}{2}}\left[-\frac{1}{2}\frac{1}{\lambda}e^{-\lambda(v_p - P)} - e^{-\lambda(v_p - P)} - \frac{1}{2}\frac{1}{\lambda}(1 - P) + 1\right] = 0.$$

From this follows that we must have $1 - \frac{1}{2}\frac{1}{\lambda}(1 - P) - e^{-\lambda(v_p - P)}\left(\frac{1}{2}\frac{1}{\lambda} + 1\right) = 0$ or equivalently

$$v_p - P = \frac{1}{\lambda}\ln\left(\frac{\frac{1}{2}\frac{1}{\lambda} + 1}{1 - \frac{1}{2}\frac{1}{\lambda}(1 - P)}\right).$$

which proves the lemma. ∎

Proof of Proposition II.2.

1. The chooser in the CCM has a dominant strategy and will always buy whenever his valuation v_c exceeds the offered price. It is straightforward to show that a risk-neutral proposer with valuation v_p will thus propose a price of $P(v_p) = 25 + \tfrac{1}{2} v_p$. According to Lemma II.A2 above a risk-averse proposer proposes a price equal to his valuation.

2. Assume that risk-neutral bidders bid according to the bidding strategy $b(\cdot)$ and risk-averse bidders bid their valuation. A risk-neutral bidder with valuation v who imitates a risk-neutral bidder of type $\hat{v}$ receives the following expected payoff

$$U(v,\hat{v}) = \alpha\left[\left(v - \frac{b(\hat{v})}{2}\right)\hat{v}\frac{1}{100} + \int_{\hat{v}}^{100}\frac{b(x)}{2}\frac{1}{100}dx\right] + (1-\alpha)\left[\left(v - \frac{b(\hat{v})}{2}\right)b(\hat{v})\frac{1}{100} + \int_{b(\hat{v})}^{100}\frac{x}{2}\frac{1}{100}dx\right]$$

Thus, in equilibrium we must have that

$$\left.\frac{\partial U(v,\hat{v})}{\partial \hat{v}}\right|_{\hat{v}=v} = \frac{1}{100}\alpha\left[(v - b(v)) - \frac{b'(v)}{2}v\right] + \frac{1}{100}(1-\alpha)\left[\left(v - \frac{3}{2}b(v)\right)b'(v)\right] = 0. \quad (1)$$

Together with the condition that $b(0) = 0$ the differential equation (1) uniquely defines the symmetric equilibrium bidding function which is given by $b(v) = \tfrac{2}{3}v$.[87]

Lemma II.A1 above shows that it is a best response for the risk-averse types to bid their valuation. ∎

---

[87] It can easily be verified that the standard single crossing condition holds and that the given (symmetric) solution to (1) is indeed a global maximum.

Proposition II.A1 *Assume that a fraction $1 > \alpha > 0$ of partners is risk neutral and the remaining partners are 'extremely' risk averse and that both partners have valuations distributed according to cdf F (with support [0,100]). Then, for every valuation, a risk-neutral partner has a strictly larger interim expected utility as chooser than as proposer.*

Proof. The proof follows the arguments in McAfee (1992, Theorem 9). The proposed price $P(v_p)$ and the interim expected utility

$$\pi_p(v_p) = \left(v_p - \frac{P(v_p)}{2}\right) F(P(v_p)) + \frac{P(v_p)}{2}(1 - F(P(v_p)))$$

of a risk-neutral proposer with valuation v_p do not depend on α and are thus the same (and have the same properties) as in McAfee, in particular we have that the derivative of the payoff is $\pi'_p(v_p) = F(P(v))$. The interim expected utility of the chooser with valuation v_c is

$$\pi_c(v_c) = \alpha E_{v_p}\left[\max\left(v_c - \frac{P(v_p)}{2}, \frac{P(v_p)}{2}\right)\right] + (1-\alpha) E\left[\max\left(v_c - \frac{v_p}{2}, \frac{v_p}{2}\right)\right]$$

and thus its derivative is given by

$$\pi'_c(v_c) = \begin{cases} (1-\alpha)F(v_c) & \text{if } v_c < P(0) \\ \alpha F(P^{-1}(v_c)) + (1-\alpha)F(v_c) & \text{if } v_c \in [P(0), P(100)]. \\ \alpha + (1-\alpha)F(v_c) & \text{if } v_c > P(100) \end{cases}$$

Denote the median valuation by v^{med}, i.e., $F(v^{med}) = \frac{1}{2}$. From the property that $P(v) < v \Leftrightarrow v > v^{med}$ and $P(v) > v \Leftrightarrow v < v^{med}$ for $v \in [P(0), P(100)]$ we have that $\pi'_p(v) > \pi'_c(v)$ if and only if $P^{-1}(v) < P(v)$ if and only if $v < P(v)$. Thus $\pi'_p(v) > \pi'_c(v)$ if and only if $v < v^{med}$ and $\pi_c(v) - \pi_p(v)$ is minimized at $v = v^{med}$. The statement follows from the fact that $\pi_c(v^{med}) > \alpha \frac{1}{2} v^{med} + (1-\alpha) \frac{1}{2} v^{med} = \pi_p(v^{med})$. ∎

Partnership Dissolution Mechanisms

Proposition II.A2 *Assume that a fraction $1 > \alpha > 0$ of partners is risk neutral and the remaining partners are 'extremely' risk averse and that both partners have valuations distributed according to the uniform distribution on $[0,100]$. Then, for every possible valuation, a risk-neutral chooser has a strictly larger interim expected utility than in the WBA whereas a risk-neutral proposer has a strictly smaller interim expected utility than in the WBA.*

Proof. The interim payoff of a (risk-neutral) proposer is

$$\pi_p = \left(v - \frac{25 + \frac{1}{2}v}{2}\right)(25 + \frac{1}{2}v)\frac{1}{100} + \frac{25 + \frac{1}{2}v}{2}\left(1 - \frac{25 + \frac{1}{2}v}{100}\right)$$

$$= \frac{1}{400}v^2 + \frac{1}{4}v + \frac{25}{4}$$

and that of a (risk-neutral) chooser is

$$\pi_c(v) = \begin{cases} \alpha \int_0^{100} \frac{1}{2}(25 + \frac{1}{2}x)\frac{1}{100}dx + (1-\alpha)\left[\int_0^v (v - \frac{x}{2})\frac{1}{100}dx + \int_v^{100} \frac{x}{2}\frac{1}{100}dx\right] & \text{if } v < 25 \\ \alpha\left[\int_0^{2v-50}(v - \frac{1}{2}(25 + \frac{1}{2}x))\frac{1}{100}dx + \int_{2v-50}^{100} \frac{1}{2}(25 + \frac{1}{2}x)\frac{1}{100}dx\right] \\ + (1-\alpha)\left[\int_0^v (v - \frac{x}{2})\frac{1}{100}dx + \int_v^{100} \frac{x}{2}\frac{1}{100}dx\right] & \text{if } v \in [25,75] \\ \alpha\int_0^{100}(v - \frac{1}{2}(25 + \frac{1}{2}x))\frac{1}{100}dx + (1-\alpha)\left[\int_0^v (v - \frac{x}{2})\frac{1}{100}dx + \int_v^{100} \frac{x}{2}\frac{1}{100}dx\right] & \text{if } v > 75 \end{cases}$$

$$= \begin{cases} \frac{1}{200}v^2 - \frac{1}{200}v^2\alpha + 25 & \text{if } v < 25 \\ \frac{25}{4}\alpha - \frac{1}{2}v\alpha + \frac{1}{200}v^2\alpha + \frac{1}{200}v^2 + 25 & \text{if } v \in [25,75] \\ v\alpha - 50\alpha - \frac{1}{200}v^2\alpha + \frac{1}{200}v^2 + 25 & \text{if } v > 75 \end{cases}$$

The interim payoff of a (risk-neutral) partner in the WBA is

$$\pi_a(v) = \alpha\left[\int_0^v \left(v - \frac{1}{2}\frac{2}{3}v\right)\frac{1}{100}dx + \int_v^{100} \frac{1}{2}\frac{2}{3}x\frac{1}{100}dx\right]$$

$$+ (1-\alpha)\left[\int_0^{\frac{2}{3}v}\left(v - \frac{1}{2}\frac{2}{3}v\right)\frac{1}{100}dx + \int_{\frac{2}{3}v}^{100} \frac{1}{2}x\frac{1}{100}dx\right]$$

$$= \frac{1}{600}v^2\alpha - \frac{25}{3}\alpha + \frac{1}{300}v^2 + 25$$

A tedious but straightforward comparison shows that $\pi_c(v) > \pi_a(v) > \pi_p(v)$. ∎

Mathematical Appendix to II.4

Proposition II.A3: *If both partners know their true valuation, the strategy $P=v_p$ always leads to efficient dissolution.*

Proof. A chooser buys if his valuation for the object subtracted by the price he has to pay exceeds the price he obtains for his share in case he sells: $s_c + \alpha s_p - \frac{P}{2} > \frac{P}{2}$. This yields $s_c + \alpha s_p > P$ which is the same as $v_c > P$. This is only efficient if $v_c > v_p$ (vice versa in case he sells). Thus for $P=v_p$ dissolution always results in an efficient allocation. ∎

Proposition II.A4: *The strategy $P=s_p$ does not always lead to efficient dissolution, even if the chooser anticipates this strategy.*

Proof. Assume that the proposer always sets $P=s_p$ and that the chooser anticipates this. First, consider the case that the chooser buys the entire object. A payoff-maximizing chooser buys if $s_c + \alpha s_p - \frac{P}{2} > \frac{P}{2}$, which is the same as $s_c + \alpha s_p - \frac{s_p}{2} > \frac{s_p}{2}$. This leads to $s_c > (1-\alpha)s_p$. Inefficiencies occur if the partner with the higher valuation does not get the object. Thus, if $s_c > (1-\alpha)s_p$ holds, an inefficient dissolution results if the proposer's valuation is higher than the chooser's ($v_c < v_p$):

$s_c + \alpha s_p < s_p + \alpha s_c$

which can be transformed into $(1-\alpha)s_c < (1-\alpha)s_p$ which leads to $s_c < s_p$. Thus, inefficient dissolution takes place if the following two conditions hold:

(1) $s_c > (1-\alpha)s_p$

(2) $s_c < s_p$,

which leads to $s_p > s_c > (1-\alpha)s_p$. This condition contains the cases in which it is profitable for a chooser to buy although his 'true' valuation is smaller than that of the proposer.

Now, consider the case that the chooser sells his share of the object. Then $s_c < (1-\alpha)s_p$ holds. Note that this can never be inefficient: Inefficiencies would result if the following two conditions hold:

(1) $s_c < (1-\alpha)s_p$

(2) $s_c > s_p$,

which leads to $s_p < s_c < (1-\alpha)s_p$. This can never be fulfilled for $\alpha \in [0,1]$. ∎

Proposition II.A5: *The sum of a partnership's net-payoffs (i.e., total gains from trade of both partners) assuming an interdependent valuations structure is half of those in the IPV benchmark case if each partnership is dissolved efficiently (or if the same partner becomes owner of the partnership).*

Proof. Consider a partnership, where i denotes the buyer and j the seller. The table below gives payoffs and net-payoffs (for the WBA as an example). If we calculate gains from trade per partnership, i.e., the partners' sum of net-payoffs, we get in the IPV case $\frac{1}{2}[v_i - v_j]$ and in the INT case $\frac{1}{4}[s_i - s_j]$. As signals in INT equal valuations in IPV in case the same partner becomes buyer in both settings we get that sum of net-payoffs are half in INT of those in IPV. Under the assumption that each partnership is dissolved efficiently the gains from trade of all partnerships should be twice as high in IPV on average. ∎

Payoffs and net-payoffs

Setting	Payoffs		Net-payoffs	
	Buyer i	Seller j	Buyer i	Seller j
IPV	$v_i - \dfrac{b_i}{2}$	$\dfrac{b_i}{2}$	$\dfrac{1}{2}v_i - \dfrac{b_i}{2}$	$\dfrac{b_i}{2} - \dfrac{1}{2}v_j$
INT	$s_i + \tfrac{1}{2}s_j - \dfrac{b_i}{2}$	$\dfrac{b_i}{2}$	$\tfrac{1}{2}s_i + \tfrac{1}{4}s_j - \dfrac{b_i}{2}$	$\dfrac{b_i}{2} - \tfrac{1}{2}s_j + \tfrac{1}{4}s_i$

Tables

Table II.A1: Panel probit regression IPV with CCM as base category

Efficient allocation	(1) Coefficient	(Std. Errors)	(2) Coefficient	(Std. Errors)
Constant	0.7729399***	(0.233446)	1.209842***	(0.3033959)
WBA	-0.5909589	(0.3817919)	-0.913102*	(0.4790707)
Round	0.0188885***	(0.0070533)	0.0182075***	(0.0070915)
Round*WBA	-0.0271209**	(0.011497)	-0.0260132**	(0.0115474)
Distance	0.0212942***	(0.0045556)	0.0106706*	(0.0060886)
Dist*WBA	0.01832**	(0.0080288)	0.0251439**	(0.0110316)
Below	-0.2550033	(0.2034501)	-0.8588609**	(0.3480503)
Below*WBA	0.5151238	(0.319235)	1.143898**	(0.5384937)
Above	-0.6138707***	(0.1872444)	-1.190707***	(0.3209465)
Above*WBA	0.6153195**	(0.2922746)	0.8532122*	(0.511318)
Dist*below			0.0236143*	(0.0134372)
Dist*below*WBA			-0.0302586	(0.0208923)
Dist*above			0.0212048**	(0.0101901)
Dist*above*WBA			-0.0018604	(0.0190349)
N	1440		1440	
$\chi^2(dF)$	130.44(9)		150.26(13)	

Standard errors are given in parentheses. *** denotes significance on the 1%-level, ** denotes significance on the 5%-level, * denotes significance on the 10%-level. Matching groups (N=24) are used as group variable. Treatment dummy variable 'CCM' is dropped. This regression measures the influence of parameters between the two treatments.

Table II.A2: Panel probit regression INT with CCM as base category

Efficient allocation	(1)		(2)	
	Coefficient	(Std. Errors)	Coefficient	(Std. Errors)
Constant	0.0972391	(0.1668456)	0.0938675	(0.169915)
WBA	-0.5461275*	(0.3285301)	-0.4763579	(0.3900817)
Round	0.0179003***	(0.0054029)	0.0178874***	(0.0054097)
Round*WBA	0.0248556**	(0.0103675)	0.025165**	(0.0104652)
Distance	0.0163093***	(0.0030749)	0.0163206***	(0.003075)
Dist*WBA	0.0166633**	(0.0065345)	0.0146573*	(0.0086435)
Below	-0.1914927	(0.147324)	-0.1903405	(0.1473716)
Below*WBA	0.1645416	(0.276828)	-0.320028	(0.4280252)
Above	-0.358637***	(0.1373184)	-0.3583632***	(0.1375603)
Above*WBA	0.0301863	(0.2528651)	0.1629963	(0.3994627)
Dist*below			0.0016572	(0.0053252)
Dist*below*WBA			0.0321998*	(0.0188901)
Dist*above			-0.0006483	(0.0046182)
Dist*above*WBA			-0.0098088	(0.0135296)
N	1440		1440	
$\chi^2(dF)$	170.79(9)		173.67(13)	

Standard errors are given in parentheses. *** denotes significance on the 1%-level, ** denotes significance on the 5%-level, * denotes significance on the 10%-level. Matching groups ($N=24$) are used as group variable. Treatment dummy variable 'CCM' is dropped. This regression measures the influence of parameters between the two treatments.

Table II.A3: Gains from trade – Different ranges of types

Mean net-payoffs	N	Low types	N	Intermediate types	N	High types
CCM_INT						
All	710	1.13	372	-0.58	838	5.95
Proposer	357	-7.09	177	-9.11	426	-6.45
Chooser	353	9.44	195	7.15	412	18.76
WBA_INT	349	3.02	183	-0.74	428	5.37

Low types (0-40), intermediate types (40-60) and high types (60-100).

Figures

Figure II.A1: Average net-payoffs of bidders and proposers over rounds

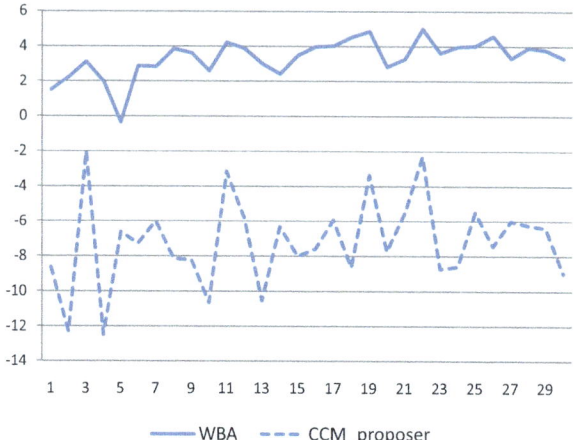

Figure II.A2: Average net-payoffs of bidders and proposers with intermediate types over rounds

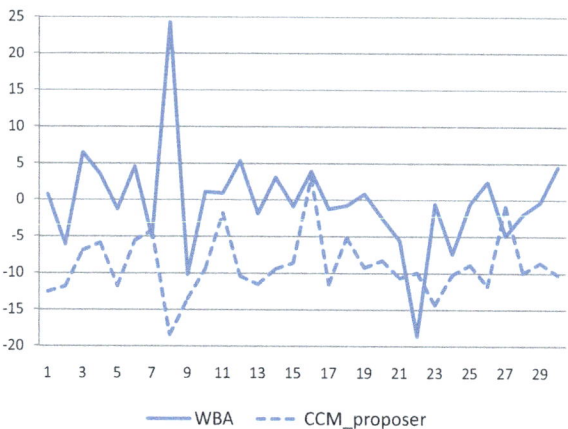

Figure II.A3: Scatter plots – True valuations and bids/proposals

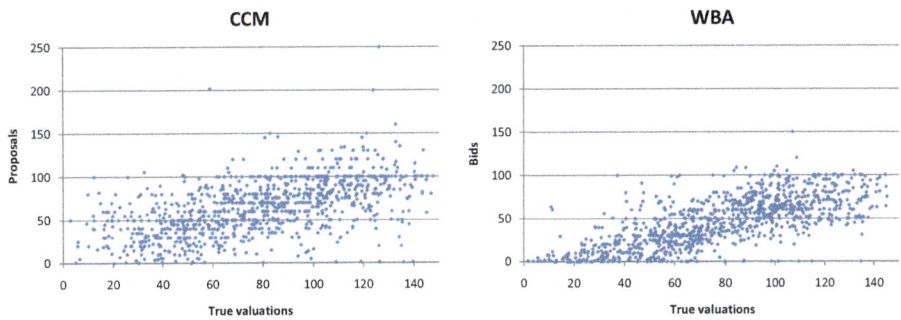

Note that in the CCM one extreme proposal of 300 is omitted.

Chapter III

The Influence of Patents and Subsidies on R&D Investment Incentives[88]

III.1 Introduction

A bulk of evidence indicates that there is a positive effect of innovative activity on firm profits, productivity, economic growth and total welfare (see e.g. Kamien and Schwartz (1975) for a survey). However, many empirical studies investigating R&D investment behavior find that firms tend to underinvest in R&D compared to the socially optimal R&D investment level, e.g. Bernstein (1996), Cohen (1995), Cohen and Levin (1989), Jones and Williams (1998, 2000), or Steger (2005). For instance, Jones and Williams (1998), p. 1133, state that "the optimal share of resources to invest in research is conservatively estimated to be two to four times larger than the actual amount invested by the U.S. economy." In general, underinvestment in R&D is mainly caused by the fact that firms' private returns of an innovation might be lower than social returns, see e.g. Griliches (1992). The reason for this inequality lies in the special properties of the good 'innovation' itself. A firm can only skim the maximal profit of an innovation if it is the exclusive owner of an innovation, e.g., if competing firms are prevented from imitating the innovation. Hence, the amount of R&D investment will depend on the degree of appropriability of an innovation and thus on the realizable profits of an investing firm.

In order to stimulate R&D spending governments use different policy instruments as incentives. Among frequently used instruments are patent protection of an innovation, subsidies for R&D investment costs, granting research joint ventures, or announcing research tournaments. All these instruments provide incentives to increase R&D investment, but they influence investment levels through very diverse channels. Patent protection is used to prohibit the imitation of the innovation by other firms (thus targeting at the

---

[88] This chapter is based on Darai, Großer and Trhal (2009).

© Springer Fachmedien Wiesbaden GmbH, part of Springer Nature 2009
N. Trhal, *Experimental Studies on Partnership Dissolution, R&D Investment, and Gift Giving*, Edition KWV, https://doi.org/10.1007/978-3-658-24667-9_3

revenue side of firms' profits), whereas subsidies are used to decrease R&D investment costs and thereby on the one hand increase incentives to innovate and on the other hand reduce the risk of an investment in case of failure (targeting at the cost side of firms' profits). Research joint ventures permit firms to cooperate in R&D (sharing risk and dividing gains) and research tournaments are competitions announced by government, often the military, in which an award is given to the company first succeeding in the wanted invention (note that in contrast to patent protection the rights of the invention are transferred to the sponsor of the tournament).[89]

Especially the first two instruments are very common in various industries like consumer electronics, pharmaceuticals, or automobile. In the fiscal year 2007, for instance, 184,376 patents were granted in the U.S. (39.37% of the applications) and the U.S. government funded 9.22% (24,450 out of 265,193 millions of US-$) of the industry's R&D expenditures (see Performance and Accountability Report 2008 by the United States Patent and Trademark Office and Info Brief 2008 of the National Science Foundation). For Germany similar results are reported: 17,884 patents were granted in 2007 (30.74% of the applications) and the German government financed 4.5% (1,723 out of 38,651 millions of €) of the business enterprise sector's R&D expenditures (see Annual Report 2007 of the German Patent and Trademark Office and Research and Innovation in Germany 2008 of the Federal Ministry of Education and Research).

Due to the extensive application and the political and practical relevance of patents and subsidies we examine the incentive effects of both instruments on firms' R&D investment decisions in this chapter.[90] Since the instruments influence investment behavior through different channels (cost vs. revenue side), we test in a controlled laboratory experiment how the induced incentives of each instrument actually perform in a direct comparison. Specifically, we compare (i) the impact of these instruments on firms' R&D investment with a benchmark situation without incentive providing instruments as well as (ii) which of the two instruments turns out to be more successful in stimulating R&D investments. However, note that we abstain from a welfare analysis, i.e., from analyzing the

---

[89] For an overview of different aspects of R&D spending and incentive instruments refer to Scotchmer (2005).
[90] According to the OECD (2004), p. 2, "(p)atenting has accelerated rapidly in the past decade, with the number of patent applications filed in Europe, Japan and the United States increasing by 40% between 1992 and 2002, from 600 000 to 850 000 per year. The effects of such patenting on incentives to innovate, on the diffusion of scientific and technical knowledge and on competition remain unclear and vary across industry sectors and technological fields." Our study is meant to shed further light on the incentive effects to innovate of the investigated instruments.

efficiency of the two instruments in terms of costs and benefits (e.g. due to difficulties in the comparability of both instruments' funding) and rather concentrate on the incentive effects of both instruments on investment behavior.

There exists a vast theoretical and empirical literature also including some experimental studies analyzing the effects, usage, design, and drawbacks of the four instruments[91] mentioned above. Patents might be one useful policy instrument to enhance R&D investment as they prohibit direct imitation which is seen as the main problem causing underinvestment compared to the socially optimal R&D investment level.[92] The impact of granting patent protection is typically analyzed in dynamic patent race models (among others see Harris and Vickers (1987)).[93] In these studies patent protection of an innovation indeed increases equilibrium R&D investment. However, by creating a the-winner-takes-all situation, patent races might systematically induce excessive spending on R&D (i.e., higher than socially optimal investment levels) with negative effects on welfare (see e.g. Dasgupta and Stiglitz (1980), or Loury (1979)). Thus, although patents set incentives to increase investment level in R&D, drawbacks of strong patent protection turn out to be the risk of creating overinvestment in R&D and furthermore socially inefficient monopoly pricing of the winner. Experimental studies on a one-stage stochastic R&D process by Isaac and Reynolds (1986, 1988) also show that subjects spend more under full[94] than under partial appropriability and they observe that R&D investment exceeds the socially optimal amount under full appropriability.

Subsidies as another policy instrument are used to stimulate investment and to decrease the risk of firms investing in R&D since the costs in case of failure are reduced. Subsidies should encourage firms either to invest more or to

---

[91] For patents please refer to e.g. Cantner et al. (2007), Reinganum (1983), or Sakakibara and Branstetter (2001); for subsidies to e.g. Spencer and Brander (1983), Hinloopen (2000, 2001), Görg and Strobel (2007), or Aerts and Schmidt (2008); for research joint venture to e.g. Suzumura (1992), Kamien et al. (1992), or Suetens (2005) and for research tournaments to e.g. Moldovanu and Sela (2006), or Fullerton et al. (1999, 2002).

[92] "The standard economic rationale for patents is to protect inventors from imitation and thereby give them the incentive to incur the cost of innovation. Conventional wisdom holds that, unless would-be competitors are restrained from imitating an invention, the inventor may not reap enough profit to cover that cost. Thus, even if the social benefit of invention exceeds the cost, the potential innovator without patent protection may decide against innovating altogether", Bessen and Maskin (2006), p. 1.

[93] Among various aspects of patent laws that have been already studied in the economic literature are the optimal length and breadth of patents (e.g. Nordhaus (1969); Gilbert and Shapiro (1990); Klemperer (1990); Gallini (1992); Chang (1995)). There exist also studies on patent races focusing on the timing of investment and the different behavior of leaders and laggards see e.g. Breitmoser et al. (2008), Zizzo (2002) and Kähkönen (2005).

[94] Full appropriability of an innovation means that the innovating firm gains the complete profits induced by the innovation, i.e., monopoly profits. Therefore full appropriability corresponds to patent protection.

overcome a threshold of investing in R&D. Theoretical work (see e.g. Hinloopen (2001)) concerning the impact of subsidies indicates that investment levels as well as welfare are increased, but that profits decrease.[95] An experimental study on the effects of subsidies and appropriability on stochastic R&D investment by Davis et al. (1995) also proves that R&D investment is increased significantly by a subsidy. Other experimental studies on subsidizing R&D like those by Buckley et al. (2003) and Cooper and Selto (1991) rather focus on the effect of different designs of the subsidy in form of tax benefits and R&D project funding (see Giebe et al. (2006)).

The existing literature provides evidence that patents as well as subsidies seem to have a substantial impact on rising R&D investment. The aim of this chapter is to make a first attempt to *directly* compare the effect of patent protection and subsidies on firms' investment in R&D by running a controlled laboratory experiment. Particularly, we investigate the questions whether patents and subsidies encourage R&D investment into a cost reducing technology (process innovation) at all compared to the baseline case without governmental incentives and which of the two instruments actually leads to higher R&D spending thus providing a stronger investment incentive in the experimental setting. Contrary to empirical research which is based on real-world data, where always a mix of instruments is present and the induced effects are not easily distinguishable, our experimental data (i) ensure that only one of the instruments is present at a time and thereby (ii) enable us to study the influence of each instrument separately and thus to compare them in a controlled setting.

The experiment consists of a two-stage game in which at a first stage subjects are asked to invest in an uncertain R&D project followed by a market stage with Bertrand price competition.[96] Investment behavior in R&D on the basis of two-stage games is investigated experimentally by e.g. Jullien and Ruffieux (2001), Suetens (2008) and Isaac and Reynolds (1992). Note that by additionally implementing a market stage (second stage of the game), a firm's private returns from R&D are determined endogenously at this Bertrand competition stage (by price setting and demand) and are not exogenously given. Following Dufwenberg and Gneezy (2000) who find that three firms are enough

---

[95] Note that a tax is used in those models to finance the subsidy.
[96] A Bertrand market is chosen for simplification in the experiment and to follow the patent race literature which often uses a the-winner-takes-all assumption, for a general model see Harris and Vickers (1987). In our setting only an exclusive innovating firm can reap all profits at the market stage, the other firms receive nothing.

to let prices converge to equilibrium prices in Bertrand games, a market is assumed to consist of three competing firms.

Three treatments are run: one with patent protection, one with subsidizing (lower investment costs), and - as a benchmark - one without incentive instruments. In order to make patent protection and subsidizing perfectly comparable, the experimental parameters for both incentive instruments are chosen in a way that in equilibrium the profit maximizing investment for firms and thus the social welfare evolving from both are equal. Specifically, in our model the patent protects the innovation during the whole market duration and the subsidy is chosen in such a way that the investment induced will equal the investment under patent protection in equilibrium. Our experiment provides evidence that subsidies and patents have a significantly positive impact on R&D investment and that the effect of both instruments on incentives to innovate is similar. However, our experiment also shows that firms seem to fail to provide their profit maximizing R&D effort as they overinvest compared to their theoretically predicted equilibrium level. This implies dissipation of rents since we observe in both treatments that welfare on the society level is smaller than in equilibrium.

The remaining part of the chapter is structured as follows. Section III.2 presents the theoretical model, which is followed by the experimental design and proceedings in Section III.3. Section III.4 encloses the experimental results and with a discussion, in Section III.5, we conclude.

III.2 The Model

Consider the following two-stage game with $i=1,...,n$ risk-neutral firms. At the first stage ('R&D investment stage'), each firm starts out with identically high marginal costs $c_i^H = c^H$, $\forall i$, and independently decides on the amount it invests in R&D, $r_i \in [0,1]$, to gain low marginal costs, $c_i^L = c^L > 0$, $\forall i$, with $0 \leq c^L < c^H$.[97] Firm i's probability of successful R&D is given by a continuous cumulative distribution, $F(r_i)$, with density $f(r_i)$, and we assume $F(0) = 0$, $F(1) = 1$, and that $F(\cdot)$ is monotone and concave (i.e., $f(r_i) > 0$ and $f'(r_i) < 0$ for $r_i \in [0,1]$, respectively). In words, we assume constant marginal costs and

---

[97] Each firm chooses privately and simultaneously an R&D investment level.

diminishing returns from R&D investment.[98] At the second stage ('market stage'), $t=1,...,T$ consecutive Bertrand market periods take place in each of which firms simultaneously set their prices, $p_{i,t}$, at which they sell a homogeneous good.[99] Consumers only buy at the lowest market price, p_t^{min}, and we assume the same (normalized) price-inelastic market demand in each period, $Q=Q_t=1$, $\forall t$.[100] In the first Bertrand market period, each firm's marginal costs, c^H or c^L, only depend on its own success in the R&D investment stage.[101] We assume, without loss of generality, that high cost firms can then imitate the production technology of low cost firms at no cost and also produce at c^L beginning in the second market period. Thus, in absence of any imitation-prohibiting policy, a firm's marginal costs in the second and all subsequent market periods depend not only on its own success but also on whether or not at least one firm has successfully innovated in the first period.

We examine two common government R&D policies that influence the firms' incentives to invest in R&D: *subsidies* and *patents*. Subsidies target at the cost side of each firm's expected profit from R&D by covering a proportion $\sigma \in [0,1]$ of its R&D costs (i.e., each firm i pays $(1-\sigma)r_i$ and government pays σr_i). Patents, in contrast, target at the revenue side of each firm's expected profit by protecting innovating firms beyond the first period. More precisely, government prohibits high cost firms to apply imitated production technologies for other $\theta=0,1,...,T-1$ market periods after the first market period. Note that each successfully innovating firm obtains patent protection in our model, i.e., more than one firm in a market might be provided with a patent. Thus, patent protection does not automatically create a monopoly. One might argue that this is no 'pure' patent protection (in the sense of 'the winner takes all'). However, it is realistic to assume that firms might invest in different technology innovations yielding a cost reduction and that these different technologies are protected. Finally, we assume that the game structure and parameters as well as the R&D success of each firm and the government R&D policy (hence the marginal cost of

---

[98] Although it is debated whether R&D investments exhibit diminishing returns in the empirical literature, we follow the theoretical papers in the tradition of d'Aspremont and Jacquemin (1988). For comments on that matter please refer, e.g., to Kamien and Schwartz (1975), Griliches (1990), and Nadiri (1993). We also refrain from modeling fix costs, FC, as we do not analyze any decisions to enter the market.
[99] For simplicity, we assume that firms only produce when they can sell.
[100] An implication of assuming price-inelastic demand is that the innovation will be automatically non-drastic since the monopoly price before and after the innovation (which equals the prohibitive price $\bar{p}$) is assumed to be higher than c^H.
[101] We assume that there are no technological spillovers at the investment stage: Each firm i's chances of a successful innovation depend only on its own investment r_i, not on a rival's investment r_j.

each firm in each market period) are common knowledge. In the next subsections we analyze our two-stage game. Due to backward induction we start the analysis with the second stage of the game followed by the first stage.

III.2.1 Market Stage

Depending on the government's R&D policy and the firms' R&D successes at the first stage, we distinguish between the following three compositions of marginal costs in each Bertrand market (for simplicity, we refrain from indexing R&D policies and market periods). We assume that among the firms which offer the lowest price those with the lowest marginal costs share the demand equally.

Proposition III.1 (*Market equilibrium*)

(i) c_i^H, $\forall i$ ('*no firm has low marginal costs*') in which case any price constellation with $p_i^* = p_j^* = c^H$, $i \neq j$, and $p_k^* \geq c^H$, $\forall k \neq i,j$ is a Nash equilibrium of the market period with market profits $\pi_i^* = 0$, $\forall i$;

(ii) c_i^L and c_{-i}^H, $\forall -i \neq i$ ('*one firm has low marginal costs*') in which case any price constellation with $p_i^* = p_j^* = c^H$, $i \neq j$, and $p_k^* \geq c^H$, $\forall k \neq i,j$ is a Nash equilibrium of the market period with market profits $\pi_i^* = p_i^* - c^L \equiv c^H - c^L > 0$ and $\pi_{-i}^* = 0$, $\forall -i \neq i$;

(iii) $c_i^L = c_j^L$, $i \neq j$, and $c_k^L \lor c_k^H$, $\forall k \neq i,j$ ('*at least two firms have low marginal costs*') in which case any price constellation with $p_i^* = p_j^* = c^L$ and $p_k^* \geq c^L$ is a Nash equilibrium with market profits $\pi_i^* = 0$, $\forall i$.

Proof of Proposition III.1. These are well-known standard results (see, for instance, Motta 2004). ∎

Note that (*i*), (*ii*), and (*iii*) may apply to the first market period and all periods that are patent protected by government, but in all other cases either no firm or all firms have low marginal costs. Moreover, note that market prices as well as Nash equilibrium profits are unique for each cost structure (though there are infinitely many Nash equilibrium price constellations) and that the only equilibrium situation in which a firm makes strictly positive market profits is in case it is the only low cost firm.

III.2.2 R&D Investment Stage

In this subsection we analyze the investment decision at the first stage. In the following we concentrate on the case that all firms' R&D investments are symmetric (i.e., $r_i \equiv r$, $\forall i$) as a benchmark case. Note that there might also exist asymmetric equilibria. We will discuss the equilibrium selection in more detail in Sections III.2.4 and III.4.1. At the R&D investment stage, each firm knows the government's R&D policy and anticipates all possible Nash equilibrium profits at the market stage.

Proposition III.2 (R&D investment levels) *The symmetric Nash equilibrium level of R&D investment, $r^*(n, \Delta c, \theta, \sigma) \in [0,1]$, is characterized by the necessary and sufficient condition*

$$f(r^*)[1 - F(r^*)]^{n-1}(1+\theta)\Delta c = 1 - \sigma. \quad (1)$$

The optimal investment level in R&D r^* is increasing in the mark-up from being the only low cost firm $\Delta c = p - c^L = c^H - c^L$, the number of patent-protected periods θ, and the subsidized proportion of the firms' R&D investment costs σ. However, r^* is decreasing in the number of firms n; and it is independent of the number of market periods T.

The proof is given in the Appendix.

Proposition III.2 implies that both policy instruments provide incentives for the firms to increase their investment levels in R&D. Moreover, as a firm can only achieve positive profits under Bertrand competition if it is the sole innovating firm in its market, the incentive to invest in R&D increases the higher this mark-up is. In our model investment levels decrease with competition (i.e., an increase in n), because it becomes less probable that a firm is the sole innovator the more competitors are in the market. Note that there is huge literature studying the impact of market structure on investment behavior providing mixed results (for studies on the different effects of competition on investment see e.g. Boone (2000), Schmutzler (2007), Vives (2006), or Sacco and Schmutzler (2008) for an experimental investigation).[102] The equilibrium value of r is independent of the number of market periods T, because without any

---
[102] Cohen and Levin (1989, p. 1075) already stated that "[e]conomists have offered an array of theoretical arguments yielding ambiguous predictions about the effects of market structure on innovation."

imitation-prohibiting policy a firm can only receive strictly positive Nash equilibrium market profits if it is the only low cost firm in the first period. The number of market periods in which this low cost firm can make such profits is in our model reduced to the first period and in the patent case determined by the additional number of patent-protected market periods θ. However, T is the upper boundary of θ and thus may have an indirect effect on r^* in case of patent protection.

III.2.3 Distributional Effects

In this subsection we distinguish the welfare shares (or rents) of the different interest groups (firms, consumers and government) in order to analyze the effects of an increase in the subsidized proportion and in the number of patent-protected periods, respectively. Thereby, we do not focus on absolute changes of the rents, but rather on rent shifting between different interest groups. Given equilibrium behavior of the firms (i.e., the symmetric Nash equilibrium investment level of $r_i^*(\sigma,\theta) = r^*(\sigma,\theta)$, $\forall i$), we investigate the impact of each policy instrument on added rents.[103] Proposition III.3 indicates that different policy instruments have different distributional consequences.

Proposition III.3 (Rent shifting)   *An increase in the subsidized proportion of the firms' R&D investment costs induces a transfer from government to firms as well as expected rent shifting between consumers and firms; an increase in the number of patent-protected market periods induces as well expected rent shifting between consumers and firms.*

Proof of Proposition III.3. If firms choose the symmetric Nash equilibrium investment level, this yields the following implications for added welfare shares of different interest groups. Note first that the investment level r is strictly increasing in σ and θ as was shown in Proposition III.2 ($\frac{dr}{d\sigma} > 0$ and $\frac{dr}{d\theta} > 0$).
In the following we first present the derivatives of welfare shares with respect to σ, then with respect to θ. The added government rent is given by

$$GR(r^*,\sigma) = -nr^*\sigma \quad (2).$$

Hence, an increase in the subsidized proportion σ yields

---

[103] Note that we use *added* rents, i.e., we consider the change of actual total rents in case firms invest in R&D in comparison to the situation in which no firm invests in R&D.

$$\frac{\partial GR(r^*,\sigma,\theta)}{\partial \sigma} = -n\sigma \frac{dr^*}{d\sigma} - nr^* < 0. \quad \}\text{ transfer to } PR$$

Moreover, expected added consumer rent is given by[104]

$$CR^e(r^*,\theta,\sigma) = nF(r^*)[1-F(r^*)]^{n-1}(T-1-\theta)\Delta c$$

$$+ \sum_{k=2}^{n} \binom{n}{k} F(r^*)^k [1-F(r^*)]^{n-k} T\Delta c,$$

which can be rewritten as

$$CR^e(r^*,\theta,\sigma) = T\Delta c - [1-F(r^*)]^n T\Delta c$$
$$- nF(r^*)[1-F(r^*)]^{n-1}(1+\theta)\Delta c. \quad (3)$$

This yields

$$\frac{\partial CR^e(r^*,\theta,\sigma)}{\partial \sigma} = T\Delta c n f(r^*) \frac{dr^*}{d\sigma}[1-F(r^*)]^{n-1}$$

$$- n(1+\theta)\Delta c f(r^*) \frac{dr^*}{d\sigma}[1-F(r^*)]^{n-2}\{[1-F(r^*)]-(n-1)F(r^*)\}\} \text{ transfer to } PR$$

Finally, expected added producer rent is given by

$$PR^e(r^*,\theta,\sigma) = nF(r^*)[1-F(r^*)]^{n-1}(1+\theta)\Delta c - n(1-\sigma)r^*. \quad (4)$$

Hence, we have

$$\frac{\partial PR^e(r^*,\theta,\sigma)}{\partial \sigma} = n(1+\theta)\Delta c f(r^*)\frac{dr^*}{d\sigma}[1-F(r^*)]^{n-2}\{[1-F(r^*)]-(n-1)F(r^*)\}\} \text{ transfer from } CR$$

$$+ nr^* + n\sigma \frac{dr^*}{d\sigma}\} \text{ transfer from } GR$$

$$- n\frac{dr^*}{d\sigma}.$$

Now we concentrate on an increase of the number of patent-protected periods θ. Concerning government rent this yields

$$\frac{\partial GR(r^*,\sigma,\theta)}{\partial \theta} = -n\sigma \frac{dr^*}{d\theta} < 0. \quad \}\text{ transfer to } PR$$

---

[104] For a derivation of the added consumer rent see the Mathematical Appendix III.D1.

Note that $\frac{\partial GR(r^*, \sigma, \theta)}{\partial \theta} = 0$ if we consider 'pure' instruments (i.e., $\sigma = 0$ if patent protection is on hand).

The derivatives of CR^e and PR^e with respect to θ are given by

$$\frac{\partial CR^e(r^*, \theta, \sigma)}{\partial \theta} = T\Delta cnf(r^*)\frac{dr^*}{d\theta}\left[1-F(r^*)\right]^{n-1}$$

$$\left.\begin{array}{l} -n(1+\theta)\Delta cf(r^*)\frac{dr^*}{d\theta}\left[1-F(r^*)\right]^{n-2}\left[\left[1-F(r^*)\right]-(n-1)F(r^*)\right] \\ -n\Delta cF(r^*)\left[1-F(r^*)\right]^{n-1} \end{array}\right\} \text{transfer to } PR$$

and

$$\frac{\partial PR^e(r^*, \theta, \sigma)}{\partial \theta} = \left.\begin{array}{l} n(1+\theta)\Delta cf(r^*)\frac{dr^*}{d\theta}\left[1-F(r^*)\right]^{n-2}\left[\left[1-F(r^*)\right]-(n-1)F(r^*)\right] \\ +n\Delta cF(r^*)\left[1-F(r^*)\right]^{n-1} \end{array}\right\} \text{transfer from } CR$$

$$\left.\begin{array}{l} +n\sigma\frac{dr^*}{d\theta} \end{array}\right\} \text{transfer from } GR$$

$$-n\frac{dr^*}{d\theta}.$$

Then, our proposition holds, because there is rent shifting both between firms and government as well as between firms and consumers as indicated by curly brackets. More precisely, the first term of PR equals the second term of CR and the decrease of GR equals the increasing second term in PR. This is valid for an increase in the subsidized proportion as well as for an increase in the number of patent-protected periods. ∎

However, note that the sign of the shifted transfers between consumers and producers depends on the concrete parameterization. Precise predictions for our experimental setup are derived in the next subsection in order to analyze which group benefits from an introduction of subsidies and patents, respectively.

III.2.4 Experimental Setup: Equilibrium Predictions and Hypotheses

Table III.1 summarizes the treatment parameters of our experimental setup.[105] Specifically, we use the continuous cumulative probability distribution of R&D

---

[105] In the following the standard case with no instrument is called *NO*, the subsidy case is called *SUB* and the patent case *PAT*.

success $F(r_i) = \frac{1}{10} r_i^{0.5}$, $\forall r_i \in \{0,99\}$, with density $f(r_i) = \frac{1}{20} r_i^{-0.5}$ and $f'(r_i) = -\frac{1}{40} r_i^{-1.5}$, and $n=3$, $c^H=500$, $c^L=100$ and $T=2$. As the market stage consists only of two market periods and a cost reduction can only be imitated in the second period, we set the patent-protected rounds equal to $\theta = 1$ ($\theta = T-1$), i.e., the patent protects the innovation during the whole market duration T. The subsidy proportion $\sigma = \frac{1}{2}$ is chosen such that for comparability reasons of the two policy instruments both instruments (patents and subsidies) induce equal symmetric Nash equilibrium investment levels.

Table III.1: Treatment parameters

Treatment	Investment costs	Cost structure 1st market period	Cost structure 2nd market period	Number of independent observations (sessions)
NO	r_i	$c_{i,1} \in \{c^L, c^H\}$	$c_{i,2} = \min[c_{1,1}, c_{2,1}, c_{3,1}]$	5(1)
SUB	$0.5 r_i$	$c_{i,1} \in \{c^L, c^H\}$	$c_{i,2} = \min[c_{1,1}, c_{2,1}, c_{3,1}]$	5(1)
PAT	r_i	$c_{i,1} \in \{c^L, c^H\}$	$c_{i,2} = c_{i,1}$	5(1)

The cost structure is given by $c_{i,t}$, where i denotes the firm and t the market period.

The continuous equilibrium predictions which will be used as a benchmark for our data analysis are given in Table III.2 for our concrete parameters.[106] The equilibrium R&D investments lead to the same added welfare in *SUB* and *PAT* which is higher than in *NO*.[107] Comparing the effect of an introduction of each R&D policy instrument with the situation without policy instruments Table III.2 indicates that an introduction of subsidies decreases the firms' expected added profits and government rent, and increases expected added consumer rent. The introduction of patent protection increases the firms' expected profits and decreases expected consumer rent. Thus, in our concrete experimental setup the

Table III.2: Experimental predictions

Treatment	Nash equilibrium investment	Added welfare	Added consumer rent	Added producer rent	Added government rent
NO	25	625	550	75	0.00
SUB	37.16	640.92	640.90	55.76	-55.74
PAT	37.16	640.92	529.40	111.51	0.00

For the derivation of welfare shares we use the continuous symmetric Nash equilibrium investment levels given in the first column of this table as well as $T=2$, $\theta=1$, $\sigma=0.5$ and $\Delta c = 400$.

---

[106] Derivations of equilibrium investment levels are given in the Mathematical Appendix III.D2. Note that the presented investment levels are the symmetric Nash equilibria. In *SUB* and in *PAT* in addition there exist three asymmetric Nash equilibria given by (56.25, 56.25, 6.25).
[107] The formula for added welfare is given in the Mathematical Appendix III.D3. The individual welfare shares (added consumer, producer and government rent) are given in the proof of Proposition III.3.

introduction of a subsidy partly shifts rents from firms to consumers and the introduction of a patent partly shifts rents from consumers to firms.

The symmetric Nash equilibrium investment level and the corresponding implications for welfare shares yield testable predictions about the incentives to invest in R&D. Let us summarize our main experimental hypothesis which will be tested in Section III.4:

Hypothesis 1: (*Investment levels*)   Investment levels increase if a policy instrument (*SUB*, *PAT*) is introduced.

Hypothesis 2: (*Welfare*)   Welfare increases if a policy instrument is introduced.

Hypothesis 3: (*Special interests*)   Consumers prefer *SUB* to *NO* to *PAT*, firms prefer *PAT* to *NO* to *SUB*.

III.3 Experimental Design and Procedures

The computerized[108] experiment was conducted at the Cologne Laboratory for Economic Research in December 2005. We ran 3 sessions (baseline (*NO*), subsidy (*SUB*) and patent (*PAT*) treatment) each with 30 subjects.[109] Each session lasted about 1.45 hours (cf. the Appendix for the instructions). Earnings in the experiment were expressed in points. At the end of a session, point earnings were transferred to cash at an exchange rate of 300 points = 1 €. Subjects earned on average 14.95 € including a 2.50 € show-up fee (average earnings amount to: 16.53 € in Session 1 (*PAT*), 13.84 € in Session 2 (*SUB*) and 14.48 € in Session 3 (*NO*)).

Each session consists of 30 decision rounds. At the beginning of the experiment, subjects are randomly divided into 5 matching groups of 6 subjects each. At the beginning of each round 3 subjects (i.e., 'firm' 1, 2, and 3, respectively) are randomly matched.[110] Though subjects know they are randomly re-matched in each round, they are not informed that this happens within matching groups. Hence, each session provides us with five independent observations.

---

[108] The experimental software was programmed using z-Tree (Fischbacher (2007)).
[109] Subjects were recruited using ORSEE (Greiner 2004). The vast majority (96%) of subjects were undergraduate students from the University of Cologne, mostly belonging to the faculty of management, economics and social sciences.
[110] We use strangers matching to avoid cooperation in a repeated game and to retain the one-shot character. Price competition experiments show that three firms are sufficient to ensure near Bertrand-equilibrium prices (see Dufwenberg and Gneezy (2000)).

Each round of the 30 rounds is divided into two phases. Phase 1 corresponds to the investment stage and phase 2 to the market stage with two consecutive market periods $T=2$ (labeled phase 2A and 2B, respectively). In the *NO* treatment, each subject receives an endowment of $B=100$ points at the beginning of each round. In phase 1, each subject has to make an investment decision by choosing an integer of $r_i \in \{0,1,...,99\}$ points, which is subtracted from his endowment B. Moreover, each subject starts with high production costs of $c_i^H = 500$ points. Depending on the investment decision r_i and chance, represented by the realization of the cumulative probability function $F(r_i) = 0.1(r_i)^{0.5}$,[111] an innovation may occur which decreases production costs to a lower level of $c_i^L = 100$ points.[112] At the beginning of phase 2, each subject is informed about whether or not he successfully innovates, i.e., achieves lower production costs, and also about the innovation success of the other two subjects in his group (but not about their investment decisions). Thereafter, the first Bertrand market (phase 2A) starts, in which each subject has to submit a price $p_{i,1} \in \{c_{i,1}, c_{i,1}+1,...,1000\}$ between his own production costs $c_{i,1} \in \{c_{i,1}^L, c_{i,1}^H\}$ and a prohibitive price of 1000 points. The $n_1 \in \{1,2,3\}$ subjects with the lowest submitted price in the market can sell their goods[113] each earning $\pi_{i,1} = \frac{1}{n_1}(p_{i,1} - c_{i,1})$ points in the first market, whereas subjects with higher prices earn nothing (zero points). Each subject is informed about the lowest price and his own profit in the first market, but no other information is given. In the second Bertrand market (phase 2B), due to costless imitation opportunities, each subject starts with the lowest production costs among the firms in the first market $c_{i,2} = \min\{c_{1,1}, c_{2,1}, c_{3,1}\}, \forall i$. The procedure in the second market is exactly the same as in the first market: Those subjects with the lowest price (n_2) obtain

---

[111] To simplify matters r_i is divided by hundred, since this allows subjects to choose integer numbers between 0 and 99 in the experiment instead of decimals. Note that by excluding an investment level of 100, cost reduction remains stochastic since the maximum feasible investment level still bears the risk of failure.
[112] In the experiment subjects are given a table which specifies the investment costs and the probability of a cost reduction (i.e., a successful innovation) for each possible investment level. Given a subject's investment decision, the computer program randomly determines based on the corresponding cumulative probability function $F(r_i)$ whether or not the subject 'innovates', i.e., achieves lower production costs (for more details of these procedures and the given table see the instructions in the Appendix).
[113] In order to make the design as simple as possible for the subjects, those subjects with the lowest price share the demand equally. Thus, we relax the assumption of our model that among those firms which offer the lowest price only those with the lowest marginal costs share the demand. Note that this implies that the achievable mark-up of a sole innovator decreases to $\Delta c = 399$, since its equilibrium price decreases to 499.

profits of $\pi_{i,2} = \frac{1}{n_2}(p_{i,2} - c_{i,2})$ points and those with higher prices zero-profits. At the end of each round, each subject i is informed about his round profits, which are given by $\pi_i = \pi_{i,1} + \pi_{i,2} - r_i + B$, and his total profits so far.

In the *PAT* treatment, exactly the same procedure as in *NO* is applied, with the only difference that imitation in the second Bertrand market is prohibited ($\theta = 1$): Each subject's production costs in the second market are equal to his own costs in the first market $c_{i,2} = c_{i,1}$, $\forall i$. Finally, the *SUB* treatment differs in only one aspect from *NO*: As half of the investment costs are subsidized ($\sigma = \frac{1}{2}$), a firm's investment costs are reduced from r_i to $0.5 r_i$ (compare also Table III.1).

III.4 Experimental Results

The presentation and analysis of our experimental data are organized as follows. We start by examining R&D investment levels (III.4.1) including investment dynamics and individual behavior. Thereafter, we investigate firms' price setting and resulting profits in the Bertrand markets (III.4.2). Finally, we analyze the effects of subsidies and patents on social welfare as well as on welfare for special interest groups, i.e., firms, consumers and government (III.4.3). In case average results are presented, the term average refers to mean value over rounds in the subsequent analyses. Laboratory findings and their comparisons with the respective Nash predictions are summarized as *experimental results* (ER) at the end of each section.

III.4.1 R&D Investments

Table III.3 shows the average R&D investment for each treatment and the predicted symmetric Nash equilibrium for continuous investment levels.[114] At first sight, there are two remarkable aspects. First, the observed investment level is higher using a policy instrument like subsidy or patent in comparison with our baseline treatment with no R&D policy: Subsidies and patents increase firms' R&D investment levels by 35.79% and 45.62%, respectively. This indicates that both instruments serve the purpose of rising investment levels supporting

---

[114] We take the continuous symmetric Nash equilibrium as a benchmark. Note that we get multiple equilibria in case of discrete investment levels (all equilibria are given in Table III.A1 in the Appendix). However, continuous and discrete equilibria do not differ (much) as long as we concentrate on symmetric equilibria (discrete symmetric equilibria are 25, 37, 37 in *NO, SUB, PAT*).

Hypothesis 1.[115] Using matching group averages as independent observations a Kruskal-Wallis test reveals that we can reject the hypothesis that the investment levels of all treatments are drawn from the same population.[116] Pair-wise Mann-Whitney-U tests reveal significant differences between *NO* and *SUB* as well as between *NO* and *PAT* whereas *SUB* and *PAT* investment levels do not differ significantly.[117] Second, the observed average R&D investment in the experiment is always higher than the predicted Nash equilibrium for each treatment. R&D investments are about 37.92% (26.00%; 35.12%) higher than theoretically predicted by the symmetric Nash equilibrium in *NO* (*SUB*, *PAT*). We will later discuss possible explanations for the surprising overinvestment result.

Table III.3: Average observed and predicted R&D investments

Investment levels	NO	SUB	PAT
Observed	34.48 (23.67)	46.82 (32.13)	50.21 (35.61)
Predicted	25	37.16	37.16

Standard deviations are given in parentheses.

III.4.1.1 Investment Dynamics

Figure III.1 depicts observed and predicted average R&D investment levels per round. These levels are higher than predicted by the symmetric Nash equilibrium

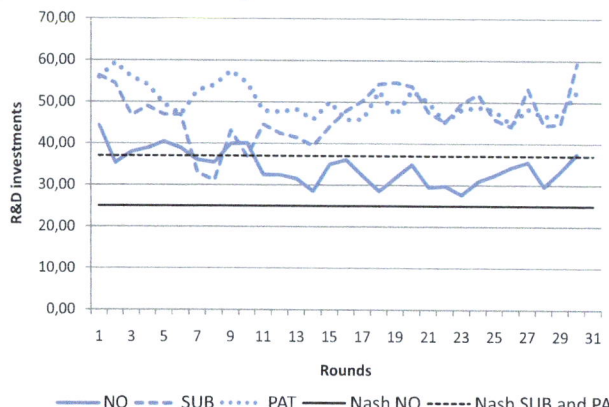

Figure III.1: Observed and predicted R&D investments over rounds

---

[115] However, note that the theoretical increase in investment levels is higher: Investment levels are predicted to be 48.64% higher in *SUB* (and *PAT* respectively) than in *NO*.
[116] In the following nonparametric tests we always use matching groups as independent observations.
[117] One-tailed Mann-Whitney-U tests reject the null hypothesis of no differences in average investments in favor of higher investment levels in *SUB* and *PAT* than in *NO* ($p=0.016$) respectively ($p=0.004$), but cannot reject the null hypothesis for the comparison of *SUB* and *PAT* ($p=0.21$).

in all rounds in each treatment (with only three exceptions in *SUB*). Considering investment behavior over time, average R&D investment levels decrease from the first to the second half of 30 rounds in *NO* and *PAT* (36.59 vs. 32.36 and 52.14 vs. 48.28, respectively), but increase in *SUB* (43.81 vs. 49.82). However, Wilcoxon Signed Rank tests yield significant results only for the decrease in investments in *NO* at the 5% significance level.

To examine the dynamics of R&D investment decisions at the individual level, we use a simple ordinary least squares regression (Table III.4). Due to dependency of the observations within matching groups we calculate clustered standard errors. As explanatory variables we consider treatment dummies and dummies for firm i's success in reducing its cost in the previous round (i.e., lagged variables) as well as round dummies. The treatment dummies (*NO, SUB, PAT*) are used to generate interaction variables with the explanatory variables. In model (1) in Table III.4 we consider dummies for a cost reduction due to successful innovation of a firm in the previous round CR_{t-1} (CR=1 for successful innovation, CR=0 for no innovation), where t denotes the round. Round dummies given for the first half of rounds (round 1-15) and the second half of rounds (round 16-30) as the base category are considered additionally in model (3). Moreover, in the estimated model (2) in Table III.4 cost reduction dummies CR are subdivided into the cases that only firm i successfully reduced its costs ($CR1_{t-1}$), that firm i and one other firm j reduced their costs ($CR2_{t-1}$), and that all three firms reduced their costs in the previous round ($CR3_{t-1}$). Note that in all these categories at least firm i successfully innovates. The reference category for the three cost reduction dummies ($CR1_{t-1}$, $CR2_{t-1}$, $CR3_{t-1}$) is the situation that firm i did not have low costs in the previous round independent of the other firms' cost levels ($CR0_{t-1}$).

Model (1) in Table III.4 shows that a successful innovation of firm i in the previous round has a positive and highly significant influence on its current investment level compared to the reference category 'no success' (CR=0). Moreover, the coefficients of all single cost reduction dummies in model (2) have a positive sign and are significantly different from zero as well: Independent of the treatment a firm i invests significantly more in the current round if at least this firm i successfully innovated in the previous round compared to the benchmark case that firm i had no success. Note that the investment level also increases if one or even both other firms in the market were also successful in cost reduction in the previous round. Note as well that being the exclusive innovator increases investment levels strongest (compare Table III.A2 in the Appendix, where we drop $CR1$ as the base category; the coefficients for all other cost reduction dummies are negative compared with $CR1$). In line with the results from above we observe a round effect in NO: We find that investment levels in NO are significantly higher being in the first half of rounds (first round excluded) compared to the last half of rounds, whereas investment levels are significantly lower in the first half of rounds in SUB and are not significantly influenced by round in PAT.

Table III.4: OLS regression results

Investment	(1) coefficient	(St. er.)	(2) coefficient	(St. er.)	(3) coefficient	(St. er.)
NO	28.26***	(2.604)	28.26***	(1.962)	26.67***	(2.347)
SUB	31.78***	(2.086)	31.78***	(1.265)	34.84***	(1.626)
PAT	27.90***	(3.671)	27.90***	(4.007)	27.33***	(3.663)
$CR_{t-1}*NO$	11.18***	(2.226)			11.09***	(2.204)
$CR_{t-1}*SUB$	23.34***	(3.096)			23.09***	(2.983)
$CR_{t-1}*PAT$	37.49***	(3.884)			37.40***	(3.906)
$CR1_{t-1}*NO$			15.82***	(2.607)		
$CR1_{t-1}*SUB$			25.63***	(2.088)		
$CR1_{t-1}*PAT$			46.84***	(3.675)		
$CR2_{t-1}*NO$			11.95***	(2.870)		
$CR2_{t-1}*SUB$			22.45***	(1.862)		
$CR2_{t-1}*PAT$			38.12***	(4.337)		
$CR3_{t-1}*NO$			6.231**	(2.581)		
$CR3_{t-1}*SUB$			23.79***	(3.652)		
$CR3_{t-1}*PAT$			31.36***	(2.896)		
round1_15*NO					3.39**	(1.511)
round1_15*SUB					-6.004***	(1.917)
round1_15*PAT					1.286	(1.838)
N	2610		2610		2610	
R^2	0.211		0.218		0.215	

Standard errors are given in parentheses and are corrected for matching group clusters. As we drop the constant in the estimated models, the reported R^2 is taken from the (analogous) models as presented in Table III.A3.
$^*p<0.1$, $^{**}p<0.05$, $^{***}p<0.01$

The above OLS regression measures the effects of the tested parameters in each treatment (i.e., whether a parameter has an influence on a firm's investment level for each treatment separately). For a comparison of effects between treatments (i.e., whether a parameter has a stronger influence in one treatment than in the other) see OLS regression results given in Table III.A3 in the Appendix. As the reference treatment we drop the treatment dummy 'SUB'. Table III.A3 clearly indicates that the positive effect of firm i's successful innovation (compared to no success) on investment levels is significantly stronger in PAT than in SUB and significantly weaker in NO than in SUB (see models (1) and (3)). Moreover, the positive effect of a successful cost reduction on the investment level if firm i is the exclusive innovator or if firm i and one other firm successfully innovate is as well in *PAT* significantly higher and in *NO* significantly lower than in *SUB* (see model (2)).

III.4.1.2 Individual Investment Decisions

In the previous sections we focused on symmetric Nash equilibrium R&D investment strategies, which specifically imply that each firm always chooses a discrete investment level of 25 in *NO* and 37 in *SUB* and *PAT*. However, the actual investment levels are very diverse: Figure III.2 specifies the frequencies of the chosen investment levels for each treatment.[118] Obviously, in the baseline treatment without policy instruments the predominant investment level is consistent with the symmetric Nash equilibrium investment level of 25 (this level is chosen in 19.11% of cases). Yet keeping the endowment and investing zero is the second most chosen behavior in this treatment. On the contrary, in the two treatments with policy instruments the Nash equilibrium of 37 is almost never

Figure III.2: Investment frequencies

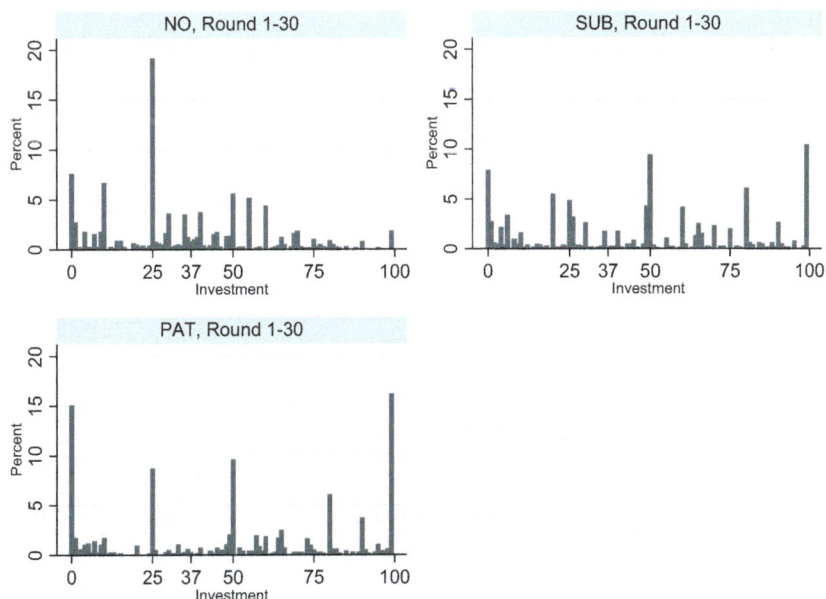

---

[118] Individual investment behavior over rounds is given in Figure III.A1 in the Appendix. A small fraction of subjects sticks to a certain investment level (or adjusts the investment level only slightly over rounds). Investment levels remaining constant over rounds are most frequently observed in the *PAT* treatment.

chosen (in less than 1% of the cases). In the *PAT* treatment the most frequently chosen investment levels are zero (15%) and the maximum of 99 (16.11%). This behavior obeys kind of an 'all-or-none law': A subject either invests his complete endowment trying to achieve low costs (and thus a possible competitive advantage in the two market periods) or a subject decides on retaining his endowment and not trying at all to reduce his costs for the market stage. A smaller percentage of investments of 9.56% is set equal to the intermediate level of 50. In the *SUB* treatment the most chosen investment levels 0, 50 and 99 are more uniformly distributed (7.78%; 9.33%; 10.33%).

Investing 99 points is the most frequently chosen strategy in both treatments with policy instruments,[119] whereas investing the maximum amount plays nearly no role in the baseline treatment. To examine these observed frequencies further, we consider asymmetric equilibria in the following. Table III.5 summarizes discrete symmetric and asymmetric Nash equilibrium R&D investment levels for our experimental parameters. Note that the discrete parameterization gives raise to asymmetric equilibria. In the continuous case there exists only a unique symmetric equilibrium investment level in *NO*, and a symmetric and three asymmetric equilibria in *SUB* and *PAT* (compare footnote 106).

Table III.5 reveals that some of the frequencies shown in Figure III.2 may be explained by asymmetric Nash equilibria. In all treatments there exist three asymmetric Nash equilibria in which two firms choose 0 and one firm chooses 99. This is consistent with the observed investment levels of 0 and 99. However, note that the predicted asymmetric equilibria of (0, 0, 99) fail to explain (i) why 99 is chosen even more often than the minimum level of zero in *SUB* and *PAT*, as opposed to half the times as predicted and (ii) why 0 and 99 are less frequently chosen in *NO* than in *SUB* and *PAT*. The first observation might hint at a possible coordination failure. The asymmetric equilibria add a substantial coordination problem to the subjects' decision task.[120] The second observation that 0 and 99 are less frequently chosen in *NO* than in *SUB* and *PAT* may be explained by additional asymmetric investment levels which exclusively occur in *NO*: In *NO*

---

[119] The accumulation of the maximum investment level in *SUB* and *PAT* might be a further indication that the introduction of either policy instrument provides stronger incentives to invest in R&D.
[120] However, there seems to be evidence that at least some subjects are aware of this coordination problem, because we observe subjects 'jumping' from very low investment levels to very high investment levels and vice versa especially in the *SUB* treatment (cf. Figure III.A1 in the Appendix). In general, a subject has an incentive to decrease his own investment if a rival increases his investment and vice versa (see comparative statics in the Mathematical Appendix III.D4).

the number of discrete asymmetric Nash equilibria is highest (in *SUB* and *PAT* there exist – besides the symmetric equilibrium – only the asymmetric equilibria in which one firm invests all and the other two firms invest nothing (0,0,99)). In *NO* there are in addition asymmetric Nash equilibria consisting of R&D investment levels from the interval [20, 21,..., 30]. Note that although in *NO* the number of discrete asymmetric Nash equilibria is highest, *NO* is nevertheless the treatment in which behavior is most consistent with the symmetric Nash equilibrium. This might be due to the fact that the additional asymmetric investment levels are oscillating around the symmetric equilibrium investment level of 25. Hence, it seems that asymmetric Nash equilibria can contribute to explain some of our data.[121]

Table III.5: Discrete symmetric and asymmetric Nash equilibrium investment levels

Treatment		Investment decision		
		r_i	r_j	r_k
NO	Symmetric	25	25	25
	Asymmetric	All combinations of investment levels [20,...,30] that add up to 75, without (25,25,25)		
		0	0	99
SUB	Symmetric	37	37	37
	Asymmetric	0	0	99
PAT	Symmetric	37	37	37
	Asymmetric	0	0	99

All asymmetric equilibria are given in Table III.A1 in the Appendix.

We also examine the dynamics of investment behavior (i.e., the time path of investment) in order to analyze whether there is a convergence to equilibrium levels over rounds. Therefore we consider investment behavior of the first round as well as investment behavior of the first third, second third and last third of rounds separately (Figures III.3-III.5). Strikingly, investment levels of 25 (which is no equilibrium strategy in *SUB* and *PAT*) and 50 are chosen frequently (50 is even the most often chosen investment level in *NO* and *PAT* in the first round). Possible explanations for this observation might be that those investment levels are prominent numbers and, moreover, that an investment of 25 gives a 50% chance of a successful innovation, which might also create a focal point. However, note that an investment level of 25 is chosen much more frequently in

---

[121] Besides behavior that is consistent with asymmetric equilibria, we observe 'local maxima' in all three treatments, which occur in 5-scale increments. By local maxima we mean investment levels which are chosen more frequently compared to investment levels slightly below and slightly above these maxima (e.g. in the range from 50 to 60 investments of 50, 55 and 60 are chosen in more cases than intermediate investment levels). This may be explained by the prominence level of numbers (see Albers (2001)) as these investment level increments seem to create focal points.

NO – where it is the symmetric equilibrium level – since the very first round. Thus, at least a part of this percentage in *NO* seems to be driven by equilibrium investment behavior. Furthermore, the fraction of the chosen symmetric Nash equilibrium level of 25 in *NO* remains constant from the first third till the last third (although it is lower in the first round in which the most often chosen

Figure III.3: Dynamic view on investment level choices – *NO*

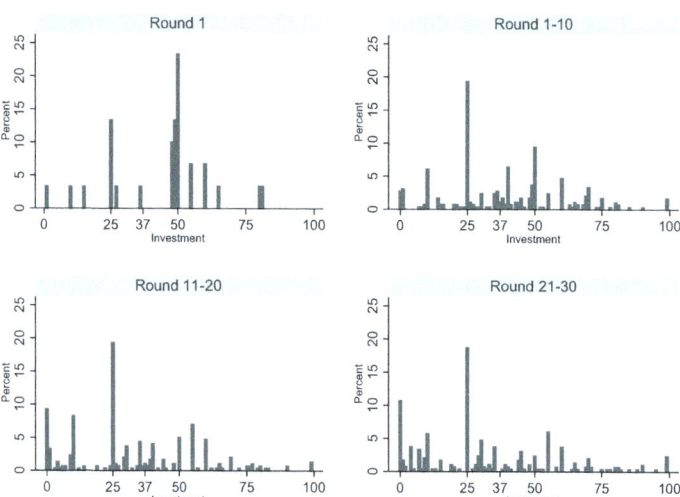

Figure III.4: Dynamic view on investment level choices – *SUB*

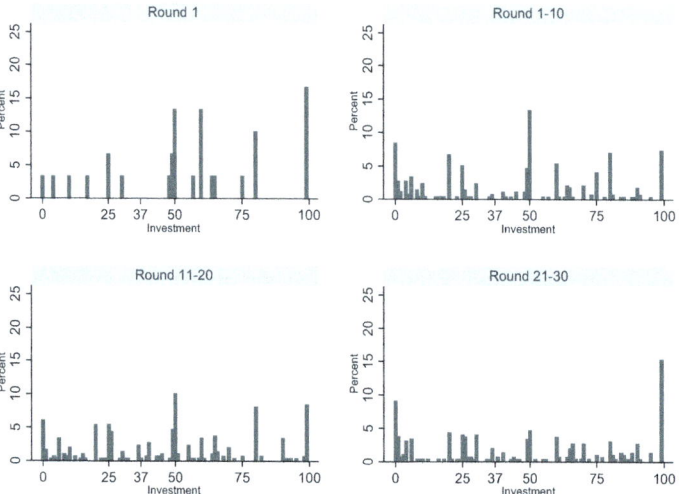

Figure III.5: Dynamic view on investment level choices – *PAT*

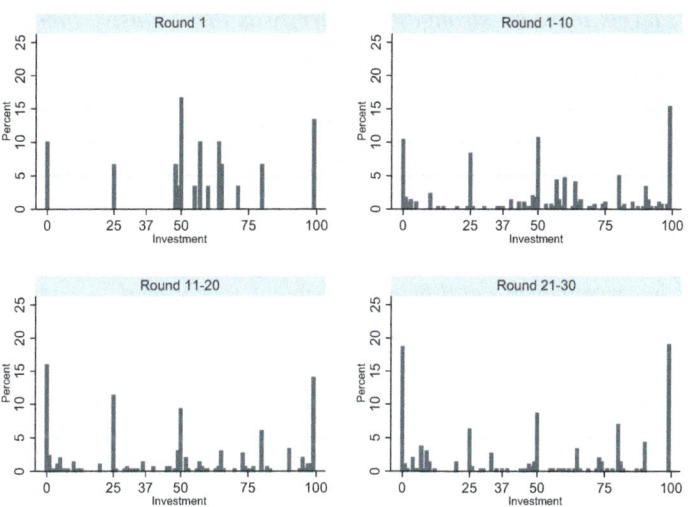

investment level is 50). In general, in all treatments non-equilibrium investment levels decrease over rounds and there seems to be a tendency to converge to the asymmetric equilibria (0, 0, 99). Especially investing zero, which belongs to an asymmetric equilibrium strategy, increases. Specifically, in *SUB* non-equilibrium levels (in particular choosing 50) decrease over rounds converging to the extreme points 0 and 99 and also the *PAT* treatment clearly indicates that the extreme investment levels 0 and 99 are chosen more frequently in later rounds (non-equilibrium levels decrease in favor of 0 and 99).

ER Investment levels:

Result 1: *Concerning the investment levels the experimental data show the following:*

- *The introduction of each policy instrument (SUB and PAT) significantly increases the investment level compared to no governmental R&D intervention (by 35.79% and 45.62% compared to a theoretical increase of 48.64%), which is in favor of Hypothesis 1.*
- *As compared to the Nash predictions, firms overinvest in R&D with and without R&D policy instruments.*

Result 2: *The dynamics of R&D investment decisions are very similar between treatments: previously successful innovation has per se a positive effect on* *current investment decisions independent of other firms' success. Moreover, investment levels increase strongest if a firm was the exclusive innovator in the previous round and if patent protection is implemented.*

Result 3: *In NO, the modal R&D investment level is indeed the predicted level of 25, whereas the modal level of 99 in SUB and PAT is different from the predicted 37. The second and third most frequently chosen levels are 0 and an intermediate level of 50 in PAT, and 50 and 0 in SUB. These observations might be (partly) explained by asymmetric equilibria. Investment levels tend to converge to the asymmetric equilibrium levels of 0 and 99 over rounds.*

III.4.2 Cost Structure, Prices and Profits

III.4.2.1 Cost Structure

The cost structure in the first Bertrand market period (i.e., the number of firms facing low costs of 100 and the number of firms facing high costs of 500) is determined by the number of successful innovations. The cost structure in the second Bertrand market period depends on the cost structure of the first market as well as on the chosen policy instrument. Table III.6 gives observed frequencies of the different cost structures in the two Bertrand market periods (and as a benchmark predicted frequencies in case of symmetric discrete equilibrium investment levels). Only in the *PAT* treatment the innovating firms are protected against imitation. Thus, in this treatment the number of low cost firms does not change in the 2*nd* market. In the other two treatments however, in the second market period there are either three firms with high costs (if in the first market period there was no low cost firm in the market) or three firms with low costs (in all other cases). Markets with two or three low cost firms occur more often in *SUB* and *PAT* than in *NO* after the investment stage. Moreover, we observe the extreme case of three high cost firms (see column 'zero' in the 1*st* period) twice as often in the baseline treatment as in *SUB* and *PAT*. The higher percentage of successfully innovating firms in a market is a result of the higher investment levels in treatments with policy instruments.

Table III.6 reveals only slight differences in observed proportions of cost structures as compared to those predicted by symmetric R&D investment strategies.[122] Specifically, predicted proportions are always higher than observed proportions if there is no low cost firm in the market in all three treatments, whereas the chances of two or three low cost firms in a market are typically higher than predicted.[123] This observation can be explained by the observed overinvestment in all three treatments. The observed frequency of a sole low cost firm is smaller than predicted in *NO* and *SUB*, but higher in *PAT*. Theoretically, *SUB* and *PAT* should result in identical frequencies of cost structures in the first market (as in both treatments the same equilibrium investment is induced by our parameterization). Note however, that in *SUB* more successful innovations occur than in *PAT* (the percentage of two and three low cost firms is higher and the percentage of no or one low cost firm is lower in *SUB*).

Table III.6: Observed (predicted) cost structure in the Bertrand markets

Bertrand markets	Treatment	Number of low cost firms 1st period				
		zero	one	two	three	Total
1st	NO	11.67% (12.5%)	32.33% (37.5%)	41.33% (37.5%)	14.67% (12.5%)	100% (100%)
	SUB	4.67% (6.01%)	24.00% (28.00%)	48.67% (43.48%)	22.67% (22.51%)	100% (100%)
	PAT	5.67% (6.01%)	29.67% (28.00%)	46.33% (43.48%)	18.33% (22.51%)	100% (100%)
		Number of low cost firms 2nd period				
		zero	one	two	three	Total
2nd	NO	11.67% (12.5%)	0% (0%)	0% (0%)	88.33% (87.50%)	100% (100%)
	SUB	4.67% (6.01%)	0% (0%)	0% (0%)	95.3% (93.99%)	100% (100%)
	PAT	5.67% (6.01%)	29.67% (28.00%)	46.33% (43.48%)	18.33% (22.51%)	100% (100%)

The number of low cost firms indicates how many of the three competing firms in each Bertrand market attain low cost of 100. Predicted cost structure taking discrete symmetric Nash equilibrium investment levels of 25 in *NO* and 37 in *SUB* and *PAT* are given in parentheses.

III.4.2.2 Prices and Mark-Ups

Figure III.6 depicts the average market price (i.e., the lowest price $p_{i,t}^{min} = \min[p_{1,t}, p_{2,t}, p_{3,t}]$ set in each market) for the three treatments for both market periods. Obviously, observed market prices in the experiment are on average close to those theoretically predicted (if subjects choose discrete symmetric equilibrium investment levels and equilibrium market prices).

---

[122] This is a surprising result. Although the majority of individual behavior is not consistent with the discrete symmetric equilibrium investment level, on average similar cost structures result as predicted by the symmetric Nash equilibrium.

[123] However, Chi-square goodness-of-fit tests yield no significant differences on the 10%-level in observed and predicted frequencies for all three treatments in the first market period (χ^2 - values are given by 4.60, 4.48 and 3.24 in *NO*, *SUB* and *PAT*). It is not possible to calculate Chi-square tests for the second period as there are parameter values equaling zero in *NO* and *SUB*.

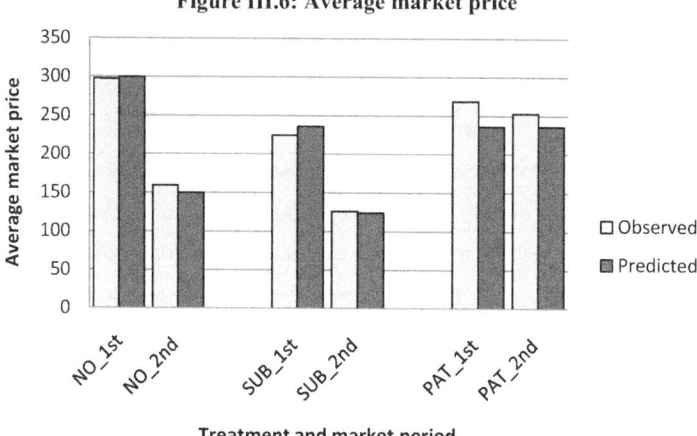

Figure III.6: Average market price

Treatment and market period

The average observed (predicted) market price was derived by taking the observed (predicted) frequency of each cost structure after the investment stage (see Table III.6) and multiplying these probabilities with the observed (predicted) average lowest prices of each cost structure. Note that the average market price thus includes all different cost structures.

Under Bertrand competition market prices are mainly driven by the underlying cost structure. Therefore, Table III.7 presents the average of actual market prices in the 1*st* and 2*nd* Bertrand markets for each cost structure separately.[124] Again, in all three treatments average market prices are close to those theoretically predicted. If there are only high cost firms in the market (column 1) prices are slightly above 500 in all three treatments (in the 1*st* market slightly higher prices are set than in the 2*nd* market). If there is one low cost firm in the first market (column 2), prices are set again close to those theoretically predicted. One low cost firm in the first market means three low cost firms in the second market due to imitation in *NO* and *SUB*. Thus, prices drop close to 100 except for the *PAT* treatment, where innovation is protected (prices stick to nearly 499). In case of two successfully innovating firms market prices in the first market period are between 127.77 and 149.20 on average, depending on the treatment (column 3). This cost structure implies that there are in the second market three low cost firms again in *NO* and *SUB* and still two low cost firms in *PAT*. The last column gives the average lowest prices if there are three low cost firms in the 1*st* and

---

[124] We proceed in the following way: After the investment stage four different states of nature may occur - the numbers of successful innovations before Bertrand market starts are either zero, one, two or three. We calculate for these four different cases the average of *lowest* prices over all rounds separately for the 1*st* and for the 2*nd* market. Note that the labeling 'Number of innovating firms' alludes only to the number of low cost firms at the beginning of the first market period, not to the second market period (where number of low cost firms might differ due to imitation).

thus also three low cost firms in the *2nd* market in all three treatments. In case of zero, two as well as three low cost firms prices are lower in the *2nd* than in the *1st* market period. Moreover, prices are higher than theoretically predicted in all cases, except the case that one firm has low costs and the other two firms have high costs.[125] Figure III.A2 in the Appendix depicts average lowest prices for each cost structure in the *1st* and *2nd* Bertrand markets for each round. The figure shows that average market prices converge to the Bertrand equilibrium prices over rounds as well as over market periods: First, average prices in general converge to the equilibrium price over rounds and second, prices in the *2nd* market are nearly always set closer to the equilibrium price than those of the corresponding *1st* market.

Table III.7: Average of lowest prices observed (predicted) in the Bertrand markets

Bertrand markets	Treatment	Number of innovating firms			
		zero	one	two	three
1st	NO	508.37 (500)	494.37 (499)	146.13 (100)	124.14 (100)
	SUB	507.36 (500)	473.00 (499)	127.77 (100)	112.69 (100)
	PAT	519.29 (500)	493.88 (499)	149.20 (100)	131.36 (100)
2nd	NO	504.66 (500)	113.39 (100)	114.23 (100)	113.55 (100)
	SUB	504.93 (500)	107.26 (100)	108.77 (100)	106.12 (100)
	PAT	504.53 (500)	494.99 (499)	124.48 (100)	111.13 (100)

The number of innovating firms indicates the successfully innovating firms after the investment stage (i.e., low cost firms in the first market period), but does not refer to imitating firms in the second market period. Note that in case of a sole low cost firm the discrete equilibrium price is 499, otherwise the sole innovator runs the risk of sharing the demand and decreasing his profits considerably.

Taking the average lowest price (market price) for each cost structure given by Table III.7 leads to the expected mark-ups of firms depicted in Table III.8.[126] *Mark-ups* of the firms are defined as *price – costs* and represent the firm's incentive to innovate. Recall that theoretically predicted mark-ups if there are zero, one, two and three innovations are 0, 399, 0, and 0 points in the first market; 0, 0, 0, and 0 in the second market for *NO* and *SUB* due to imitation, and 0, 399, 0, and 0 in the second market for *PAT*. Table III.8 shows that mark-ups deviate to some extent from Nash predictions. Hence, observed mark-ups are higher when zero-mark-ups are predicted if there are no, two, or three low cost firms and slightly lower when mark-ups of 399 points are predicted if there is a

---

[125] Slightly higher prices in these cases might be explained by the fact that in the discrete case firms can achieve positive profits even if they are not the only innovating firm with low costs. Note that in the discrete case 501(and 101) are also equilibrium prices for zero (two and three) innovating firms.
[126] Note that only those firms benefit from the mark-up who set the lowest price in their market.

sole low cost firm. Moreover, deviations appear to be systematic. First, observed average mark-ups are always larger in the first than the second market period for a given cost structure and treatment, except when there is only one low cost firm in *PAT*.[127] Second, mark-ups rank in a specific ascending order of cost structures: Three low cost firms achieve somewhat higher mark-ups than three high cost firms, and two low cost firms have somewhat higher mark-ups than three low and high cost firms, i.e., it holds *zero* < *three* < *two* < *one* low cost firms for a given market period and treatment. The finding that prices and thus mark-ups are higher if there are only two low cost firms in the market is consistent with what has been observed in previous Bertrand market experiments: E.g. Dufwenberg and Gneezy (2000) find that the number of competing firms with identical marginal costs influences the fierceness of competition in a Bertrand oligopoly experiment. Their data provide evidence that prices converge towards the theoretical prediction when there are groups of three or four competitors, whereas prices are much higher than predicted when only two competitors are matched. Hence, these observations can be explained by the influence of market concentration (of firms with identical low costs) on price setting.

Table III.8 shows that in terms of providing incentives to invest in R&D *PAT* is not only the best policy for a sole innovating firm as the observed (theoretically predicted) sum of mark-ups of both periods amounts to 788.87 (798) compared to 407.76 and 380.26 (both 399) in *NO* and *SUB*, but

Table III.8: Average mark-ups in the Bertrand markets

Bertrand markets	Treatment	Number of innovating firms			
		zero	*One*	*two*	*three*
1st	*NO*	8.37	394.37	46.13	24.14
	SUB	7.36	373.00	27.77	12.69
	PAT	19.29	393.88	49.20	31.36
2nd	*NO*	4.66	13.39	14.23	13.55
	SUB	4.93	7.26	8.77	6.12
	PAT	4.53	394.99	24.48	11.13
Both periods	*NO*	13.03	407.76	60.36	37.69
	SUB	12.29	380.26	36.54	18.81
	PAT	23.82	788.87	73.68	42.49

The number of innovating firms indicates the successfully innovating firms after the investment stage (i.e., low cost firms in the first market period), but does not refer to imitating firms in the second market period.

---

[127] This result is driven by the higher price setting in the first market.

furthermore it also yields the highest sum of mark-ups for all other cost structures (zero, two and three). In *SUB* mark-ups over both periods are lowest. Note that here incentives to innovate refer to a 'pure' mark-up effect (and target solely at the revenue side of firms) neglecting incentives which arise from a reduction of investment costs.

III.4.2.3 Profits

This subsection surveys the profits of the firms. We differ between profits achieved solely at the market stage and profits over both stages of the game: *Market profits* (given separately for the *first period*, *second period*, and *both periods*) refer to the actually realized profit per firm at the market stage and *round profits* defined as *endowment - investment cost + market profits over both periods* give profits over both stages (including the investment and the market stage). Table III.9 gives average market profits over rounds for both periods separately and in sum.[128]

Table III.9: Average market profits per high and low cost firms

Treatment	Number of innovating firms							
	zero	one			two			three
	$\pi_i(c_{i,1}^H) =$ total	$\pi_i(c_{i,1}^L)$	$\pi_i(c_{i,1}^H)$	total	$\pi_i(c_{i,1}^L)$	$\pi_i(c_{i,1}^H)$	total	$\pi_i(c_{i,1}^L) =$ total
NO_1^{st}	2.79	390.25	0.00	130.08	21.45	0.00	14.30	8.05
SUB_1^{st}	2.45	367.44	0.00	122.48	13.89	0.00	9.26	4.23
PAT_1^{st}	6.43	389.38	0.00	129.79	24.60	0.00	16.40	10.45
NO_2^{nd}	1.55	5.49	3.95	4.46	3.99	6.25	4.74	4.52
SUB_2^{nd}	1.64	1.76	2.75	2.42	2.33	4.10	2.92	2.04
PAT_2^{nd}	1.51	389.93	0.28	130.16	12.24	0.00	8.16	3.71
NO_both	4.34	395.74	3.95	134.55	25.44	6.25	19.05	12.56
SUB_both	4.10	369.21	2.75	124.90	16.22	4.10	12.18	6.27
PAT_both	7.94	779.31	0.28	259.96	36.84	0.00	24.56	14.16

---

[128] Note that there is a difference between mark-ups and market profits. Mark-up refers to the potential profit margin in a market with a specific cost structure, thus measuring a firm's profit margin if a single firm sets the lowest price. Since mark-ups present the potential profit margin they can be interpreted as incentives to innovate in order to encourage a firm to set the lowest price in the market. Average market profits, however, refer to the sum of actually realized profits in a market *divided by the number* of firms, thus measuring the average profit per firm (including also the 'losing' firms). Hence, average market profits can be seen as the expected profit a firm could obtain ex ante.

For each specific cost structure after the investment stage $\pi_i(c_{i,1}^H)$ and $\pi_i(c_{i,1}^L)$ denote firm i's profits depending on its marginal costs (e.g. $c_{i,1}^H$ refers to firm i starting with high marginal costs after the investment stage in market period $t=1$). Note that in *NO* and *SUB* in case of one and two low cost firms after the investment stage all three firms face low costs in the *2nd* market period due to imitation. Table III.9 summarizes average total market profits per firm for all cost structures as well as market profits per firm separately for low and high cost firms if both types share a market. Total market profits give the average profit of a market per firm for each cost structure (which naturally equals profits of solely high (low) cost firms in zero (three)). Concentrating on average total market profits over both market periods (which can be interpreted as a firm's expected profit at the market stage before it gets to know if it successfully innovates or not) it holds again for each possible cost structure that firms benefit most from *PAT* and achieve lowest profits in *SUB* as theoretically predicted (for this matter refer also to the following subsection).

Now we take a look on firms' average round profits including the investment stage. We can interpret the average round profits as the expected profits a firm can gain in general in a specific treatment per round (regardless of a specific cost structure). As round profits measure the ex ante expected profit, they indicate which treatment is most profitable for firms. Table III.10 summarizes the average (predicted) profits of all firms over all rounds for the three treatments. Note that round profits (observed as well as predicted) are smallest in *SUB*, however profits do not differ significantly between treatments. A Kruskal-Wallis test as well as pair-wise Mann-Whitney-U tests reveal no significant differences in average profits across treatments using matching groups.[129]

Table III.10: Average observed and predicted round profits

Round profits	NO	SUB	PAT
Observed	119.25 (119.92)	114.11 (102.85)	141.34 (226.07)
Predicted	124.88	118.74	137.48

Standard deviations are given in parentheses. To calculate predicted levels we use the discrete symmetric equilibrium (25 in *NO* and 37 in *SUB* and *PAT*) and $\Delta c = 399$.

---

[129] Kruskal-Wallis test yields $p=0.171$ and pair-wise one-tailed Mann-Whitney-U tests yield $p=0.274$ (*NO-SUB*), $p=0.075$ (*NO-PAT*) and $p=0.075$ (*SUB-PAT*).

ER Cost structure, prices and profits:

Result 4: *The predicted and observed proportions of cost structures show only slight differences.*

Result 5: *Average market prices converge to predicted Bertrand market prices (over rounds as well as over subsequent market periods). This results in mark-ups (and thus the incentive to invest in R&D) being highest in PAT (over the two market periods). Observed mark-ups of a sole low cost firm are somewhat lower than in Nash equilibrium and mark-ups are somewhat higher when there are zero, two, or three low cost firms.*

Result 6: *Firms' profits are highest in PAT and lowest in SUB (although we find no significant difference between treatments), which confirms the tendency of firms' interest as stated in Hypothesis 3.*

III.4.3 Welfare and Distributional Effects

In this subsection, we examine the effects of subsidies and patents on welfare at the society level and at the level of interest groups (i.e., consumers, firms,[130] and government). For each treatment Table III.11 gives observed and predicted (in parentheses) added welfare as compared to a benchmark situation in which all firms make zero-R&D investments. There are three main observations: First, in comparison to zero-investments in R&D, total social welfare (as well as total consumer surplus and total firms' profits) increases intensely if firms invest in R&D with and without R&D instruments (which is shown by the fact that all added values in all treatments are positive). Second, if firms invest in R&D, added social welfare (*NO*: 600.56; *SUB*: 620.88; and *PAT*: 601.38) does not differ significantly between our treatments,[131] which implies that added social welfare cannot be enhanced by the introduction of policy instruments. However, subsidies and patents have very different consequences for the distribution of welfare within society. As compared to the situation without R&D policy (*NO*), on the one hand subsidies increase consumer welfare by 105.95 points and on the other hand they reduce industry profits by 15.42 points and government budget

---

[130] Note that we refrain from including the firms' experimental endowment of 100 in the producer rent in contrast to round profits presented in Table III.10 in the last subsection. Here we use instead the formula of rents given in Section III.2.
[131] Using added welfare per matching group a Kruskal-Wallis test yields $p>0.5$ and two-tailed Mann-Whitney-U tests $p>0.1$ for each comparison. Note however, that a replication of the experiment would be reasonable in order to check the robustness of results by getting more independent observations.

by 70.23 points. In contrast, patents decrease consumer welfare by 65.47 points, leave the government budget unaffected, and increase firms' profits by 66.29 points.[132] Third, observed added social welfare and added welfare shares are lower than the theoretically predicted values (besides consumer rent in *SUB* and producer rent in *PAT*),[133] which can be explained by the overinvestment mentioned above. This result implies that those interest groups which are anyway privileged by a policy instrument (consumers in *SUB* and firms in *PAT*), realize even higher rents than predicted at the expense of the already disadvantaged group.

However, it remains the problematical question what practical implications can actually be derived. Our welfare results have to be interpreted with caution as our model and experimental setting are subject to some limitations which deserve mention: We neglected the funding of subsidies (for instance, in our model government budget is not linked to consumers by tax) and further patent costs (which occur due to the possible monopoly position of an innovating firm with patent protection: E.g. future welfare might decrease as firms' incentives decrease to invest in future R&D projects). For these reasons a complete welfare analysis is beyond the scope of this chapter. But even in our simplified framework it can be shown that the decisions of whether and which R&D policy should be introduced seem to be sensitive to the political interests.

Table III.11: Average welfare effects

Treatment	Added welfare – observed (predicted)			
	Social welfare	Consumers	Producers	Government
NO	600.56 (623.25)	542.83 (548.63)	57.74 (74.63)	0.00 (0.00)
SUB	620.88 (639.03)	648.78 (638.31)	42.32 (56.23)	-70.23 (-55.50)
PAT	601.38 (639.03)	477.36 (526.58)	124.03 (112.45)	0.00 (0.00)

To calculate predicted levels we use the discrete symmetric equilibrium (25 in *NO* and 37 in *SUB* and *PAT*) and $\Delta c = 399$.

---

[132] The increase in consumer rent if *SUB* is introduced compared to *NO* is significant at the 1%-level (one-tailed Mann-Whitney-U test). All other comparisons do not yield significant differences. This result might be partly driven by a small sample size of only 5 independent observations.
[133] *CR* in *SUB* is higher than expected, because more successful innovations take place than theoretically predicted (compare Table III.6: Theoretically, *SUB* and *PAT* should provide identical cost structures (due to the Nash equilibrium of 37 in both treatments), however more successful innovations occur in *SUB* for two and three firms). In *PAT* we observe a higher than predicted frequency of one low cost firm in the market which might explain the higher *PR*.

ER Welfare effects:

Result 7: *R&D subsidies and patents do not increase social welfare significantly (due to overinvestment), thus we question Hypothesis 2. However, we observe an (although not significant) tendency that both policy instruments cause redistribution within society. With subsidies, consumers gain welfare at the expense of industry profits and government budget. With patents, the industry increases profits at the expense of consumer welfare. These results seem to support Hypothesis 3.*

III.5 Conclusions

This chapter investigates the performance of two prominent policy instruments used to enhance firms' investments in R&D: subsidies and patents. A successful R&D innovation entails lower marginal costs for the innovating firm. We use a two-stage stochastic R&D model with an investment stage followed by a Bertrand price competition stage with two market periods and derive equilibrium investments and prices for our experimental parameters. In equilibrium, both patents and subsidies induce the same amount of R&D investment, which is higher than the investment without governmental incentives. To test these theoretical predictions we run an experiment comparing a baseline treatment without any policy instrument with two treatments in which either subsidies are paid to investing firms or in which innovating firms are granted patent protection respectively. Our main finding at the investment stage is a significant increase in investment levels if a policy instrument is implemented. Thus, our experiment provides evidence that both instruments are effective in promoting investments in R&D.[134] However, we observe overinvestment in all three treatments. This overinvestment might be on the one hand explained by asymmetric discrete equilibrium investment levels (especially those in which one firm invests the maximal amount and two other firms refrain from investing) and a simple coordination failure of the subjects. On the other hand, this result might be (also) due to the specific properties of a Bertrand market: A Bertrand market leads to 'aggressive' interaction among vigorous competitors. Competition in a Bertrand market is very strong in the sense that a firm makes zero-profits for sure if it does

---

[134] Theoretically both introducing a subsidy as well as patent protection should increase the investment level by the same amount compared to the situation in which no policy instrument is used. This is supported by our experimental results as the investment level does not differ significantly across the treatments *SUB* and *PAT*.

not become the only innovator in the market.[135] Maybe this all-or-none property tempts subjects into overinvesting in R&D.

Concerning the market stage we observe that although prices are set slightly above the marginal costs, they converge to the theoretically predicted Bertrand equilibrium prices both over rounds as well as over market periods. In general, note that despite the complex experimental setting (like implementing a two-stage game with endogenously determined profits), theory predicts outcomes *on average* quite well although individual investment behavior diverges from the predicted symmetric Nash equilibrium: E.g. cost structures, average market prices, and average profits are close to the theoretically predicted levels.

Our data show that R&D investment increases added social welfare compared to no R&D investment, but also exposes that R&D subsidies as well as patents do not strongly affect social welfare compared to no policy instrument. This result is driven by the observed overinvestment discussed above. However, both policy instruments cause substantial redistribution within society. Firms fare better under patents than under no policy, the latter still yields higher profits than subsidies. The investigation of different 'interest groups' is important for policy analysis, because it reveals where support and opposition can be expected. Nevertheless, the described results should be interpreted carefully. Due to several limitations of our model an extensive welfare analysis is beyond the scope of this chapter. Limitations of our analysis are the following: We do not include funding of the instruments, i.e., taxes would change the consumer surplus, for instance, nor do we take the costs of granting patent protection into account. Patents have two effects on social welfare: On the one hand they provide incentives to innovate in R&D, but on the other hand they might create monopolies. If a firm holds a monopoly position this may hinder intertemporal innovations.[136] These intertemporal aspects are neglected in our static framework analysis. Thus, as it is shown by Bessen and Maskin (2006), patents may be desirable to encourage innovation in a static setting (e.g. in their static model a patent protection leads to higher profits of a firm undertaking R&D as well as to higher welfare), but they might actually inhibit complementary innovation in a sequential setting in which

---

[135] Expecting Bertrand competition at the second stage creates a kind of the-winner-takes-all situation at the investment stage. Patent race literature suggests that non-colluding firms invest excessively in R&D (for a seminal paper see Loury (1979)). Doraszelski (2008) shows that this result strongly hinges on the winner-takes-all assumption. If this assumption is relaxed and patent protection becomes less effective firms might even underinvest in R&D.

[136] Note however, that this effect is alleviated by our design as it is possible that more than one firm successfully innovates. Therefore, patent protection in our experiment does not automatically imply monopoly power of an innovating firm.

imitation might even become a spur to innovation. Scotchmer (1991) also notes that including positive externalities and intertemporal knowledge spillovers, which early innovators confer on later innovators, poses new problems for the optimal design of patent law. Furthermore, our model lacks R&D coordination and cooperation (like cross-licensing agreements and joint ventures), which is very common in R&D intensive markets (compare e.g. Morasch (1995)). All these factors might have an essential influence on the impact of policy instruments on R&D investment and their successful implementation and should be investigated in future research.

Hence, further research is to be done on the robustness of our results concerning the effects of the policy instruments on investment behavior. Of course, our results cannot yield conclusive evidence for policy implications as we simplified the model a lot. However, our experiment is a first step and its insights might contribute to a broader research agenda on R&D investment promoting policy instruments: Our findings suggest that the tested policy instruments serve the purpose of rising investments and that the choice of an appropriate instrument depends on the political process of interests.

III.6 Appendix to Chapter III

Short Instructions

Written instructions (translation from German)

Welcome and thank you very much for participating in this experiment. You receive 2.50 € for participating. Depending on your and other participants' decisions you can earn additional money. You collect points during the experiment with **300 points equaling 1 €**. At the end of the experiment your accumulated points will be converted into € and together with the 2.50 € paid out to you in cash. Payoffs remain *anonymous*. During the whole experiment, starting now, communication with other participants is strictly forbidden. If you have a question, please raise your hand. An experimenter will come to your place and answer your questions.

The Experiment

The experiment consists of **30 rounds**. At the beginning of *each* round all participants are randomly divided into groups of 3 participants, i.e., the composition of your group changes in each round. In the following we refer to the 3 participants of your group as firm 1, 2, and 3. Your firm number is randomly drawn anew in each round. You do not interact with other groups in a respective round. Your identity is not revealed at any time before, during or after the experiment.

At the beginning of *each* round each participant receives an **endowment of 100 points** which is credited your personal account of points.

Each round consists of 2 phases ("phase 1" and "phase 2"). In addition phase 2 consists of two sub-phases ("phase 2A" and "phase 2B"). You make three decisions in each round, one in phase 1 and one in each of the phases 2A and 2B.

R&D INVESTMENT INCENTIVES

Phase 1 – 1st Decision

In phase 1 you and the two other firms in your group can make an investment. Each firm can influence the level of its costs in the *current round* by its investment. You can have either *high* or *low costs*. You invest by choosing an amount of points (integer) between 0 and 99 (0, 1, 2, ..., 98, 99). Only you know your own investment (chosen points), it cannot be observed by any other firm. The same applies to the other firms.

PAT and NO:

Your investment induces **investment costs; they are equal to your investment (= chosen points) and will be subtracted from your endowment of 100 points.**

SUB:

Your investment induces **investment costs; they are equal to half of your investment (= chosen points) and will be subtracted from your endowment of 100 points.**

Your investment level determines the **probability** of having costs of **100 points** ("low costs") or of **500 points** ("high costs") in the *current* round. The higher your investment, the higher the probability that you have low costs (100 points). The same applies to the two other firms in your group.[137]

After you and the other two firms in your group made their investment decision, the computer separately draws a random number for *each* firm. The number is in the range of 0.1 and 100 whereby all numbers (0.1, 0.2, ..., 99.8, 99.9, 100) have an equal chance to be drawn.

Two alternatives arise:

1) **Your random number is *smaller than or equal* to your probability of obtaining costs of 100 points:** In this case your costs amount to 100 points.
2) **Your random number is *higher than* your probability of obtaining costs of 100 points:** In this case your costs amount to 500 points.

The same applies to both other firms in your group. Thus, your costs only depend on your own investment level which yields the probability of obtaining certain costs and chance. Four different situations can arise: Either none, 1, 2 or all 3

---

[137] All participants received a table containing all possible investment levels, the according investment costs, and the resulting probabilities of obtaining costs of 100 or 500 points. The probabilities are calculated by the formula $\sqrt{i/100}$, i stands for the investment of one firm.

firms of your group have low costs of 100 points (the rest of the firms in the group faces high costs of 500 points).

Phase 2A – 2nd Decision

At the beginning of phase 2A each firm within your group gets to know the costs of *all three* firms.

Each firm in your group is asked to choose a price between your own costs in phase 2A and 1000, i.e., a price either between <u>100</u>, 101, 102, ... 999, 1000, if you have low costs or between <u>500</u>, 501, 502, .., 999, 1000, if you have high costs. Each firm only knows its own price and cannot observe the prices of the other two firms.

After all firms made their decisions, the computer identifies the *lowest* price within your group which all three firms get to know. There are three possibilities for your group in phase 2A with the according profits:

1) **<u>One</u> firm in your group has chosen the lowest price:**

The profit in points of the firm with the lowest price in phase 2A is calculated by *subtracting the costs of this firm in phase 2A from its chosen price*. Both firms with the higher prices receive *nothing* (0 points) in phase 2A, independent of their prices and costs in phase 2A.

2) **<u>Two</u> firms in your group have chosen the same lowest price:**

The profit in points of each firm with the same lowest price in phase 2A is calculated by *subtracting the costs from the chosen price and <u>dividing the result by two</u>*. The firm with the higher price receives *nothing* (0 points) in phase 2A, independent of its price and costs in phase 2A.

3) **All <u>three</u> firms in your group have chosen the same price:**

The profit in points of each firm in phase 2A is calculated by *subtracting the costs from the chosen price and <u>dividing the result by three</u>*.

If you have not chosen the lowest price of your group in phase 2A, you will not bear any costs. At the end of phase 2A your profit, which can either be positive or zero, is credited your personal account of points.

Phase 2B – 3rd Decision

PAT:

The 3rd decision is identical to the 2nd decision. **Each firm's costs have not changed compared to phase 2A.**

NO and SUB:

The 3rd decision just differs slightly from the 2nd decision in phase 2A. The decision procedure and the computation of profits in phase 2B are the same as in phase 2A. But compared to phase 2A there is an important difference: **In phase 2B the costs of all firms in one group are the same. The equal cost level in phase 2B corresponds to the lowest costs within the group in phase 2A.** The costs in phase 2B which are identical for all three firms in your group are announced within your group before you have to choose your price.

After a round (consisting of phase 1, phase 2A, and phase 2B) is finished you are informed again about your decisions and the results of this round. Afterwards the next round starts.

Profit per Round

Profit per round =
Phase 1   endowment per round – investment costs in phase 1
Phase 2   + profit in phase 2A
          + profit in phase 2B

Probabilites and costs (for *NO* and *PAT*, in *SUB* investment costs are halved)

Your investment (chosen points)	Your investment costs	Probability of getting costs of 100 points in %	Probability of getting costs of 500 points in %
0	0	0,0	100,0
1	1	10,0	90,0
2	2	14,1	85,9
3	3	17,3	82,7
4	4	20,0	80,0
5	5	22,4	77,6
6	6	24,5	75,5
7	7	26,5	73,5
8	8	28,3	71,7
9	9	30,0	70,0
10	10	31,6	68,4
11	11	33,2	66,8
12	12	34,6	65,4
13	13	36,1	63,9
14	14	37,4	62,6
15	15	38,7	61,3
16	16	40,0	60,0
17	17	41,2	58,8
18	18	42,4	57,6
19	19	43,6	56,4
20	20	44,7	55,3
21	21	45,8	54,2
22	22	46,9	53,1
23	23	48,0	52,0
24	24	49,0	51,0
25	25	50,0	50,0
26	26	51,0	49,0
27	27	52,0	48,0
28	28	52,9	47,1
29	29	53,9	46,1
30	30	54,8	45,2
31	31	55,7	44,3
32	32	56,6	43,4
33	33	57,4	42,6
34	34	58,3	41,7
35	35	59,2	40,8
36	36	60,0	40,0
37	37	60,8	39,2
38	38	61,6	38,4
39	39	62,4	37,6
40	40	63,2	36,8
41	41	64,0	36,0
42	42	64,8	35,2
43	43	65,6	34,4
44	44	66,3	33,7
45	45	67,1	32,9
46	46	67,8	32,2
47	47	68,6	31,4
48	48	69,3	30,7
49	49	70,0	30,0
50	50	70,7	29,3
51	51	71,4	28,6
52	52	72,1	27,9
53	53	72,8	27,2
54	54	73,5	26,5
55	55	74,2	25,8
56	56	74,8	25,2
57	57	75,5	24,5
58	58	76,2	23,8
59	59	76,8	23,2
60	60	77,5	22,5

61	61	78,1	21,9
62	62	78,7	21,3
63	63	79,4	20,6
64	64	80,0	20,0
65	65	80,6	19,4
66	66	81,2	18,8
67	67	81,9	18,1
68	68	82,5	17,5
69	69	83,1	16,9
70	70	83,7	16,3
71	71	84,3	15,7
72	72	84,9	15,1
73	73	85,4	14,6
74	74	86,0	14,0
75	75	86,6	13,4
76	76	87,2	12,8
77	77	87,7	12,3
78	78	88,3	11,7
79	79	88,9	11,1
80	80	89,4	10,6
81	81	90,0	10,0
82	82	90,6	9,4
83	83	91,1	8,9
84	84	91,7	8,3
85	85	92,2	7,8
86	86	92,7	7,3
87	87	93,3	6,7
88	88	93,8	6,2
89	89	94,3	5,7
90	90	94,9	5,1
91	91	95,4	4,6
92	92	95,9	4,1
93	93	96,4	3,6
94	94	97,0	3,0
95	95	97,5	2,5
96	96	98,0	2,0
97	97	98,5	1,5
98	98	99,0	1,0
99	99	99,5	0,5

Mathematical Appendix

Proof of Proposition III.2. Firm i's expected total profit is given by

$$\pi_i^e(r_i, r_{-i}) = F(r_i)[1 - F(r_{-i})]^{n-1}(1+\theta)\Delta c - (1-\sigma)r_i,$$

where Δc gives i's mark-up if it is the only low cost firm, which occurs with probability $F(r_i)[1 - F(r_{-i})]^{n-1}$ for $1+\theta$ periods, and $(1-\sigma)r_i$ gives its R&D costs net of subsidy.[138]

Maximization of i's expected total profit with respect to r_i yields

$$\frac{\partial \pi_i^e(r_i, r_{-i})}{\partial r_i} = f(r_i^*)[1 - F(r_{-i})]^{n-1}(1+\theta)\Delta c - (1-\sigma) \stackrel{!}{=} 0, \forall i.$$

Rearranging and assuming symmetry, i.e., $r_i = r$, $\forall i$, yields condition (1) as stated in our proposition:

$$f(r^*)[1 - F(r^*)]^{n-1}(1+\theta)\Delta c = 1 - \sigma,$$

where the left-hand and right-hand sides (henceforth *LHS* and *RHS*, respectively) give the expected marginal revenues MR^e and marginal costs MC of R&D investment, respectively. Comparative static analysis with each of the parameters Δc, θ and n is conducted like follows: We can rewrite condition (1) as $g(x, r(x)) = c$, where the *LHS* is a function of $x \in (\Delta c, \theta, n)$, which is the parameter of interest, and the investment level r. The *RHS* is a constant c. A marginal change in x leads to $\frac{dg}{dx} + \frac{dg}{dr}\frac{dr}{dx} = 0$. We are interested in $\frac{dr}{dx}$. Note that *LHS* is strictly decreasing in r ($\frac{dg}{dr} < 0$), because:

$$\frac{\partial LHS}{\partial r} = \left[f'(r)[1-F(r)]^{n-1} - (n-1)f(r)^2[1-F(r)]^{n-2}\right](1+\theta)\Delta c < 0 \quad \text{for } r \in (0,1),$$

with $f'(r)[1-F(r)]^{n-1} < 0$ and $(n-1)f(r)^2[1-F(r)]^{n-2} > 0$.

We derive for each specific x the derivative $\frac{dg}{dx}$ and thus can conclude whether $\frac{dr}{dx}$ must be increasing or decreasing. The procedure is analogous for the comparative statics with the parameter σ: Here we use the first order condition:

---

[138] A discount factor for the profits realized in subsequent rounds is neglected.

$f(r_i^*)[1-F(r_{-i})]^{n-1}(1+\theta)\Delta c - (1-\sigma) \stackrel{!}{=} 0$, which can be rewritten as $g(x,r(x)) = c$ again.

This analysis exposes the following influence of each parameter on the optimal investment level r:

- *Mark-ups:* For a change in Δc, $\dfrac{dg}{d\Delta c} > 0$ and $\dfrac{dg}{dr} < 0$ and thus $\dfrac{dr}{d\Delta c} > 0$ which implies that the equilibrium value of r increases if Δc increases.

- *Patent-protected market periods:* For a change in θ, $\dfrac{dg}{d\theta} > 0$ and $\dfrac{dg}{dr} < 0$ and thus $\dfrac{dr}{d\theta} > 0$ which implies that the equilibrium value of r increases if θ increases.

- *Subsidy:* For a change in σ, $\dfrac{dg}{d\sigma} > 0$ and $\dfrac{dg}{dr} < 0$ and thus $\dfrac{dr}{d\sigma} > 0$ which implies that the equilibrium value of r increases if σ increases.

- *Number of firms:* For a change in n, $\dfrac{dg}{dn} < 0$. Since $\dfrac{dg}{dr} < 0$ it holds that $\dfrac{dr}{dn} < 0$ which implies that the equilibrium value of r decreases if n increases.

- *Number of market periods:* Finally, the equilibrium value of r is independent of the number of market periods, T, because a firm can only receive strictly positive Nash equilibrium market profits if it is the only low cost firm. In our model the number of market periods in which this low cost firm can make such profits is entirely determined by the first period and the additional number of patent-protected market periods θ. However, T is the upper boundary of θ and thus may have an indirect effect on r^*. ∎

III.D1: Derivation added consumer rent

Expected total consumer rent if firms invest is given by:

$$\text{Total } CR^e(r,\theta,\sigma) = nF(r)[1-F(r)]^{n-1}(T-1-\theta)(\bar{p}-c^L)$$
$$+ nF(r)[1-F(r)]^{n-1}(1+\theta)(\bar{p}-c^H)$$
$$+ \sum_{k=2}^{n}\binom{n}{k}F(r)^k[1-F(r)]^{n-k}T(\bar{p}-c^L) \quad \text{(A1)}$$
$$+ (1-F(r))^n(\bar{p}-c^H)T$$

Total consumer rent if no firm invests in R&D (benchmark situation) is given by: $(\bar{p}-c^H)T$. Thus, subtracting the benchmark situation from the expected total CR results in an expected added consumer rent of:

$$CR^e(r,\theta,\sigma) = nF(r)[1-F(r)]^{n-1}(T-1-\theta)(\bar{p}-c^L)$$
$$+ nF(r)[1-F(r)]^{n-1}(1+\theta)(\bar{p}-c^H)$$
$$+ \sum_{k=2}^{n}\binom{n}{k}F(r)^k[1-F(r)]^{n-k}T(\bar{p}-c^L) \quad \text{(A2)}$$
$$+ (1-F(r))^n(\bar{p}-c^H)T$$
$$- (\bar{p}-c^H)T$$

This expression can be rewritten as:

$$CR^e(r,\theta,\sigma) = nF(r)[1-F(r)]^{n-1}(T-1-\theta)((\bar{p}-c^L)-(\bar{p}-c^H))$$
$$+ nF(r)[1-F(r)]^{n-1}(1+\theta)((\bar{p}-c^H)-(\bar{p}-c^H))$$
$$+ \sum_{k=2}^{n}\binom{n}{k}F(r)^k[1-F(r)]^{n-k}T((\bar{p}-c^L)-(\bar{p}-c^H)) \quad \text{, (A3)}$$
$$+ (1-F(r))^n((\bar{p}-c^H)-(\bar{p}-c^H))T$$

because $nF(r)[1-F(r)]^{n-1} + \sum_{k=2}^{n}\binom{n}{k}F(r)^k[1-F(r)]^{n-k} + (1-F(r))^n = 1$ and $(T-1-\theta)+(1+\theta) = T$. (A3) yields expected added consumer rent given in Proposition III.3.

III.D2: Derivation of the optimal investment for our parameterization

The profit function of firm i ($i=\{1, 2, 3\}$) with an endowment $B=100$ at the market stage in each of the 30 rounds is given by:

$$\pi_i(r_i, r_j, r_k) = (p - c^L)(1+\theta)F(r_i)(1-F(r_j))(1-F(r_k)) - (1-\sigma)r_i + B$$

Taking the equilibrium price $p=c^H$, $F(r_i) = \frac{1}{10}r_i^{0.5}$, $T=2$, $\sigma = 0.5$ and $\theta = 1$ yield the following first order conditions (FOC):

FOC general:

$$\frac{\partial \pi_i(r_i, r_j, r_k)}{\partial r_i} = \frac{\frac{1}{20}(c^H - c^L)(1+\theta)(1-\frac{1}{10}r_j^{0.5})(1-\frac{1}{10}r_k^{0.5})}{r_i^{0.5}} - (1-\sigma) = 0$$

FOC NO ($\sigma = 0, \theta = 0$):

$$\frac{\partial \pi_i(r_i, r_j, r_k)}{\partial r_i} = \frac{\frac{1}{20}(c^H - c^L)(1-\frac{1}{10}r_j^{0.5})(1-\frac{1}{10}r_k^{0.5})}{r_i^{0.5}} - 1 = 0.$$

FOC SUB ($\sigma = 0.5, \theta = 0$):

$$\frac{\partial \pi_i(r_i, r_j, r_k)}{\partial r_i} = \frac{\frac{1}{20}(c^H - c^L)(1-\frac{1}{10}r_j^{0.5})(1-\frac{1}{10}r_k^{0.5})}{r_i^{0.5}} - \frac{1}{2} = 0.$$

FOC PAT ($\sigma = 0, \theta = 1$):

$$\frac{\partial \pi_i(r_i, r_j, r_k)}{\partial r_i} = \frac{\frac{1}{10}(c^H - c^L)(1-\frac{1}{10}r_j^{0.5})(1-\frac{1}{10}r_k^{0.5})}{r_i^{0.5}} - 1 = 0.$$

Solving these equation systems for each treatment leads to the equilibrium investments presented in Table III.2.

SOC general case:

$$\frac{\partial^2 \pi_i(r_i, r_j, r_k)}{\partial r_i^2} = -\frac{\frac{1}{40}(c^H - c^L)(1+\theta)(1-\frac{1}{10}r_j^{0.5})(1-\frac{1}{10}r_k^{0.5})}{r_i^{1.5}} < 0.$$

For the given parameters SOC is always negative.

III.D3: Added welfare

In general, expected added welfare through R&D is given by

$$W^e(r) = (1 - \prod_{i=1}^{n}[1 - F(r_i)])T\Delta c - \sum_{i=1}^{n} r_i,$$

where Δc gives the increase in welfare if at least one firm succeeds in R&D,[139] which occurs with probability $1 - \prod_{i=1}^{n}[1 - F(r_i)]$, and $\sum_{i=1}^{n} r_i$ gives the total R&D investment costs in the industry.

Expected added welfare for symmetric R&D investment levels $r_i=r$ is given by

$$W^e(r) = (1 - [1 - F(r)]^n)T\Delta c - nr.$$

III.D4: Comparative statics of the optimal investment

The optimal investment is characterized by the first order condition:

$$\frac{\partial \pi_i(r_i, r_j, r_k)}{\partial r_i} = Q(c^H - c^L)(1+\theta)f(r_i)(1 - F(r_j))(1 - F(r_k)) - (1-\sigma) = 0$$

With the implicit function theorem $\left(\dfrac{dr_i}{dr_j} = -\dfrac{\frac{\partial^2 \pi_i(r_i, r_j, r_k)}{\partial r_i r_j}}{\frac{\partial^2 \pi_i(r_i, r_j, r_k)}{\partial r_i^2}} \right)$ we can show that

the firm's investment decreases with an increase in the rival's investment:

$$\frac{\partial^2 \pi_i(r_i, r_j, r_k)}{\partial r_i r_j} = -Q(c^H - c^L)(1+\theta)f(r_i)f(r_j)(1 - F(r_k))$$

$$\frac{\partial^2 \pi_i(r_i, r_j, r_k)}{\partial r_i^2} = Q(c^H - c^L)(1+\theta)f'(r_i)(1 - F(r_j))(1 - F(r_k))$$

$$\frac{dr_i}{dr_j} = \frac{f(r_i)f(r_j)}{f'(r_i)(1 - F(r_j))} < 0.$$

---

[139] The additional welfare of a lower market price if at least one firm's innovation is successful compared to the initial higher price is given by $(\bar{p} - c^L) - (\bar{p} - c^H) = c^H - c^L \equiv \Delta c$.

Tables

Table III.A1: Discrete symmetric and asymmetric Nash equilibrium investment levels

Treatment	Investment decision		
	r_i	r_j	r_k
NO	0	0	99
	20	25	30
	20	26	29
	20	27	28
	21	24	30
	21	25	29
	21	26	28
	21	27	27
	22	23	30
	22	24	29
	22	25	28
	22	26	27
	23	23	29
	23	24	28
	23	25	27
	23	26	26
	24	24	27
	24	25	26
	25	25	25
SUB	0	0	99
	37	37	37
PAT	0	0	99
	37	37	37

$\Delta c = 399$ is taken for the computation of equilibria (compare footnote 113).

Table III.A2: OLS regression results with *CR1* as base category

	(1)	
Investment	coefficient	(St. er.)
NO	44.08***	(5.057)
SUB	57.41***	(3.272)
PAT	74.74***	(0.748)
$CR0_{t-1}*NO$	-15.82***	(2.870)
$CR0_{t-1}*SUB$	-25.63***	(1.862)
$CR0_{t-1}*PAT$	-46.84***	(4.337)
$CR2_{t-1}*NO$	-3.872*	(2.169)
$CR2_{t-1}*SUB$	-3.171	(2.543)
$CR2_{t-1}*PAT$	-8.722***	(2.585)
$CR3_{t-1}*NO$	-9.592**	(4.391)
$CR3_{t-1}*SUB$	-1.834	(2.590)
$CR3_{t-1}*PAT$	-15.49***	(1.304)
N	2610	
R^2	0.218	

Standard errors in parentheses are corrected for matching group clusters. Cost reduction dummy variable '*CR1*' is dropped as base category. As we drop the constant in the estimated model, the reported R^2 is taken from the (analogous) model (2) as presented in Table III.A3.
*$p < 0.1$, **$p < 0.05$, ***$p < 0.01$

Table III.A3: OLS regression results with *SUB* as base category

Investment	(1) coefficient	(St. er.)	(2) coefficient	(St. er.)	(3) coefficient	(St. er.)
NO	-3.521	(3.336)	-3.521	(3.340)	-8.171**	(2.855)
PAT	-3.881	(4.222)	-3.881	(4.227)	-7.511*	(4.008)
_cons	31.78***	(2.086)	31.78***	(2.088)	34.84***	(1.626)
$CR_{t-1}*NO$	-12.16***	(3.813)			-11.994***	(3.709)
$CR_{t-1}*PAT$	14.14**	(4.967)			14.316**	(4.915)
CR_{t-1}	23.34***	(3.096)			23.088***	(2.983)
$CR1_{t-1}*NO$			-9.803**	(3.422)		
$CR1_{t-1}*PAT$			21.22***	(4.720)		
$CR1_{t-1}$			25.63***	(1.862)		
$CR2_{t-1}*NO$			-10.50**	(4.472)		
$CR2_{t-1}*PAT$			15.67***	(4.660)		
$CR2_{t-1}$			22.45***	(3.652)		
$CR3_{t-1}*NO$			-17.56***	(4.201)		
$CR3_{t-1}*PAT$			7.564	(5.153)		
$CR3_{t-1}$			23.79***	(3.160)		
round1_15*NO					9.393***	(2.441)
round1_15*PAT					7.290**	(2.840)
round1_15					-6.004***	(1.888)
N	2610		2610		2610	
R^2	0.211		0.218		0.215	

Standard errors in parentheses are corrected for matching group clusters. Treatment dummy variable '*SUB*' is dropped as base category.
 * $p < 0.1$, ** $p < 0.05$, *** $p < 0.01$

Figures

Figure III.A1: Individual investment behavior

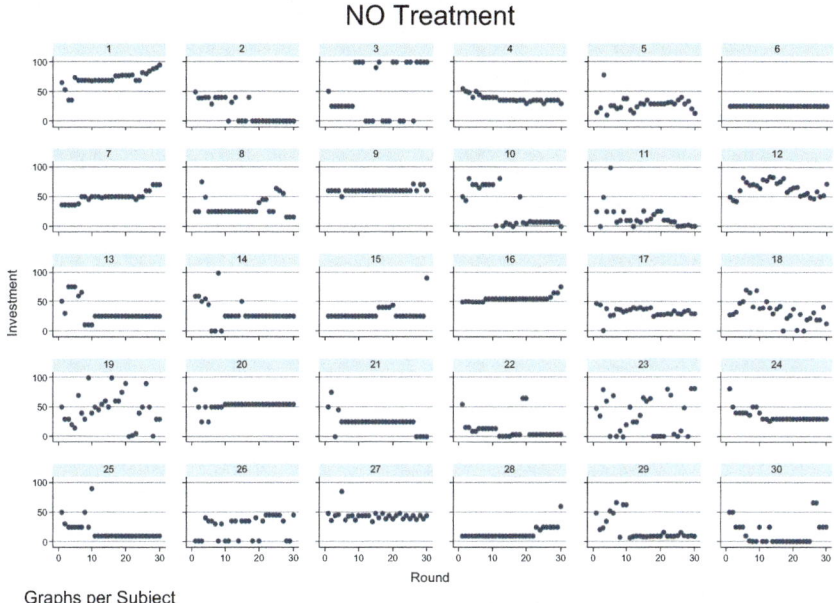

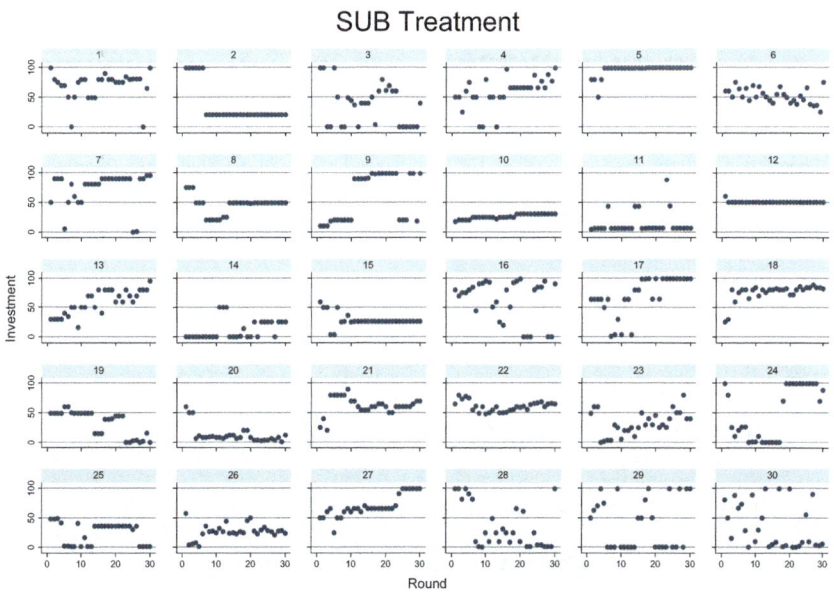

PAT Treatment

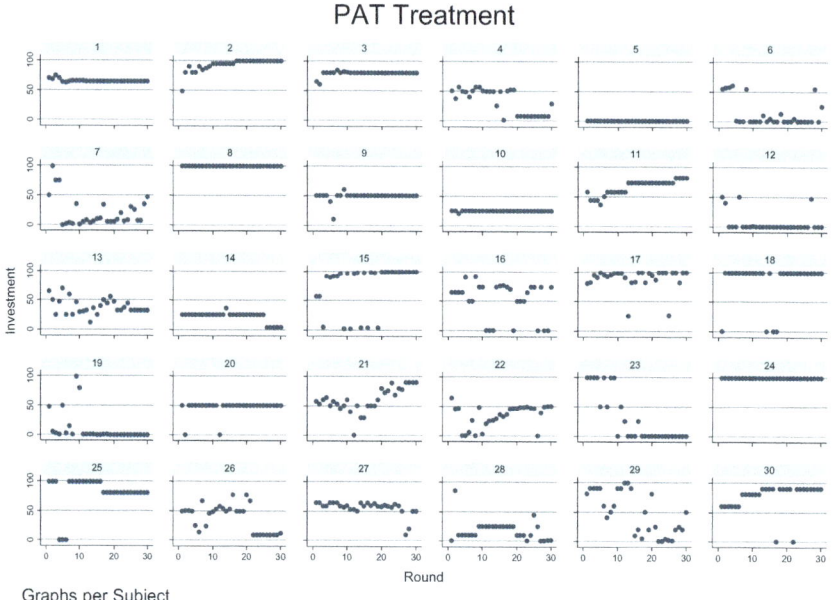

Graphs per Subject

Figure III.A2: Average lowest prices for each cost structure over rounds

NO Treatment

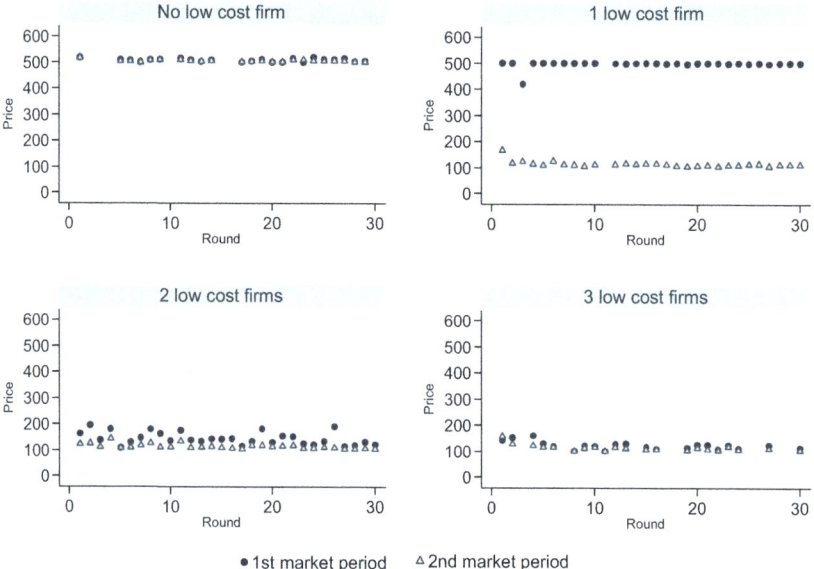

● 1st market period   △ 2nd market period

R&D INVESTMENT INCENTIVES 127

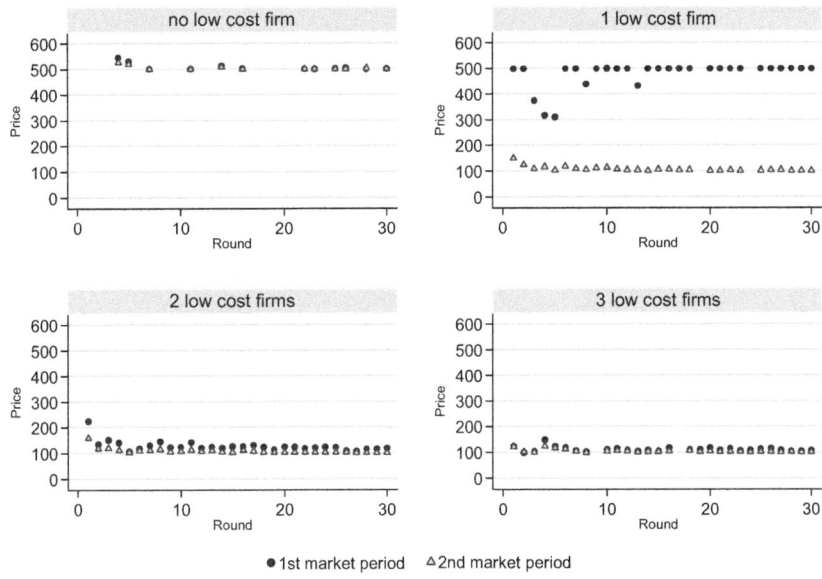

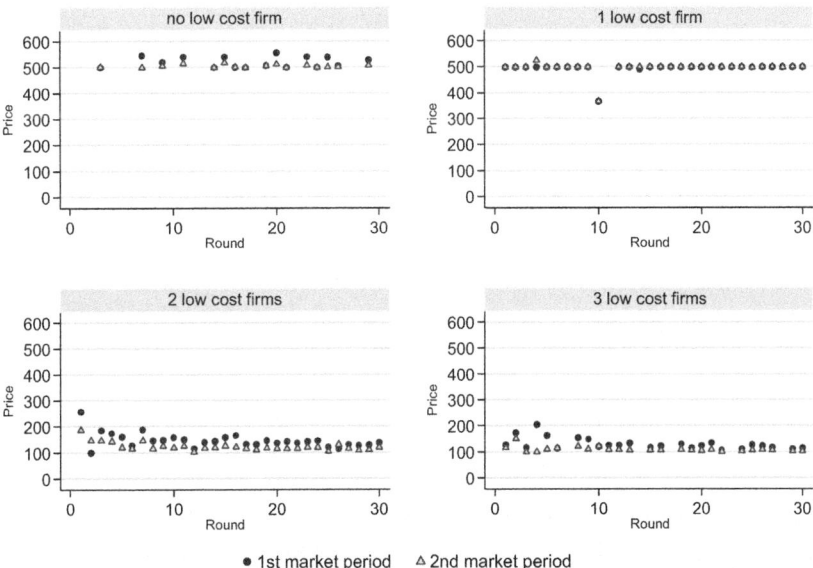

Figure III.A2 gives average lowest prices for each cost structure in the 1*st* and 2*nd* Bertrand market periods for each round. In case there is no entry there was no group consisting of that special number of low cost firms in that specific round. Note that the number of low cost firms only refers to the cost structure in the first market period (i.e., it refers to the number of initially successfully innovating firms). The labeling specifies different cost structures after the investment stage and gives prices for both periods of the Bertrand market.

Chapter IV

The Impact of Responsibility on Gift Giving[140]

IV.1 Introduction

Insurance is the upfront agreement that the 'lucky' compensate the loss of the 'unlucky'. Thus, in health insurance payment for the sick is provided by the healthy. In this context the question arises whether people feel the limits of their solidarity reached if the neediness is contingent upon the risk one takes (e.g. smokers, people practicing risky sports like paragliding, etc.). In this chapter we experimentally investigate if the willingness to transfer money to needy subjects is associated with whether their neediness is self-inflicted through deliberate risk-taking or exogenously determined. In more general terms, we experimentally examine the impact of responsibility for one's own actions on the solidarity of others.

The investigation of judgments of responsibility and their behavioral and emotional consequences has attracted a lot of attention in the psychological and sociological literature in recent decades (compare e.g. Bernts (1988), Weiner (1980, 1993) or Schopler and Matthews (1965)). A general finding is that causal controllability is a major determinant of perceptions of responsibility (e.g. one is considered responsible for failure due to lack of effort but not due to lack of ability). In turn perceived responsibility plays an essential role in help-giving: If people are not personally responsible for being in need prosocial behavior increases (see e.g. Betancourt (1990) or Meyer and Mulherin (1980)).

The concept of insurance i.e. the lucky compensating the loss of the unlucky in risk pools[141] is to a considerable extent driven by reciprocity

---

[140] This chapter is based on Trhal and Radermacher (2007). Subsection IV.4 is a brief summary based on Radermacher and Trhal (work in progress).

[141] A broad body of literature exists about risk-sharing which deals for instance with situations in which individuals have joint ownerships of some uncertain financial prospect. Bone et al. (2004) conclude that less risk-averse partners should bear a greater share of the risk but also of the expected value. Closely related to the solidarity game experiment is Charness and Genicot's (forthcoming) experimental test of risk-sharing arrangements. In their risk-sharing experiment without commitment using a solidarity game with positive continuation probability they find strong evidence of risk sharing in the laboratory – a

considerations: As insurance is a repeated game, subjects agree to compensate people in need as they expect to be compensated themselves in case they will be in need some day as well. Reciprocity thus includes a time component or is at least contingent on the action others take with regard to oneself. Solidarity is different.[142] It is based on empathy with people in need, i.e. the ability to 'put oneself in the other's shoes'. "Solidarity means a willingness to help people in need who are similar to oneself but victims of outside influences such as unforeseen illness, natural catastrophes, etc." (Selten and Ockenfels 1998, p. 518).[143] When compensation of people in need is neither enforced by society (like in compulsory insurance arrangements) nor contingent on personal ties to the needy person nor motivated by expectations of reciprocity, the question arises whether individuals agree at all to compensate others in need.

Selten and Ockenfels (1998) examined this question experimentally (later applied by Ockenfels and Weimann (1999) and Büchner et al. (2007)). In a randomly composed group of three people the ex ante probability of becoming needy is the same for each participant. Winners in this one shot game are given the option to compensate needy losers, and indeed they do so. The experiment shows that winners express their solidarity with those in need, i.e. gain utility from a more equal distribution.

In this chapter we explore whether solidarity is – at least partly – crowded out if neediness is self-inflicted and subjects are responsible for being in this state. Our experiment demonstrates that people do not only *judge* the same outcome distribution differently, but that they also *change* their action depending on the perceived responsibility although the final decision they have to take is exactly the same. The three-person solidarity game of Selten and Ockenfels described above is our workhorse and used as a reference treatment. Additionally, we introduce another treatment in which subjects first have to choose between a sure payment and a risky lottery. Thus, when choosing the lottery, in this treatment a person's neediness is entirely self-inflicted, and a needy person is completely responsible for his state. In a dictator game

---

higher continuation probability as well as a higher degree of risk aversion both considerably increase the level of risk sharing.

[142] It does not even seem that solidarity is driven by implicit reciprocity. Testing implicit reciprocity considerations, Büchner et al. (2007) find out that most people just give a certain amount to other people (due to social preferences or altruism) as was already shown e.g. in dictator experiments, but not due to implicit reciprocity considerations.

[143] Büchner et al. (2007, p. 294) use this definition of solidarity: "'Solidarity' [...] means voluntary gift giving by lucky winners to needy losers in a group. The interaction is characterized by an unfavorable situation that could potentially affect everybody but will eventually affect only one part of the population (the needy person(s))."

experiment in which the distribution phase was preceded by a production phase, Cappelen et al. (2005) demonstrated that people are held responsible for factors that are fully under individual control. Letting the subjects choose between two possibilities only, we create the simplest possible task in which people are held to be fully responsible as we exclude other factors like effort, ability, external factors etc. which could be – at least partly – beyond a subject's individual control. Then we compare the transfer payments subjects give to needy subjects between these treatments. We consider the following main research questions: Are people willing to donate the same transfer payments to needy people whether or not the inequality in payoffs is self-inflicted? How do cautious, risk-avoiding people react to self-inflicted neediness of others? How do risk-taking people react to self-inflicted neediness of others? In general, our experiment provides a better understanding of how people evaluate the neediness of others depending on whether this neediness is self-inflicted or not.

It is a well-known fact that people do not act like a rational homo oeconomicus only taking into account their own monetary payoffs, but that they also have concerns for fairness.[144] Latterly, a bulk of evidence exists indicating that people do not care exclusively about final monetary payoffs (their own and others), but that they are also strongly affected by the process and the conditions which lead to these final outcomes. The concept of procedural utility[145] tries to grasp the motivations which underlie individual decision making by incorporating that individuals do actually care about non-monetary procedures.[146] The term 'procedural utility' refers not only to utility people get from institutions as such but as well to utility which is evoked by interactions between people: People evaluate actions towards them not only by the instrumental outcomes, but also by how they feel treated by other persons (Frey et al. (2004)). Thus, our experimental study concerning the impact of responsibility on conditional gift giving contributes to the latter definition of procedural utility.

Closely related to the literature about procedural utility is an experiment run by Bolton et al. (2005) investigating fair procedures. They studied biased and

---

[144] Fairness models can be subdivided in a) models with distributional concerns like the inequity aversion models of Bolton and Ockenfels (2000); Fehr and Schmidt (1999) and b) intention based models like the reciprocity models of Rabin (1993), Dufwenberg and Kirchsteiger (2004) and Falk and Fischbacher (2006). In contrast to the outcome-based inequality aversion models, reciprocity models also take into account the intentions underlying a decision process.

[145] "The economic concept of utility as generally applied today is outcome-oriented: individual utility is seen as a result of benefits and costs associated with instrumental outcomes. In contrast, procedural utility refers to the noninstrumental pleasures and displeasures of processes." Frey et al. (2004, pp. 377 ff)

[146] Sen (1995, p. 12) stated that "it is hard to be convinced that we can plausibly judge any given utility distribution ignoring *altogether* the process that led to that distribution".

unbiased allocations and procedures in Ultimatum and Battle of the Sexes Games. Their experiment indicates a) that unbiased random procedures are deemed fair and b) that biased allocations are more acceptable if they are the result of an ex ante fair procedure. The pivotal point of fair procedures like lotteries is that they provide equal opportunity to everyone and that ex ante each player should have the same chance. We compare subjects' conditional gift giving in two treatments in which the ex post outcome is identical, but the ex ante processes differ. In the reference treatment subjects have equal probability of becoming needy, in the other treatment equal probability is ruled out by the subjects themselves.

The existing evidence of solidarity behavior is based on experiments conducted in Germany.[147] In section IV.4 we briefly summarize the experimental results of solidarity behavior between countries with a totally different cultural background, namely in Germany and India.[148] This study serves as a robustness check of the observed results in Germany by investigating to what extent different cultures[149] are driven by solidarity and procedural utility considerations and how they respond to responsibility. Schokkaert and Devooght (2003, p. 208) state that "…some authors […] have argued that the dividing line between responsibility and compensation can be seen as culture-dependent", because it is influenced by the dominant physiological, psychological or social theories of man. To scrutinize whether Indian students' actions are based (to the same extent) on allocative and process-related fairness considerations as those of German students, we run the same treatments with Indian students and compare the conditional gift giving behavior between the two cultures.

---

[147] A first cross-cultural approach is Ockenfels' and Weimann's (1999) study between East and West German students.

[148] The cultural differences between India and Germany are enormous. India is still a developing country where traditional and religious customs are deeply enmeshed in daily life whereas Germany is a highly industrialized country with a society emphasizing individuality. Traditional background, mentality and religious affiliation differ intensely. Regarding the economic situation of people, in India the gap between rich and poor is dramatically bigger than in Germany and there is also a huge gap between the urban highly skilled personnel and the rural population in India, concerning income, medication etc. Estimations attest that in India the percentage of illiterate people (over 15) adds up to 43% (see Borooah and Iyer (2005)). According to the World Bank (2007) 33.5% of Indian inhabitants have less than 1 US-$ per day at their disposal. More than 25% of Indians are too poor to be able to afford adequate alimentation. Yet nearly 60% of the Indians earn their living in the agricultural sector and women still face the additional struggle for equal rights and opportunities. Another important aspect – especially in the light of our experiment – is the fact that the concept of insurance is much less common in India; first and foremost family members help each other if someone is in distress. Although the economy is growing, India still belongs to the developing countries. Thus, contrasts are much bigger in many respects in India and conditions for rural and urban, male and female workers divide sharply.

[149] Cultural differences are defined as "socially transmitted rules about how to behave in certain circumstances (economic or otherwise) that may vary from group to group as a consequence of different cultural evolutionary trajectories" (Henrich (2000), p. 973).

So far economic theory is based on generalized assumptions (e.g. the assumption that preferences are theoretically exogenous) regarding human behavior that exclude cultural differences. However, the question arises to what extent actual decision-making and fairness concerns are dependent on a specific cultural background. A bulk of cross-cultural studies has empirically examined the question whether preferences over economic choices are exogenous or whether these preferences are due to economic and social interactions of everyday life, thus underlying a cultural influence (for instance, see for anthropological, psychological and economic literature on cultural differences Henrich et al. (2001), Mann et al. (1998), Kachelmeier and Shehata (1992), or Guiso et al. (2006)). Specifically, much progress has been made by experimental researchers in studying behavior in the ultimatum game (UG) (see e.g. Anderson et al. (2000), Roth et al. (1991), Henrich (2000), Chuah et al. (2007), or Ferraro and Cummings (2007)), in public good environments (see Burlando and Hey (1997), Brandts et al. (2004), Cadsby et al. (2007), or Cason et al. (2002)) and in trust games (see e.g. Buchan and Croson (2004), Croson and Buchan (1999), or Carpenter et al. (2004)).[150]

Our study on the impact of responsibility on solidarity behavior should gain a first insight whether procedural utility concerns are robust between cultures. The data provide evidence that the level of gift giving indeed differs significantly between Indian and German students (we observe higher gifts in India), however, results are driven by the same motivation: If a group member is responsible for being in need significantly less solidarity is shown.

The following Section IV.2 introduces the experimental design and procedures. The results are presented in Section IV.3 (German data) and IV.4 (cross-cultural comparison), with special emphasis on the impact of responsibility, which is followed by discussion and conclusions in Section IV.5.

---

[150] For instance, note that the results of bargaining behavior in UG experiments in which the subject pool consists of students are very robust across many different places among which are e.g. Taiwan, Israel, Tokyo, Pittsburgh, Slovenia and Java (see e.g. Roth et al. (1991) and Cameron (1999)) which indicates that students as subjects from all over the world behave quite similarly in the UG. In contrast, Henrich (2000) has found significant differences between behavior among American students and the Machiguenga in Peru in a UG experiment indicating that economic decisions and economic reasoning may be influenced by cultural differences. However, one has to be aware that in this study Henrich used different subject pools (Indians versus students). Thus, it is not completely clear if differences in behavior are due to cultural differences or if subject pool effects might also play a considerable role.

IV.2 Experimental Design and Procedures

The experiment was conducted in the Cologne Laboratory for Economic Research using pen and paper in October 2005 and August 2008.[151] Subjects were undergraduate students from the University of Cologne and recruited with ORSEE (Greiner 2004). We ran four sessions (three sessions with 24 subjects each and one with 27).

Our design consists of two treatments. Due to a within subject design, each subject takes part in both treatments. To control possible order effects we alternate the order of the two treatments in the sessions. Furthermore, we use the strategy method as usual in the solidarity game:[152] Subjects have to take their decisions for both parts of the experiment without getting any feedback on the decisions of the others or their own payoffs until the end of the experiment. Learning or experience effects are thus excluded. Therefore, in the second part of the experiment subjects are influenced only by the first part, but not by the decisions made by other subjects.[153]

The procedure is the following: first we hand the subjects general instructions which explain a) that the experiment consists of two independent parts about which they will receive further information in later instructions; b) that only one part of the experiment will be paid with equal probability. Then the first part starts including instructions for the specific treatment, followed by a questionnaire to control whether each subject has understood the instructions. The experimenters check if the answers of each subject are correct. These control questions are followed by a decision form. Afterwards subjects have to fill in an expectation form. The second part is organized analogously. Finally subjects are asked to fill in a questionnaire.[154]

In both treatments each subject is a member of a randomly formed three-person-group, the composition of which is not revealed to the members.[155] In each treatment of a session the random groups are formed anew.

---

[151] We use pen and paper for comparability reasons, as the same experiment is run at an Indian University without laboratory. In contrast to Selten and Ockenfels (1998) and Büchner et al. (2007) we do not apply a double-blind procedure in order to make the design as simple as possible.

[152] Büchner et al. (2007) discover that the strategy method does not lead to different results than the partial play method. We apply the strategy method in our specific within subject design because it creates a no feedback design. Thus, decisions of the subjects are independent from the decisions of their group members even in the second part of the experiment.

[153] This is very important as e.g. Charness and Genicot (forthcoming) find that subjects adjust the size of their transfer payments to that of their partners (strong positive effect).

[154] The instructions are given in the Appendix.

[155] Tajfel et al. (1970) show that creating group identity works very well. They find that subjects treat people who have been defined to be members of their own 'group' quite differently from 'outsiders'.

In one treatment (solidarity treatment = ST) the standard solidarity game is played as first introduced by Selten and Ockenfels (1998). In the ST each subject has a two-thirds probability of winning 10 € (winner) and a one-third probability of obtaining 0 € (loser). Before being informed whether they are winners or losers, subjects are asked how much they will give to losers in their group if they obtain 10 €. Two cases are distinguished: a) how much will they give to one loser in case only one group member loses; b) how much will they give to each loser in case both other group members lose.

In the other treatment (risk treatment = RT) we augment the solidarity game by letting each subject first decide whether to choose a secure payment of 10 € (option A) or whether to participate in a lottery (option B). The decision of every subject only affects his own probabilities and payoffs. As illustrated in Figure IV.A1 in the Appendix, the lottery entails a 50% probability of receiving 0 €, 40% of receiving 10 € and 10% of winning 60 €. Having made their decision concerning option A or B, the subjects are asked for their conditional gifts to group members who receive 0 €, only in case that they receive 10 € themselves. Subjects who receive 60 € cannot pay anything to other group members.[156] That means only subjects who choose option A and receive 10 € for sure or subjects who choose option B and win 10 € can give money to those members of their group who choose option B and receive 0 €. Subjects choosing option A play a simple dictator game, knowing that they will receive 10 € and that they will definitely pay for losers in their group (although they do not know beforehand how many losers there will be in their group). Subjects choosing option B do not know if they will be a winner and pay a gift or a loser and receive a gift from other group members. Contrary to the ST subjects have to indicate their conditional gifts in the RT for three different cases regardless of the chosen option: How much money will a subject give to group members who receive 0 €, if this subject receives 10 € himself, and:

- *one* member of the group receives 0 € and the other member receives 10 € as well (i.e. the loser receives money from two group members),
- *one* member of the group receives 0 € and the other member receives 60 € (i.e. the loser receives money only from one group member),
- *both* group members receive 0 €.

---

[156] As the high payoff in the risky choice is meant to reflect a gambling for personal benefit alone, the 60 € cannot be shared with other members of the group. If the 60 € could be shared the decision for option B could create extra gains for the whole group and thus being seen as (potentially advantageous) risk taking for the benefit of the entire group.

In the RT each subject has to choose between a 'safe' payment and a 'risky' lottery.[157] If a subject chooses option B, he 'damages' his group in so far as there is quite a high probability that he will lose and his group members will have to help him, but he creates no extra gains for his group (as the 60 € cannot be shared). A subject choosing option A 'insures' for sure losers in his group, whereas a player choosing option B is less likely to win 10 € (only in this case he pays for losers in his group). That means that someone who chooses option A is likely to have to insure someone who chooses option B, whereas someone who chooses option B never pays for anyone who chooses option A (at most an option B chooser winning the small prize of 10 € pays for another needy option B chooser).

The difference between the RT and the ST is that losing in the ST is determined exclusively by chance whereas losers in the RT must voluntarily and consciously have chosen the risky lottery to become a needy person. Thus, in the RT losing could have been prevented and subjects are responsible for their needy status, but in the ST losing is not self-inflicted and not the fault of the subjects. Nevertheless, the decisions subjects have to take are the same: What conditional gifts do I pay to needy persons (0 €) in my group in case I receive 10 €? Subjects face the same question, but the underlying process differs.[158]

In the first two sessions (October 2005) of the experiment, the RT is randomly chosen for payment, in the last two the ST (August 2008). Subjects in session 1 and session 2 receive average earnings of 10.83 € and of 14.58 €, and in session 3 and session 4 average earnings amount to 8.33 € and to 10.28 € (including a show-up fee of 2.50 €). A session lasts about one hour.

IV.3 Results

In this section we start with a brief description of our data and the behavioral types as they were first classified in Selten and Ockenfels (1998). Then we discuss the impact of responsibility on the decision-making of subjects and compare gift giving behavior between and within setups; finally, we analyze the expectations of participants regarding other subjects' gift giving behavior.

---

[157] Note that the expected values are the same for both options before potential transfers are made (safety choosers cannot receive transfers, risk choosers might).

[158] More precisely, point 1 and point 3 in the RT are absolutely identical to both questions in the ST. In the RT subjects have to answer additionally only the second point ("in case you win 10 € how much will you give to one loser in your group if the other subject receives 60 €?").

In the following we pool the data of sessions 1 and 3 (sessions 2 and 4) and refer to them as setup 1 (as setup 2) as the treatments were run in the same order in the two sessions of each setup. In setup 1, the RT was played first followed by the ST, whereas in setup 2 the sequence was reversed.

IV.3.1 Gift Giving and Behavioral Types – Allocation Matters

The classic game theoretic solution for a risk-neutral homo oeconomicus is to give zero in both treatments. As it was already shown in numerous experiments before subjects do not behave purely egoistically, but allow fairness to play a role in their considerations as they actually do care for their group members' final outcomes. Our experiment confirms voluntarily gift giving in case of one loser as well as in case of two losers regardless of the treatment. Table IV.1 below shows the means of gift giving.

Table IV.1: Means of gift giving

	N	x_1^{ST}	x_2^{ST}	$x_{1/10}^{RT}$	$x_{1/60}^{RT}$	x_2^{RT}
Setup 1	48	0.95 (1.05)	0.71 (0.88)	0.76 (0.96)	0.86 (1.16)	0.54 (0.75)
Setup 2	51	1.33 (1.38)	0.99 (1.12)	0.67 (1.15)	0.84 (1.50)	0.39 (0.79)

x_1^{ST}: ST 1 loser, x_2^{ST}: ST 2 losers, $x_{1/10}^{RT}$: RT 1 loser (other winner: 10 €), $x_{1/60}^{RT}$: RT 1 loser (other winner: 60 €), x_2^{RT}: RT 2 losers, standard deviations in brackets

In the ST one loser gets an average conditional gift of each winner of 0.95 € (1.33 €) in setup 1 (setup 2). Thus, in total a loser receives 1.90 € (2.66 €) if he is the only loser in his group. By contrast, if there are two losers, the transfer payment to each loser amounts to 0.71 € (0.99 €).[159] In the RT gifts decrease: In setup 1 (setup 2) one loser receives on average 0.76 € (0.67 €) from each winner in case he is the only loser and both others win 10 €. However, if he is the only one to lose, but the third group member wins the high prize of 60 € he receives from the 10 € winner on average 0.86 € (0.84 €). Of two losers in the group each loser receives 0.54 € (0.39 €). A loser receives most if he is the only loser in the group and if there are two members receiving 10 €, i.e. in total he receives an average gift of 1.52 € (1.34 €).[160]

---

[159] Although using only single blind procedure the results for the ST were similar to those found in previous studies. E.g. Büchner et al. (2007) find a gift giving for one loser of $x_1^{ST} = 1.39$ and for each of two losers of $x_2^{ST} = 0.96$ in the standard solidarity game where a winner also receives 10 €.

[160] We observe higher means of gift giving for one loser in the RT if the third group member wins the high prize of 60 € in both setups than if the third member also receives 10 €. However, the differences are

The following investigation concentrates on the two comparable conditional gift giving situations in both treatments: a) the average gift giving in case there is one loser and the third member wins also 10 € and b) the average gift giving in case of two losers. For the time being, we neglect the conditional gifts paid in the RT in case of one member losing and one other member receiving the high prize of 60 €.

Selten and Ockenfels (1998) distinguish the following types of conditional gift giving behavior: egoistic behavior, fixed total sacrifice, fixed gift to loser and intermediate behavior. We follow the classification used by Selten and Ockenfels (1998) and Büchner et al. (2007) to categorize the behavioral types observed in each setup. Table IV.2 shows the results, whereas setup 1 (setup 2) is referred to as S1 (S2). Egoistic behavior occurs if $x_1=x_2=0$. Fixed total sacrifice is defined by $x_1=2x_2>0$. The behavioral pattern $x_1=x_2>0$ is called fixed gift to loser. If the level of the observed gifts lies between fixed total sacrifice and fixed gift to loser the behavior is classified as intermediate ($2x_2>x_1>x_2>0$).

Analyzing the two STs, our sample does not support a predominance of fixed total sacrifice behavior as was found by Selten and Ockenfels (1998). They find that 52% of subjects behave according to fixed total sacrifice. Our results are more balanced. In both STs the percentage of fixed total sacrifice is indeed at least as high as fixed gift to the loser or intermediate behavior, but these differences are quite small. However, the predominant type is egoistic behavior.[161] Obviously, the accumulation of zero-gifts expands in the RT where the percentage of egoistic behavior increases to 45.83% and 64.71% in the two setups. Taken together with the fact that means of conditional gift giving are higher in the ST than in the RT, this observation already suggests that responsibility is a decisive factor in subjects' considerations.

We also consider the question if types of behavior remain stable over time: How many subjects of each type maintain their type during each setup? A certain percentage of subjects stick to their respective type: In our first setup,

---

only weakly significant (a two-tailed Wilcoxon Signed Rank test yields $p=0.102$ in setup 1 and $p=0.063$ in setup 2.
[161] In the standard solidarity experiments Büchner et al. (2007) and Selten and Ockenfels (1998) observed only 27% and 21% egoistical behavior respectively. We do not have an explanation yet for the higher frequency of egoistic types in our ST treatments.

60.42% of the subjects always show the same type; in setup 2, 54.90% do not change their type.[162]

Let us now define consistent behavior in the following way: We call a behavior consistent over time if a subject either does not change his type at all or if he changes his type exclusively in so far as he does not give any amount to losers in the RT when losing is self-inflicted. We observe consistent behavior in setup 1 for 70.83% of the subjects and in setup 2 even for 86.27% of the subjects. The great majority of subjects behaves consistently over time.

Table IV.2: Types of gift giving behavior

	N	Egoistical	Fixed total sacrifice	Fixed gift to loser	Intermediate	Other types
S1 – RT	48	22 (45.83%)	6* (12.5%)	9 (18.75%)	6 (12.5%)	5 (10.42%)
S1 – ST	48	18 (37.5%)	13* (27.08%)	6 (12.5%)	8 (16.67%)	3 (6.25%)
S2 – ST	51	20 (39.22%)	10 (19.61%)	6 (11.76%)	10 (19.61%)	5 (9.8%)
S2 – RT	51	33 (64.71%)	5 (9.8%)	2 (3.92%)	7 (13.73%)	4 (7.84%)

Note: The sequence of treatments refers to the procedure in the two experimental setups (S1: RT-ST; S2: ST-RT). * $n-1$ subjects behave exactly according to $x_1=2x_2>0$, 1 subject up to rounding according to the prominence theory (compare for example Keser and Vogt (2000)).

IV.3.2 The Impact of Responsibility – Process Matters

Both, the higher conditional gift giving in the solidarity treatment[163] and the higher proportion of subjects behaving egoistically in the risk treatment indicate the influence of perceived self-inflictedness on the action of subjects. Now we examine the different levels of gift-giving contingent on the treatment. We expect subjects to be well aware of the fact that losing in the RT is someone's own fault. In the RT subjects who chose option *B* are perceived as selfish in the sense that they accept a high risk of becoming dependent on transfer payments from other group members. Thus, subjects' gift giving to group members who are responsible for their loss can be conjectured to be lower in the RT; whereas we suppose by contrast subjects being willing to give a needy person a much higher conditional gift if the person had no choice and just bad 'luck' in the ST.

Figure IV.1 illustrates the direction of the means in both setups and applies to one as well as to two losers.[164] A within subject analysis for both

---

[162] Note that we investigate only the *type* of behavior, not the *level* of gift giving. A subject's type remaining constant does not mean that the amount he gives to losers is the same. The type refers only to the relation between x_1 and x_2.

[163] If one takes the median instead of the mean conditional gift higher gift giving becomes even more obvious: Setup 1: $x_1^{ST}=0.8$ and $x_2^{ST}=0.5$ vs. $x_1^{RT}=x_2^{RT}=0.1$; Setup 2: $x_1^{ST}=1.0$ and $x_2^{ST}=0.5$ vs. $x_1^{RT}=x_2^{RT}=0$.

[164] In the following we cannot pool the data of the two setups as we observe an order effect. The gift giving for two losers in the RT treatments differ significantly (two-tailed Mann-Whitney-U test, $p=0.054$), whereas in all other cases gifts are not significantly different in the two setups (pair-wise two-

setups shows that conditional gifts are significantly lower in the RT – in which losing is self-inflicted – than in the ST – in which losing is due to chance. This is valid for one loser as well as for two losers.[165] Moreover, not only are the means significantly lower in the RT, but also a comparison of each subject's gift giving between the treatments yields that in setup 1 (setup 2) 19 subjects (22 subjects) give a higher gift in the ST. This proves that at least to a considerable fraction of subjects considerations of responsibility and the underlying process matter.[166]

Figure IV.1: Directions of the means

	1st part		2nd part
Setup 1:	RT	<	ST
	∧		∨
Setup 2:	ST	>	RT

A between subjects analysis of the statistically independent first part of each setup – namely a comparison of the gift giving in the RT (of setup 1) and the ST (of setup 2) – also reveals significantly higher means of gifts in the ST (a one-tailed Mann-Whitney-U test delivers $p=0.035$ for one loser and $p=0.046$ for two losers).[167] Significant lower gifts in the RT – even in the case in which subjects do not have a reference treatment – obviously indicate that subjects perceive losing being strongly self-inflicted in the RT.

Thus, our analysis supports the hypothesis that process-related fairness plays an important role for the gift giving behavior of subjects in a within subjects analysis as well as in a between subjects analysis: Subjects pay in principle lower gifts to losers who are responsible for their situation in the RT than to 'unlucky' losers in the ST.

---

tailed Mann-Whitney-U test, $p>0.1$). A two-tailed Kolmogorov-Smirnov-Z test yields $p>0.1$ for all comparisons except for the RT for two losers indicating that there exist differences between the means and distributions in this one case.

[165] Means are given in Table IV.1. A one-tailed Wilcoxon Signed Rank test provides for setup 1 $p=0.036$ for one loser and $p=0.021$ for two losers. The p-values in setup 2 are $p<0.001$ for one loser as well as for two losers.

[166] Note that there is also a substantial fraction of subjects (totally egoistic type) who do not show any concerns of solidarity whatever treatment they face. We observe that there are 17 persons (35.4%) in the first setup and 17 persons (33.33%) in the second setup giving zero to losers in their group in both treatments.

[167] This result is very robust as comparing the second part of both setups yields even more significant results (one-tailed Mann-Whitney-U test $p=0.016$ for one and $p=0.001$ for two losers).

IV.3.3 The Impact of Responsibility on Safety Choosers and Risk Choosers

Having seen that the perception of responsibility influences conditional gift giving in the different treatments in general, we now examine the effects on subjects choosing the safe option A (safety choosers) and the risky option B (risk choosers) in the RT. In setup 1 31 subjects out of 48 decide in favor of option A and in setup 2 27 subjects out of 51 choose option A. The remaining subjects in each setup choose option B. The average conditional gifts of A- and B-players are given in Table IV.3 below.

Table IV.3: Means of gift giving of A-players and B-players

	N	x_1^{ST}	x_2^{ST}	$x_{1/10}^{RT}$	$x_{1/60}^{RT}$	x_2^{RT}
S1: A-players	31	0.81 (0.97)	0.58 (0.79)	0.60 (0.88)	0.65 (1.03)	0.39 (0.63)
S1: B-players	17	1.20 (1.16)	0.94 (1.02)	1.04 (1.06)	1.25 (1.31)	0.82 (0.89)
S2: A-players	27	1.17 (1.28)	1.06 (1.18)	0.19 (0.68)	0.19 (0.68)	0.12 (0.42)
S2: B-players	24	1.52 (1.49)	0.91 (1.06)	1.21 (1.34)	1.56 (1.82)	0.70 (0.99)

$x_{1/10}^{RT}$: RT 1 loser (other winner: 10 €), $x_{1/60}^{RT}$: RT 1 loser (other winner: 60 €), x_2^{RT}: RT 2 loser, x_1^{ST}: ST 1 loser, x_2^{ST}: ST 2 loser, standard deviations in brackets

Safety Choosers' Behavior

Focusing first on subjects choosing the safe state in the RT, we suppose that subjects who choose option A in the RT deem it very unfair to 'insure' other subjects who were not as cautious as themselves. Thus, we inquire if those safety choosers transfer less to those who decided to take risk compared to transfers to subjects in the ST in which loss is due to bad luck.

First, we conduct a within subject analysis which solely concentrates on safety choosers' gift giving. We compare gift giving of subjects choosing option A in the RT with their gift giving in the ST (excluding gift giving of subjects choosing option B). In setup 1, those subjects choosing option A in the RT ($N=31$) give on average less in the RT than in the ST (Table IV.3 indicates means of gift giving in the RT and in the ST of $x_1^{A-RT} = 0.60$ € and $x_1^{A-ST} = 0.81$ € for one loser and of $x_2^{A-RT} = 0.39$ € and $x_2^{A-ST} = 0.58$ € for two losers). In setup 2, we observe $x_1^{A-RT} = 0.19$ € and $x_1^{A-ST} = 1.17$ € for one loser and $x_2^{A-RT} = 0.12$ € and $x_2^{A-ST} = 1.06$ € for two losers ($N=27$). The differences between the treatments are significant in all cases except in setup 1 for one loser (one-tailed Wilcoxon Signed Rank tests yields $p=0.087$ for one loser, and $p=0.039$ for two losers in setup 1 and in setup 2 $p<0.001$ for one as well as for two losers).

Second, we consider the between subjects analysis of the first part of each setup, i.e. we compare the gift giving of subjects choosing option A in the RT (in the first part of the first setup) and of the gift giving of *all* subjects in the ST (in the first part of the second setup). In setup 1 subjects choosing option A in the RT ($N=31$) give on average $x_1^{A-RT} = 0.60$ € to one loser and $x_2^{A-RT} = 0.39$ € to two losers (see Table IV.3). Subjects in setup 2 playing the ST ($N=51$) in the first part give on average $x_1^{ST} = 1.33$ € to one loser and $x_2^{ST} = 0.99$ € to two losers (compare Table IV.1).[168] These differences are highly significant (one-tailed Mann-Whitney-U test results in $p=0.014$ for one as well as for two losers).[169]

The above analyses show that subjects who are cautious and choose the safe option A give significantly less to losers in case their needy state is due to self-selected risk taking than in case it is due to 'bad luck'.

Risk Choosers' Behavior

If we isolate the gift giving of subjects choosing option B, we observe higher means of gift giving in general except in the ST of setup 2 for two losers (see Table IV.3). For a within subject analysis we pool the data of the two setups as there are no order effects for B-players: Pooled data (setup 1+2) yield ($N=41$): $x_1^{B-RT} = 1.14$ € and $x_1^{B-ST} = 1.39$ € for one loser and $x_2^{B-RT} = 0.75$ € and $x_2^{B-ST} = 0.92$ € for two losers. Concerning the B-players the difference in gift giving between treatments for one loser as well as for two losers is significant (one-tailed Wilcoxon Signed Rank test $p=0.018$ for one loser and $p=0.042$ for two losers). This indicates that B-players give also significantly less in the RT. This result is quite surprising. Although these subjects voluntarily take a higher risk themselves, they do not want to pay for others acting in the same way. Thus, a loser's responsibility for becoming needy plays an important role for gift giving behavior even of those subjects bearing the risk themselves. However, a between subject analysis of the independent first part of both setups (see Table IV.1 and

---

[168] Note that in both setups the average conditional gift giving of A-choosers is lower than the overall average gift in the RT.

[169] Analyzing the second part of the experiment (means of gift giving in the RT ($N=27$) and in the ST ($N=48$): $x_1^{A-RT} = 0.19$ €; $x_2^{A-RT} = 0.12$ € and $x_1^{ST} = 0.95$ €; $x_2^{ST} = 0.71$ € for one loser and for two losers respectively) yields again even more significant results (one-tailed Mann-Whitney-U test: $p<0.001$ for one as well as for two losers).

Table IV.3) shows no significant results – neither for one nor for two losers.[170] This result provides further evidence that conditional gifts of B-players are in general higher than average gifts. We investigate this in more detail in the next subsection.

Comparison of Safety and Risk Choosers' Behavior

Do people who choose risk themselves pay more to losers in the RT than people who choose the safe state in the same treatment? Subjects who choose the lottery and not the safe state are all in the same boat. There is an equal possibility of losing for all of them and after having decided in favor of the lottery, they play the 'standard' solidarity game again. Table IV.3 summarizes the means of gift giving for subjects choosing option A or B respectively for both setups. Subjects choosing option B give higher gifts in all cases except one than subjects choosing option A. In both setups gift giving in the standard solidarity treatment ST does not differ significantly between A- and B-players (one-tailed Mann-Whitney-U test provides $p>0.1$ for one loser as well as for two losers). However, in the RT a one-tailed Mann-Whitney-U test yields (at least weakly) significant differences in gift giving of A- and B-players (setup 1: $p=0.069$ for one loser and one other 10 €-winner, all other cases $p<0.05$). B-players give at least as much to losers as A-players in the treatment, in which losing is partly self-inflicted. These are very intuitive results: A- and B-players both give similar transfer payments to losers if they are not held responsible for their neediness (ST) (if losing is only due to chance then there are no significant differences in gift giving of A- and B-players). However, if subjects are given the possibility of avoiding risk, subjects who choose a safe payment pay significantly less to losers who are responsible for their neediness compared to subjects taking the risk themselves (RT).[171] Thus, risk takers show a slightly higher solidarity with other risk takers than subjects having chosen the secure payment.

---

[170] A one-tailed Mann-Whitney-U test yields $p=0.33$ for one loser and $p=0.43$ for two losers. (First part setup 1 risk choosers ($N=17$): $x_1^{B-RT} = 1.04$ € for one loser and $x_2^{B-RT} = 0.82$ € for two losers and first part setup 2 all subjects ($N=51$): $x_1^{ST} = 1.33$ € to one loser and $x_2^{ST} = 0.99$ € to two losers.) This result seems to be robust as a comparison of the second part also does not yield significant differences in conditional gift giving (one-tailed Mann-Whitney-U test: $p=0.30$ for one loser and $p=0.26$ for two losers). (Second part setup 2 risk choosers ($N=24$): $x_1^{B-RT} = 1.21$ € for one loser and $x_2^{B-RT} = 0.70$ € for two losers and second part setup 1 all subjects ($N=48$): $x_1^{ST} = 0.95$ €; $x_2^{ST} = 0.71$ € for one loser and for two losers respectively.)

[171] Nevertheless, the means of B-players are almost always higher, albeit not significant in the ST. This might indicate that more risk averse subjects (A-players) are self-selecting and more egoistical.

IV.3.4 Impact of Responsibility on Expectations of Actions

When subjects express their expectations regarding the gift giving behavior of others they implicitly estimate how the perception of responsibility influences their fellows' actions. If most subjects assume that others are as well sensitive to process-related fairness one can expect that one's expectations and one's own actions somehow correspond. First, we concentrate on the preciseness of expectations in the ST. Means of gift giving and means of expected gifts in the solidarity treatment are illustrated in Table IV.4.

Table IV.4: Means of gift giving and means of expected gifts in the ST

	N	x_1^{ST}	x_2^{ST}	e_1^{ST}	e_2^{ST}
Setup 1 – ST	48	0.95 (1.05)	0.71 (0.88)	1.14 (0.93)	0.86 (0.81)
Setup 2 – ST	51	1.33 (1.38)	0.99 (1.12)	1.82 (1.19)	1.26 (1.12)

Average gifts (x_1 and x_2) and expectations (e_1 and e_2) in €, standard deviations in brackets

The average of expected gifts is higher than the average of actual conditional gifts. Nevertheless, Spearman rank correlations show a strong and significant correlation (one-tailed $p<0.01$ for one as well as for two losers) among gifts and expected gifts for both setups (setup 1: $\rho = 0.72$ for x_1^{ST} and e_1; and $\rho = 0.80$ for x_2^{ST} and e_2; setup 2: $\rho = 0.55$ for x_1^{ST} and e_1; and $\rho = 0.57$ for x_2^{ST} and e_2). One-tailed Wilcoxon Signed Rank tests yield significant differences between conditional gifts and expectations in both setups ($p<0.05$ for one as well as for two losers). These results correspond to the findings of Büchner et al. (2007).[172]

Now, we consider gift giving and expectations in the RT of our experiment. First, we concentrate on gifts of subjects choosing option A and their expectations. Table IV.5 summarizes the results. Spearman rank tests show again a high and significant correlation among gifts and expectations for A-players in setup 1 ($\rho = 0.66$ for $x_{1(A)}^{RT}$ and $e_{1(A)}$, $p<0.01$; and $\rho = 0.67$ for $x_{2(A)}^{RT}$ and $e_{2(A)}$, $p<0.01$). In setup 2, there is no correlation, which is driven by the fact that only 3 A-players contribute a positive amount. One-tailed Wilcoxon Signed Rank tests

---

[172] Büchner et al. show that the results are driven by a false consensus effect of those subjects, who give more than average gifts ('altruistic' type). Our data for the ST support their hypothesis. Subjects giving less than the average gift ('greedy' type) expect others to give more (setup 1: greedy subjects ($N=24$): $x_1=0.08$ and $x_2=0.05$; $e_1=0.53$ and $e_2=0.33$), however the more altruistic subjects expect too high gifts ($x_1=2.22$ and $x_2=1.79$; $e_1=2.08$ and $e_2=1.78$, $N=16$). The same holds for setup 2: greedy subjects ($N=26$): $x_1=0.21$ and $x_2=0.12$; $e_1=1.29$ and $e_2=0.75$; altruistic subjects ($N=21$): $x_1=2.71$ and $x_2=2.06$; $e_1=2.35$ and $e_2=1.78$.

show that subjects expect significantly higher gifts from others than they actually transfer themselves ($p<0.05$ for one as well as for two losers), except in setup 1 for one loser ($p=0.168$).

Table IV.5: Means of gift giving and of expected gifts in the RT of A-players

	N	$x_{1(A)}^{RT}$	$x_{2(A)}^{RT}$	$e_{1(A)}^{RT}$	$e_{2(A)}^{RT}$
Setup 1 – RT	31	0.60 (0.88)	0.39 (0.63)	0.75 (0.69)	0.62 (0.54)
Setup 2 – RT	27	0.19 (0.68)	0.12 (0.42)	0.35 (0.45)	0.30 (0.39)

Average gifts (x_1 and x_2) and expectations (e_1 and e_2) in €, standard deviations in brackets

Table IV.6 contains the conditional gifts on average and the expected gifts of B-players (pooled data as there are no order effects). Spearman rank tests find a significant but weak correlation (pooled setups: $\rho = 0.35$ for $x_{1(B)}^{RT}$ and $e_{1(B)}$, $p<0.05$; and $\rho = 0.36$ for $x_{2(B)}^{RT}$ and $e_{2(B)}$, $p<0.01$). However, one-tailed Wilcoxon Signed Rank tests show only weak significance that expectations are higher than conditional gifts ($p=0.054$ for one loser and $p=0.018$ for two losers).

Table IV.6: Means of gift giving and of expected gifts in the RT of B-players

	N	$x_{1(B)}^{RT}$	$x_{2(B)}^{RT}$	$e_{1(B)}^{RT}$	$e_{2(B)}^{RT}$
Setup 1+2 – RT	41	1.14 (1.22)	0.75 (0.94)	1.41 (1.17)	1.06 (0.89)

Average gifts (x_1 and x_2) and expectations (e_1 and e_2) in €, standard deviations in brackets

In summary, although means of expectations are higher than actual gift-giving, they predict quite well actual gifts[173] and thus indicate that subjects expect other individuals to be sensitive to allocative and process-related fairness as well.

All in all, additional to allocative fairness we found evidence for our hypothesis that the responsibility of one's own actions plays an important role and actually has a strong influence on the solidarity of subjects. The questionnaire distributed after the experiment further corroborates our assumptions: Many subjects state explicitly that they do not want to pay for

---

[173] Interestingly, this indicates that cheap talk does not influence the accuracy of expected means. Although we did not pay subjects for correct expectations and therefore these expectations are just cheap talk, the predictions in the ST of our experiment are as precise as in Büchner et al. (2007) who paid the subjects for correct answers.

others if losing is their own fault, whereas they are willing to help others if losing is only due to 'bad luck'. Some of their statements are given in the Appendix.[174]

IV.4 A Cross-Cultural Comparison – Evidence from Germany and India

We conducted the experiment at Birla Institute of Management Technology in New Delhi (BIMTECH)[175] in December 2005 using pen and paper. Subjects were undergraduate students from BIMTECH. We ran two sessions; session 1 consisted of 30 subjects and session 2 of 18 subjects.[176] In session 1 the RT was randomly chosen for payment and in session 2 the ST. Subjects earned on average 81.13 rupees in session 1 and 40.28 rupees in session 2 including the show-up fee. Show-up fee was 12.5 Rps. The stake size in India amounts to German stake size times 5.[177] Indeed, this is not the actual exchange rate, but with respect to purchasing power this is nearly comparable to a student's average hourly earnings in India. In the ST each subject has a two-thirds probability of winning 50 Rps. (winner) and a one-third probability of obtaining 0 Rps. (loser); in the RT each subject chooses between option A (50 Rps. for sure) and option B (0 Rps., 50 Rps. or 300 Rps. with identical probabilities as in the German experiment) as depicted in Figure IV.A2 in the Appendix. In each treatment a 50 Rps.-winner has to indicate how much he would give to a loser in his group (0 Rps.). We proceed in exactly the same way as in Cologne, first handing out the subjects general instructions about the experiment followed by the first part including instructions for the specific treatment and a sheet with control questions. After the experimenters controlled whether the answers were correct, the subjects receive the decision sheet followed by an expectation form. The second part is organized analogously. Finally subjects are asked to fill in a questionnaire.

---

[174] Note that even a substantial fraction of totally egoistic subjects clearly distinguishes the two situations: They also state in the accompanying questionnaire that needy subjects in the risk treatment do not deserve compensation as they choose the risk of losing voluntarily. Thus, these subjects *judge* the two situations differently as well.
[175] BIMTECH is characterized by a student community coming from almost all states of India and it ranks in Top 25 B-schools in India in various surveys.
[176] The unequal amount of subjects in our two sessions is due to no shows.
[177] Concerning the experimental currency we used the corresponding currency of the country as a fictive currency might confuse the Indian students who had never taken part in an experiment before. Note that steps were equal (in Germany 10 cent steps and in India 0.5 rupee steps).

Table IV.7 gives means of gift giving in India[178] and for comparability reasons the scaled gift giving in Germany (German gifts are multiplied by 5). A comparison of gift giving between countries shows that means of conditional gift giving are always higher in India than in Germany. These differences are significant except for the comparison of the gifts in the ST between Indian gifts and the German gifts in setup 2 for one as well as for two losers ($p>0.1$, two-tailed Mann-Whitney-U test).[179] Thus, allocative fairness considerations seem to be even stronger in India than in Germany.[180]

Table IV.7: Means of gift giving in India and Germany (in rupees)

	N	x_1^{ST}	x_2^{ST}	$x_{1/50}^{RT}$	$x_{1/300}^{RT}$	x_2^{RT}
Indian data	45	8.12 (7.54)	5.19 (5.30)	6.38 (7.28)	6.61 (7.81)	4.10 (4.55)
Germany Setup 1	48	4.73 (5.24)	3.53 (4.42)	3.78 (4.79)	4.31 (5.81)	2.72 (3.76)
Germany Setup 2	51	6.67 (6.90)	4.93 (5.59)	3.35 (5.77)	4.19 (7.48)	1.95 (3.96)

$x_{1/50}^{RT}$: RT 1 loser (other winner: 50 Rps.), $x_{1/300}^{RT}$: RT 1 loser (other winner: 300 Rps.), x_2^{RT}: RT 2 loser, x_1^{ST}: ST 1 loser, x_2^{ST}: ST 2 loser, standard deviations in brackets. Means of gift giving in Germany are multiplied by 5. We exclude in session 1 one subject and in session 2 two subjects from the Indian data set. One subject did not fill in the form completely so data points are missing for this subject, one subject gives more than his endowment and one subject does not understand the instructions (expecting payments from group members of 300 Rp.)

Just as the German data the Indian data also provide evidence that group members' self-inflicted neediness leads to a reduction of conditional gift giving. Means of Indian gifts are higher in the ST than in the RT for one as well as for two losers. This is significant for one loser ($p=0.012$ one-tailed Wilcoxon Signed Rank test) but not for two losers ($p=0.051$ one-tailed Wilcoxon Signed Rank test) on the 5% significance level. Thus, procedural utility has (at least a slight) impact on decision making, but this result is not as strong as in our German data.

Separately investigating the gift giving behavior of safety and risk choosers (subjects choosing option *A* or *B*) yields again qualitatively similar results as it is observed in the German data. Table IV.8 shows the means of

---
[178] Testing for order effects yields no differences due to the order of the treatment in each session ($p>0.1$ two-tailed Mann-Whitney-U tests). Thus we can pool the data of both sessions.
[179] The comparison of gifts between German students in setup 1 and Indian students is significant on the 1% significance level for the ST one loser, on the 5% significance level for the RT and on the 10% level for the ST two losers using a two-sided Mann-Whitney-U test. For setup 2 the differences between Indian and German data are highly significant on the 1% level in the RT.
[180] However, we have to interpret these results carefully as German students have to divide an amount of 10 whereas in India the subjects get an amount of 50. The level of gift giving might also be influenced by number effects.

conditional gifts differentiating between safety (*A*-players) and risk choosers (*B*-players).

Examining the gift giving between the ST and the RT for the two types of subjects separately, yields for *A*-players significantly higher gift giving in the ST than in the RT ($p=0.026$ (one loser) and $p=0.044$ (two losers), one-tailed Wilcoxon Signed Rank test), whereas *B*-players' gifts in the ST are not significantly different from *B*-players' gifts in the RT ($p=0.112$ (one loser) and $p=0.256$ (two losers), one-tailed Wilcoxon Signed Rank test). Indian subjects avoiding the risky choice give significantly less to group members if they are considered to be responsible for losing, whereas subjects deciding to take the risk themselves do not give significantly higher gifts to losers whose losing is due to bad luck and not to a voluntarily borne risk.

However, gift giving between *A*- and *B*-players does not vary significantly all in all. Comparing *A*-players' with *B*-players' means of gift giving we find always higher gifts for *B*-players for joint data, but the difference is not significant ($p>0.1$, two-tailed Mann-Whitney-U test).

Table IV.8: Means of gift giving of *A*-players and *B*-players in India

Joint data	N	x_1^{ST}	x_2^{ST}	$x_{1/50}^{RT}$	$x_{1/300}^{RT}$	x_2^{RT}
A-players	25	6.66 (7.39)	4.76 (5.67)	5.00 (7.12)	4.90 (7.21)	3.54 (4.83)
B-players	20	9.95 (7.51)	5.73 (4.89)	8.10 (7.29)	8.98 (8.00)	4.80 (4.18)

Our experimental data from India provide evidence once again that allocative fairness as well as procedural utility concerns matter. Although the overall gift giving level differs between the Indian and the German subjects quantitatively, allocative fairness and procedural utility concerns seem to be robust besides the cultural differences of our investigated subject pools. Moreover, as it has already been shown in the German data subjects even *expect* differences in conditional gift giving: Expectations of Indian subjects are a good predictor for actual gift giving behavior (mean gifts and mean expected gifts are given in Table IV.A1 and IV.A2 in the Appendix).[181] Hence, in our experiment culture indeed seems to influence economic outcomes indicating that preferences and beliefs might be endogenous and are thus likely to vary between

---

[181] Spearman rank correlations show strong and significant correlations among gifts and expected gifts and two-tailed Wilcoxon Signed Rank tests yield no significant differences between gifts and expectations (this holds for all cases except *A*-players, whose expectations are significantly higher than their gifts).

environments. However, we find the same fairness motives having a driving force in our cross-cultural study.

IV.5 Discussion and Conclusions

We ran an experiment to examine the influence of responsibility on solidarity. The experiment provides strong evidence for our hypothesis that the process plays an important role in the decision-making process and obviously has a strong impact not only on the *judgment* but also on the *actions* of subjects. We found conditional gift giving to be highly dependent on whether subjects are thought to be responsible or not: The experimental data provide evidence that, controlling for payoff distributions, subjects are less generous towards those whose bad outcome is a result of their own risk-taking actions compared to those who had no role in their bad outcome. Furthermore, although showing a slightly higher solidarity than safety choosers, even risk choosers were less generous to other risk choosers than to those who had no role in their bad outcome.

There already exist some studies on distributive justice which deal with responsibility for one's own actions. Schokkaert and Devooght (2003) conclude that one has to distinguish "[...] between two sets of individual characteristics: those for which individuals have to be compensated and those for which they are to be held responsible. Differences in natural talent could be an obvious example of the former category, effort an example of the latter. [...] (T)he degree of control is crucial: people can only be held responsible for (the consequences of) the individual characteristics which follow from their own voluntary choice."[182] In our view the degree of control and responsibility is the pivotal point. Subjects in our experiment pay significantly more money to losers in the treatment in which losers are not responsible for being in their state, while subjects who voluntarily choose a risk and thus are to be held fully responsible for losing receive significantly less. Many subjects even expressed these considerations in the questionnaire after the experiment explicitly. Could this imply for health insurances that people consider it as fair if e.g. smokers and people doing risky sports like paragliding should pay for themselves if they fall ill or are injured (e.g. by paying higher premium rates)? In our abstract experiment we found evidence that subjects' willingness to pay for others actually depends on whether need of others arise from chance or a voluntarily taken risk. Schokkaert and

---

[182] Schokkaert and Devooght (2003), p. 208.

Devooght (2003) achieved even more extreme results using specific questionnaires: "if our respondents really feel that individuals are responsible for their behavior (smoking and working hard are obvious examples) [...] not only should people not be compensated for the consequences of this behavior, they should even be punished if they smoke or are lazy."[183, 184] Note that smoking and not working hard are examples in which also the payoffs of other people are reduced (passive smoking enhances health disadvantages and employees have to work for their free-riding colleagues). In our experiment, payoffs of *other* subjects were not reduced if one subject chose the risky option. Although subjects were not harmed directly by their risk-taking group members they nevertheless did not want to pay for their neediness. Thus, we suppose these results to become even stronger if the risk taking of their group members have a negative externality on them (besides the possible transfer payments they have to pay).

The data show that subjects' solidarity is at least partly crowded out if needy group members are responsible for their state. The robustness of this result is tested in a cross-cultural study which yields qualitatively the same results and thus supports the findings on the relevance of allocative fairness as well as procedural utility. The procedural utility concept tries to take process-related fairness considerations into account. Procedural utility differs from intention-based reciprocity models in so far as in reciprocity models utility depends on outcomes (or, at least, the reference points depend on allocations). Intentions can be measured, but only in terms of payoffs. By contrast, in procedural utility concepts "utility is reaped from the process itself, over and above the outcome generated".[185] Thereby the *non-instrumental* aspect of procedural utility is emphasized, an aspect which is not covered by reciprocity models, although these do incorporate intentions (but only measured in terms of payoffs). Bolton et al. (2005) and Sen (1995) also emphasize the importance of incorporating

---

[183] Schokkaert and Devooght (2003) p. 223.
[184] Other studies on distributive justice provide similar results. Fleurbaey and Maniquet (2003, p. 5) speak of a 'sphere of individual responsibility' and Cohen (1989, p. 914) states "(w)e should [...] compensate only for those welfare deficits which are not in some way traceable to the individual's choices". Arneson (1990, p. 176) says that "(d)istributive justice does not recommend any intervention by society to correct inequalities that arise through the voluntary choice or faulty behavior that gives rise to the inequalities." Yaari and Bar-Hillel (1984) already pointed to the impact of different processes by "showing that the traditional welfarist solutions perform badly because different contexts seem to call for different choices of allocation rules" Fleurbaey and Maniquet (2003, p. 72).
[185] Frey and Stutzer (2005), p. 91.

procedure-sensitive behavior in social utility models.[186] Our data (which is also successfully tested for robustness in a cross-cultural comparison) provide strong evidence both for allocative fairness *and* for process-related fairness thus further corroborating the statement of Frey et al. (2004):

> *"procedural utility is an important determinant of human well-being that has to be incorporated more widely into economic theory and empirical research."*

---

[186] Bolton et al. (2005, p. 1067): "Social utility models – whether distribution or attribution based or both – will not capture this sort of procedure-sensitive behavior so long as they only incorporate allocation-driven reference points." Bolton et al. (2005, p. 1066): "[…] a satisfactory explanation of the experiment need incorporate elements of both procedural and allocation fairness". Sen (1995, p. 18): "Procedural concerns can, however, be amalgamated with consequential ones by recharacterizing states of affairs appropriately, and the evaluation of states can then take note of the two aspects together."

IV.6 Appendix to Chapter IV

Instructions[187]

General Instructions:

Welcome and thank you very much for participating in this experiment. Please read the instructions carefully. If you have any questions please do not ask aloud but raise your hand and wait until an experimenter will come to your place. Then you can discuss your question with him personally. During the whole experiment, starting now, communication with other participants is strictly forbidden. Following this rule is very important. In case of non-compliance, we must exclude you from the experiment and all pay offs.

THE EXPERIMENT

- You receive 2.50 € for your participation irrespective of your decisions during this experiment. Additionally, you can earn more money in this experiment. How much you earn depends on both your decisions and the decisions of other participants.
- The experiment consists of two independent parts. First, the first part is conducted, followed by the second part. At the end of the experiment only one part will be paid out; it will be the same part for all participants. Either the first or the second part is chosen for payment with an equal probability (50%) **after both parts were conducted**. A six sided dice will be thrown at the end of the experiment:
    - if the dice shows one of the numbers 1, 2, or 3, the **first part** of the experiment will be paid out
    - if the dice shows one of the numbers 4, 5, or 6, the **second part** of the experiment will be paid out
- Your interaction partners in the experiment will be randomly assigned to you in the first as well as in the second part of the experiment.
- Please follow the instructions in both parts; all instructions are identical for each participant. This is also true for the questionnaires you have to fill in during this experiment: they are identical for everybody as well.

The first part of the experiment starts now.

---

[187] Translated from German. These are the instructions of session 1, where the first part consists of the RT and the second part consists of the ST. The instructions of session 2 are analogous.

Instructions for the first part of session 1:
1ST PART OF THE EXPERIMENT

Each participant is a member of a randomly formed group of three persons. At no time before, during or after the experiment the identity of your group members is revealed to you. In this part of the experiment you have to make two decisions.

FIRST DECISION

Each participant has the choice between two options A or B. This choice and the two options are identical for each participant. The chosen option will be separately conducted for each participant.

Please choose an option:

  Option A: You receive **10 €** for sure

  Option B: A ten-sided dice will be thrown (0-9)

  - if the dice shows one of the numbers 1, 2, 3, 4 or 5 you receive **0 €**

    (probability of 50%).

  - if the dice shows one of the numbers 6, 7, 8 or 9 you receive **10 €**

    (probability of 40%).

  - if the dice shows 0 you receive **60 €**

    (probability of 10%).

Thus, the following results are possible for each participant:
- You receive **10 €** (You chose either option A or option B)
- You receive **0 €** (You chose option B)
- You receive **60 €** (You chose option B)

SECOND DECISION

The pay offs of each participant are ascertained. Participants who chose option A receive 10 €. For *each* participant who chose option B a dice will be thrown separately.

Before the dice is thrown all participants have to make the following decision: In case you **receive 10 €**, and only in this case, how much would you give voluntarily to other members of your three-person-group who receive 0 €.

Participants who won 60 € **cannot give any money** to group members. Each participant has to make his decision on three cases: How much money would you give to group members who receive 0 € if **you receive 10 € yourself** and:

- *one* member of the group receives 0 € and the other member receives 10 €
- *one* member of the group receives 0 € and the other member receives 60 €
- *both* group members receive 0 €

The total amount you give to your group members has to be between 0 € and 10 €.

Your group members have to make the same decision. The other participants will not get to know your decisions.

This means:

- In case you choose option *A* (you receive **10 €** for sure), you can give money to your group members who choose option *B* and receive 0 €.
- In case you choose option *B* and win **10 €**, you can give money to your group members who choose option *B* and receive 0 €.
- In case you choose option *B* and receive **60 €**, you *cannot give any money* to your group members.
- In case you choose option *B* and you receive **0 €**, you *cannot give any money* to your group members. You receive money which your group members might give to you in case they receive 10 €.

YOUR PAY OFFS

Your final pay off depends on your decision and on the decisions of the other participants in the experiment. If the first part of the experiment will be paid out you receive additional to 2.50 €:

•	In case you receive 10 €:	10 € **minus** the amount you decided to give to potential losers (0 €) in your group
•	In case you receive 0 €:	0 € **plus** the amount you get from potential winners of 10 € in your group
•	In case you receive 60 €:	60 €

PROCEDURE

1. Now the experimenters distribute a control sheet to make sure that every participant understood the instructions.
2. Afterwards, the experimenters will distribute an envelope containing a decision form to each participant. Please open your envelope and check your control number **top right** on the form. Fill in the decision form completely and write **on top of the envelope** which option (*A* or *B*) you decided for. If you forget to write down your decision you will *not* be paid after the experiment! After you filled in the form, put the form back into the envelope and close it. After all participants having filled in their decision forms the experimenters will collect all the envelopes in a box.
3. Then the experimenters will distribute a further form with your control number top right on the form. Please check your number and fill in the form completely. As soon as all participants filled in their forms, the experimenters will collect them.
4. The experimenters will then draw the envelopes containing the decision forms one by one from the box. If option *B* is chosen the experimenters will throw a ten-sided dice to acquire how much each particular control number wins. The experimenters know which option you chose, because of your decision on the envelope. The experimenters will write down on each envelope how much money each control number won. Afterwards all envelopes will be put back into the box and will be mixed properly.
5. The experimenters draw envelopes from the box again. The envelopes will be randomly arranged in groups of three. For each group the experimenters will open the envelopes and calculate the pay offs each participant gets if the first part of the experiment will be paid out.
6. After this, the second part of the experiment begins.

Are there any further questions?

Instructions for the second part of session 1:
2ND PART OF THE EXPERIMENT

Again, each participant is a member of a *new* randomly formed group of three persons. The probability that you are in exactly the same group as in the previous part of the experiment is smaller than 1%. At no time before, during or after the experiment the identity of your group members is revealed to you.

Each member of the group can win 10 € with a certain probability or receive 0 € with the counter probability.

A six-sided dice will be thrown for *each* participant:

- If the dice shows one of the numbers 1 or 2 you receive **0 €**

  (probability of 1/3)

- If the dice shows one of the numbers 3, 4, 5, or 6 you receive **10 €**

  (probability of 2/3)

A dice will be thrown for *each* participant of the group individually defining whether the person receives 0 € or 10 €. One of the following four scenarios will occur:

1. All three members of the group win 10 €.
2. One member of the group wins 10 € and the other two lose (0 €).
3. Two members of the group win 10 € and the third one loses (0 €).
4. All three members of the group lose (all receive 0 €).

YOUR DECISION

Before you get to know whether you win (10 €) or lose (0 €) you decide how much you would voluntarily give to losers in your group in case you win. You have to distinguish between two possible situations: You have to decide how much you would give to *one* member of your group in case that only *one* other member receives 0 €. And you have to decide how much you would give to *two* members of your group in case both receive 0 €. The total amount you give to your group members has to be between 0 € and 10 €. Your group members have to make the same decision. The other participants will not get to know your decisions.

YOUR PAY OFFS

Your final pay off depends on your decision and on the decisions of the other participants in the experiment. If the second part of the experiment will be paid out you receive additional to 2.50 €:

• In case you receive 10 €	10 € **minus** the amount you decided to give to potential losers (0 €) in your group
• In case you receive 0 €	0 € **plus** the amount you get from potential winners in your group

THE PROCEDURE

1. Now the experimenters distribute a control sheet to make sure that every participant understood the instructions.
2. Afterwards, the experimenters will distribute an envelope containing a decision form to each participant. Please open your envelope and check your control number **top right** on the form. Fill in the decision form completely, put it back into the envelope and close it. After all participants having filled in their decision forms the experimenters will collect all the envelopes in a box.
3. Then the experimenters will distribute a further form with your control number top right on the form. Please check your number and fill in the form completely. As soon as all participants filled in their forms, the experimenters will collect them.
4. Subsequently, the experimenters distribute another short questionnaire. Please check again your control number and complete the form.
5. The experimenters will then draw the envelopes containing the decision forms one by one from the box. For each envelope they will throw a six-sided dice to acquire whether the particular control number wins or loses. The experimenters will write down on each envelope whether the control number won or lost. Afterwards all envelopes will be put back into the box and will be mixed properly.
6. The experimenters draw envelopes from the box again. The envelopes will be randomly arranged in groups of three. For each group the experimenters will open the envelopes and calculate the pay offs each participant gets if the second part of the experiment will be paid out.

7. Now, the experimenters throw a six-sided dice to define the part that will be paid out. Afterwards, they will call on the control numbers separately and disburse the pay offs to the participants.

Are there any further questions?

Tables

Table IV.A1: Means of gift giving and means of expected gifts in the ST (India)

ST	N	x_1^{ST}	x_2^{ST}	e_1	e_2
Indian joint data	45	8.12 (7.54)	5.19 (5.30)	8.02 (7.03)	5.52 (4.74)

Average gifts (x_1 and x_2) and expectations (e_1 and e_2) in Rps., standard deviations in brackets

Table IV.A2: Means of gift giving and of expected gifts in the RT (India)

RT	N	$x_{1(i)}^{RT}$	$x_{2(i)}^{RT}$	$e_{1(i)}$	$e_{2(i)}$
Indian joint data A-players	25	5.00 (7.12)	3.54 (4.83)	7.16 (6.48)	5.74 (5.01)
Indian joint data B-players	20	8.10 (7.29)	4.80 (4.18)	7.50 (5.15)	5.20 (3.61)

Average gifts (x_1 and x_2) and expectations (e_1 and e_2) in Rps., standard deviations in brackets. $i = \{A, B\}$

Figures

Figure IV.A1: Options in the RT (Germany)

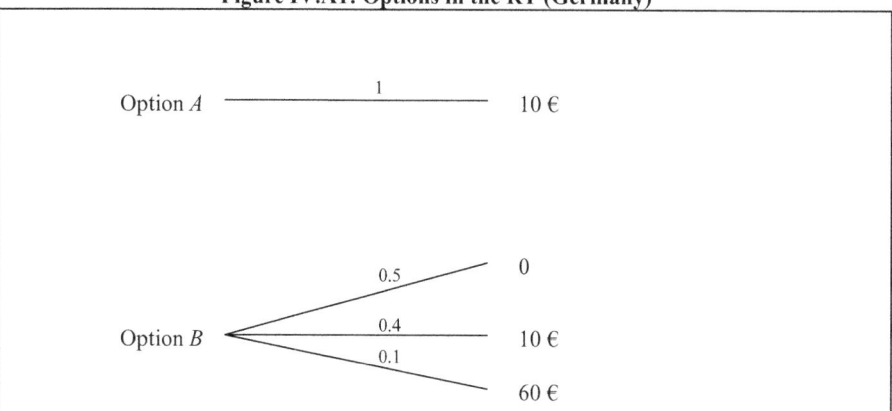

If option B was chosen we throw a ten-sided dice for each subject. The subjects who chose option B lose if the dice shows one of the numbers 1, 2, 3, 4 or 5, they win 10 € if one of the numbers 6, 7, 8 or 9 occurs and they win the big prize of 60 € if the number 0 occurs.

Figure IV.A2: Options in the RT (India)

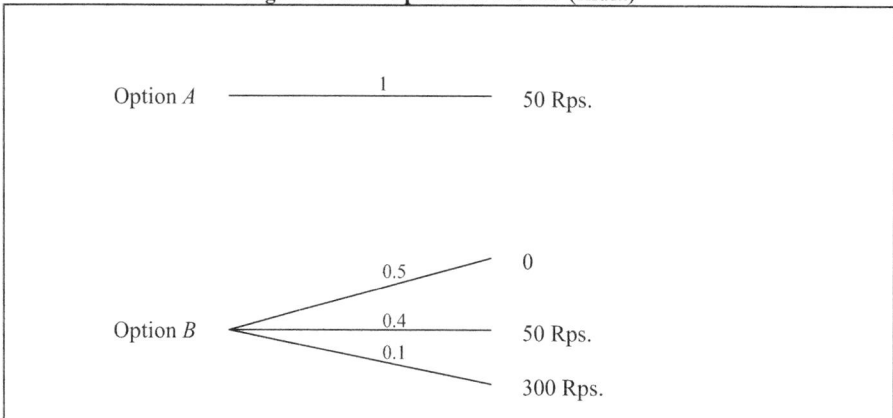

If option B was chosen we throw a ten-sided dice for each subject. The subjects who chose option B lose if the dice shows one of the numbers 1, 2, 3, 4 or 5, they win 50 Rps. if one of the numbers 6, 7, 8 or 9 occurs and they win the big prize of 300 Rps. if the number 0 occurs.

Some selected statements from the questionnaire:[188]

RT:

"I decided to take possibility *A*. I give 0 € to other participants, because everybody had the free choice to choose the secure possibility. Those choosing possibility *B* nevertheless, have to bear their risk alone/themselves."

"I give less, because the others decided for the lottery and therefore choose the risk consciously."

"All participants wanting a secure payment could have chosen possibility *A*. All participants choosing *B* as myself, are soldiers of fortune and let luck/chance decide. Therefore they receive nothing."

"Those who are greedy and therefore take risks, have to take the responsibility for it."

"Choosing possibility *A* I have no chance to get something from others and therefore I do not give anything, too. Moreover, I do not want to support others' risk loving behavior, if I decided for the safe state."

"I give nothing to other participants choosing possibility *B*, because they took a chance by playing the lottery. Therefore it is their own fault."

ST:

"In this case one could not control his own risk and therefore I decided in case I win to pay an amount as consolation."

"Here I give more, because it is no one's fault if he loses."

"Game of chance, now I give a minimal amount to my group members."

"I want all three group members to receive similar amounts, because winning is only due to the dice."

"Because I also lose with a probability of 1/3, I am probably dependent on the pity of others and therefore I am also generous myself."

"I share, because everybody has the same chance."

---

[188] Translated from German.

Chapter V

Conclusions

This thesis deals with the importance of behavioral aspects in various economic applications. The main results of the experimental studies presented in this thesis are summarized as follows: The studies on partnership dissolution in Chapter II show that, although the investigated dissolution mechanisms in general perform well, their efficient performance strongly depends on the specific setting. In general, the assumption of interdependent valuations gives rise to a more complex decision situation which yields more allocative inefficiencies and which in turn changes the ranking of the mechanisms. The experimental results of the first part of this chapter contradict theoretical predictions of a standard independent private values model assuming homogenous agents and can rather be explained by a model with heterogeneous agents with respect to risk attitudes. In the second part of this chapter the robustness of results is tested for different assumptions on partnership valuations structure. If the valuations structure is characterized by an interdependent valuations structure in contrast to a framework with independent private values, we observe the reverse results concerning efficiency: With independent private values the cake-cutting mechanism performs better in terms of efficiency, whereas with interdependent valuations the winner's bid auction achieves higher efficiency results. However, in the independent private values case management deadlocks could occur in the better-performing cake-cutting mechanism, because no partner has an incentive to start proposing a price. As we find partners' payoff expectations to differ substantially in the cake-cutting mechanism, the specification of roles in this mechanism (see also de Frutos and Kittsteiner (2008)) still remains an interesting object for future research. Furthermore, in the interdependent valuations case the reluctance to propose is even considerably worsened by proposers achieving negative gains from trade on average. Non-participation proves to be a new arising problem with interdependent valuations – not only for proposers. The problem of non-participation in dissolution mechanisms if participation is not forced (e.g. by previous contracts) is caused by adverse selection effects (i.e., winner's and loser's curses). Further empirical examination of the extent of these adverse selection effects should be analyzed in future research. For this purpose, the degree of interdependence could be varied for instance. The robustness check concerning different assumptions on the underlying valuation structure could also be extended in order to learn more about the selection and the design of a 'well-performing' dissolution mechanism. For instance one could consider the situation in which one partner receives a private signal for the value of the asset while the other partner holds only public information (e.g. an active partner and a sleeping partner only sharing profits).

Chapter III investigates the impact of two prominent policy instruments on incentives to innovate. Both instruments serve the purpose of rising investment levels (albeit overinvestment is on hand in all treatments). Consistent with our simple theoretical model we find very different distributional effects of policy instruments on welfare shares of firms and consumers: Although both policy instruments increase investment levels by a similar amount, the implications for firms and consumers differ substantially. These interacting incentives of different interest groups who benefit from and who are hampered by a specific instrument should be subject to further research as they might have a decisive influence on the approval of a chosen instrument and thus on the political interests. However, it remains the problematic question what practical implications can actually be derived from the experiment. As we have simplified our model and for instance neglected positive externalities and intertemporal knowledge spillovers, the relevance and the robustness of our results should be tested in future research, since these factors are expected to have an essential impact on incentives to innovate as well.

The investigation of gift giving in Chapter IV shows strong influence of self-inflicted neediness on the solidarity of group members indicating that procedural utility plays a role besides allocative fairness. The latter result – which has already been shown by Selten and Ockenfels (1998), Ockenfels and Weimann (1999), and Büchner et al. (2007) – is another demonstration in favor of the necessity to incorporate human motivations like social preferences and fairness aspects into theoretic modeling. Chapter IV in addition provides evidence of procedural fairness concerns: If the same decision situation is evoked by different procedures, subjects' behavior changes substantially in the laboratory. Specifically, we observe that conditional gift giving is dependent on whether subjects are thought to be responsible or not. These findings cannot be explained by standard economic theory. A further investigation not only of economic but also of psychological aspects of decision-making (like the interrelation of responsibility and perceived fairness) that shape actual behavior still remains an open and interesting research area.

Another lesson from this experiment in more general terms might be that judgments on social welfare outcomes ought not to be made independently of the procedures by which a society achieves these outcomes. Institutions should not only be evaluated by the outcome they produce (e.g., by efficiency criteria), but moreover by their framing of decision-making procedures as they also generate procedural utilities and disutilities. The procedural utility of an institution has a strong impact on the acceptance of this specific institution which should also be included in policy implications (compare Frey et al. (2004)). The result that procedural fairness increases compliance with rules and authorities has already been documented in social psychology literature (see e.g. Thibaut and Walker (1975) or Lind and Tyler (1988)). Thus, future research should further tackle the question which role these procedural fairness concerns play in actual decision-making and real-existing institutions.

In summary, the results of the four experiments presented in this thesis further demonstrate that behavioral components do have a decisive influence on actual economic decision-making which cannot be explained by standard economic theory. Thus, this thesis shows that a combination of theoretical, experimental and empirical research methods is essential for a systematical prediction of decision-making in order to take the complexity of human behavior into account and to deal with all its aspects.

Bibliography

Aerts, K. and Schmidt, T. (2008): Two for the Price of One? Additionality Effects of R&D Subsidies: A Comparison between Flanders and Germany. *Research Policy*, 37 (5), pp. 806-822.

Albers, W. (2001): Prominence Theory as a Tool to Model Boundedly Rational Decisions. In: Gigerenzer, G. and Selten, R. (Eds.), Bounded Rationality: The Adaptive Toolbox. MIT Press, Cambridge, MA, pp. 297-318.

Anderson, L. R., Rodgers, Y. V. and Rodriguez, R. R. (2000): Cultural Differences in Attitudes toward Bargaining. *Economics Letters*, 69 (1), 45-54.

Arneson, R. J. (1990): Liberalism, Distributive Subjectivism, and Equal Opportunity for Welfare. *Philosophy and Public Affairs,* 19 (2), pp. 158-194.

Barbanel, J. B. (2004): The Geometry of Efficient Fair Division. Cambridge University Press, New York.

Bernstein, J. I. (1996): International R&D Spillovers between Industries in Canada and the United States, Social Rates of Return and Productivity Growth. *Canadian Journal of Economics*, 29 Special Issue Part 2, pp. 463-467.

Bernts, T. (1988): Sanctioning Risky Life-Styles: Attitudes Toward Solidarity or Equitable Distribution of Health Care. *Social Justice Research*, 2 (4), 249-262.

Bessen, J. and Maskin, E. (2006): Sequential Innovation, Patents, and Imitation. NajEcon Working Paper Reviews, 321307000000000021.

Betancourt, H. (1990): An Attribution-Empathy Model of Helping Behavior: Behavioral Intentions and Judgments of Help-Giving. *Personality and Social Psychology Bulletin*, 16 (3), 573-591.

Bolton, G., Brandts, J. and Ockenfels, A. (2005): Fair Procedures: Evidence from Games Involving Lotteries. *The Economic Journal*, 115 (506), pp. 1054-1076.

Bolton, G. and Ockenfels, A. (2000): ERC – A Theory of Equity, Reciprocity and Competition. *American Economic Review*, 90 (1), pp. 166-193.

Bone, J., Hey, J. and Suckling, J. (2004): A Simple Risk-Sharing Experiment. *Journal of Risk and Uncertainty*, 28 (1), pp. 23-38.

Boone, J. (2000): Competitive Pressure: The Effects on Investments in Product and Process Innovation. *RAND Journal of Economics*, 31 (3), pp. 549-569.

Borooah, V. and Iyer, S. (2005): Vidya, Veda, and Varna: The Influence of Religion and Caste on Education in Rural India. *The Journal of Development Studies*, 41 (8), pp. 1369-1404.

Brams, S. and Taylor, A. (1996): Fair Division: From Cake-Cutting to Dispute Resolution. Cambridge University Press, New York.

Brams, S. and Taylor, A. (1999): The Win-Win Solution: Guaranteeing Fair Shares to Everybody. Norton: New York.

Brandts, J., Saijo, T. and Schram, A. (2004): How Universal is Behavior? A Four Country Comparison of Spite and Cooperation in Voluntary Contribution Mechanisms. *Public Choice*, 119 (3-4), 381-424.

Breitmoser, Y., Tan J. H. W. and Zizzo, D. J. (2008): Understanding Perpetual R&D Races. CeDEx Discussion Paper No. 2008-04.

Brooks, R. and Spier, K. E. (2004): Trigger Happy or Gun Shy? Dissolving Common-Value Partnerships with Texas Shootouts. Yale Law and Economics Research Paper No. 298.

Buchan, N. R. and Croson, R. T. A. (2004): The Boundaries of Trust: Own and Others Actions in the U.S. and China. *Journal of Economic Behavior and Organization*, 55 (4), 485-504.

Buckley, N., Mestelman, S. and Shehata, M. (2003): Subsidizing Public Inputs. *Journal of Public Economics*, 87 (3-4), pp. 819-846.

Büchner, S., Coricelli, G. and Greiner, B. (2007): Self Centered and Other Regarding Behavior in the Solidarity Game. *Journal of Economic Behavior and Organization*, 62 (2), pp. 293-303.

Burlando, R. and Hey, J. D. (1997): Do Anglo-Saxons Free-Ride More? *Journal of Public Economics*, 64 (1), 41-60.

Cadsby, B., Hamaguchi, Y., Kawagoe, T., Maynes, E. and Song, F. (2007): Cross-National Gender Differences in Behavior in a Threshold Public Goods Game: Japan versus Canada. *Journal of Economic Psychology*, 28 (2), 242-260.

Camerer, C. F. (2003): Behavioral Game Theory: Experiments in Strategic Interaction, Princeton University Press, Princeton, New Jersey.

Cameron, L. (1999): Raising the Stakes in the Ultimatum Game: Experimental Evidence from Indonesia. *Economic Inquiry*, 37 (1), pp. 47-59.

Cantner, U., Güth, W., Nicklisch, A. and Weiland, T. (2007): Competition in Product Design: An Experiment Exploring Innovation Behavior, Jena Economic Research Papers 2007-014.

Cappelen, A., Sørensen, E. and Tungodden, B. (2005): Responsibility for What? An Experimental Approach to Fairness and Responsibility. Discussion Papers of the Norwegian School of Economics and Business Administration.

Carpenter, J. P., Daniere, A. G. and Takahashi, L. M. (2004): Cooperation, Trust, and Social Capital in Southeast Asian Urban Slums. *Journal of Economic Behavior and Organization*, 55 (4), 533-551.

Cason, T. N., Saijo, T. and Yamato, T. (2002): Voluntary Participation and Spite in Public Good Provision Experiments: An International Comparison. *Experimental Economics*, 5 (2), 133-153.

Chang, H. F. (1995): Patent Scope, Antitrust Policy, and Cumulative Innovation. *RAND Journal of Economics*, 26 (1), pp. 34-57.

Charness, G. and Genicot, G. forthcoming: An Experimental Test of Risk-Sharing Arrangements. *The Economic Journal*.

Chien, H.-K. (2007): Incentive Efficient Mechanisms for Partnership Dissolution, Mimeo.

Chuah, S.-H., Hoffmann, R., Jones, M. and Williams, G. (2007): Do Cultures Clash? Evidence from Cross-National Ultimatum Game Experiments. *Journal of Economic Behavior and Organization*, 64 (1), 35-48.

Cohen, G. A. (1989): On the Currency of Egalitarian Justice. *Ethics*, 99, pp. 906-944.

Cohen, W. M. (1995): Empirical Studies of Innovative Acitivity. In: Stoneman, P. (Ed.), Handbook of the Economics of Innovation and Technological Change, Basil Blackwell, Oxford, pp. 182-264.

Cohen, W. M. and Levin, R. C. (1989): Empirical Studies of Innovation and Market Structure. In: Schmalensee, R. and Willig, R. (Eds.), Handbook of Industrial Organization, Amsterdam, North Holland, pp. 1059-1107.

Cooper, L. C. and Selto, F. H. (1991): An Experimental Examination of the Effects of SFAS No.2 on R&D Investment Decisions. *Accounting Organizations and Society*, 16 (3), pp. 227-242.

Cramton, P., Gibbons, R. and Klemperer, P. (1987): Dissolving a Partnership Efficiently. *Econometrica*, 55 (3), pp. 615-632.

Croson, R. T. A. and Buchan, N. R. (1999): Gender and Culture: International Experimental Evidence from Trust Games. *American Economic Review, Papers and Proceedings*, 89 (2), 386-391.

Darai, D., Großer, J. and Trhal, N. (2009): Patents vs. Subsidies: A Laboratory Experiment. Working Paper.

Dasgupta, P. S. and Stiglitz, J. E. (1980): Uncertainty, Industrial Structure, and the Speed of R&D. *Bell Journal of Economics*, 11 (1), pp. 1-28.

D'Aspremont, C. and Jacquemin, A. (1988): Cooperative and Noncooperative R&D in Duopoly with Spillovers. *American Economic Review*, 78 (5), pp. 1133-1137.

Davis, J. S., Quirmbach, H. C. and Swenson, C. W. (1995): Income Tax Subsidies and Research and Development Spending in a Competitive Economy: An Experimental Study. *Journal of the American Taxation Association*, 17 Supplement, pp. 1-25.

de Frutos, M. A. and Kittsteiner, T. (2008): Efficient Partnership Dissolution under Buy-Sell Clauses. *RAND Journal of Economics*, 39 (1), pp. 184-198.

Doraszelski, U. (2008): Rent Dissipation in R&D Races. In: Cellini, R. and Lambertini, L. (Eds.), The Economics of Innovation: Incentives, Cooperation, and R&D Policy, Emerald, Bingley, pp. 3-13.

Dufwenberg, M. and Gneezy, U. (2000): Price Competition and Market Concentration: An Experimental Study. *International Journal of Industrial Organization*, 18 (1), pp. 7-22.

Dufwenberg, M. and Kirchsteiger, G. (2004): A Theory of Sequential Reciprocity. *Games and Economic Behavior*, 47 (2), pp. 268-298.

Dyer, D., Kagel, J. and Levin, D. (1989): A Comparison of Naïve and Experienced Bidders in Common Value Offer Auctions: a Laboratory Analysis. *The Economic Journal*, 99 (394), pp. 108-115.

Falk, A. and Fischbacher, U. (2006): A Theory of Reciprocity. *Games and Economic Behavior*, 54 (2), pp. 293-315.

Federal Ministry of Education and Research (2008): Research and Innovation in Germany 2008, forthcoming (German Version "Bundesbericht Forschung und Innovationen 2008").

Fehr, E. and Schmidt, K. (1999): A Theory of Fairness, Competition and Cooperation. *Quarterly Journal of Economics*, 114 (3), pp. 817-868.

Ferraro, P. J. and Cummings, R. G. (2007): Cultural Diversity, Discrimination, and Economic Outcomes: An Experimental Analysis. *Economic Inquiry*, 45 (2), 217-232.

Fieseler, K., Kittsteiner, T. and Moldovanu, B. (2003): Partnerships, Lemons and Efficient Trade. *Journal of Economic Theory*, 113 (2), pp. 223-234.

Fischbacher, U. (2007): z-Tree: Zurich Toolbox for Ready-Made Economic Experiments. *Experimental Economics*, 10 (2), pp. 171-178.

Fleurbaey, M. and Maniquet, F. (2003): Compensation and Responsibility. In: Arrow, K. J., Sen, A. and Suzumura, K. (Eds.), Handbook of Social Choice and Welfare, 2, Amsterdam.

Frey, B., Benz, M. and Stutzer, A. (2004): Introducing Procedural Utility: Not Only What, but Also How Matters. *Journal of Institutional and Theoretical Economics*, 160 (3), pp. 377-401.

Frey, B. and Stutzer, A. (2005): Beyond Outcomes: Measuring Procedural Utility. *Oxford Economic Papers*, 57 (1), pp. 90-111.

Fullerton, R., Linster, B. G., McKee, M. and Slate, S. (1999): An Empirical Investigation of Research Tournaments. *Economic Inquiry*, 37 (4), pp. 624-636.

Fullerton, R., Linster, B. G., McKee, M. and Slate, S. (2002): Using Auctions to Reward Tournament Winners: Theory and Experimental Investigations. *RAND Journal of Economics*, 33 (1), pp. 66-84.

Gallini, N. T. (1992): Patent Policy and Costly Imitation. *RAND Journal of Economics*, 23 (1), pp. 52-63.

German Patent and Trademark Office (2008): Annual Report 2007.

Giebe, T., Grebe, T. and Wolfstetter, E. (2006): How to Allocate R&D (and Other) Subsidies: An Experimentally Tested Policy Recommendation. *Research Policy*, 35 (9), pp. 1261-1272.

Gilbert, R. and Shapiro, C. (1990): Optimal Patent Length and Breadth. *RAND Journal of Economics*, 21 (1), pp. 106-112.

Goeree, J. and Offerman, T. (2002): Efficiency in Auctions with Private and Common Values: An Experimental Study. *American Economic Review*, 92 (3), pp. 625-643.

Goeree, J. and Offerman, T. (2003): Competitive Bidding in Auctions with Private and Common Values. *The Economic Journal*, 113 (489), pp. 598-613.

Görg, H. and Strobel, E. (2007): The Effect of R&D Subsidies on Private R&D. *Economica*, 74 (294), pp. 215-234.

Greiner, B. (2004): An Online Recruitment System for Economic Experiments. In: Kremer, K. and Macho, V. (Eds), Forschung und wissenschaftliches Rechnen 2003, GWDG Bericht 63, Göttingen: Gesellschaft für Wissenschaftliche Datenverarbeitung, pp. 79-93.

Griliches, Z. (1990): Patent Statistics as Economic Indicators: A Survey. *Journal of Economic Literature*, 28 (4), pp. 1661-1707.

Griliches, Z. (1992): The Search for R&D Spillovers. *Scandinavian Journal of Economics*, 94 Supplement, pp. 29-47.

Güth, W., Ivanova-Stenzel, R., Königstein, M. and Strobel, M. (2002): Bid Functions in Acutions and Fair Division Games: Experimental Evidence. *German Economic Review*, 3 (4), pp. 461-484.

Güth, W., Ivanova-Stenzel, R., Königstein, M. and Strobel, M. (2003): Learning to Bid – An Experimental Study of Bid Function Adjustments in Auctions and Fair Division Games. *The Economic Journal*, 113 (487), pp. 477-494.

Guiso, L., Sapienza, P. and Zingales, L. (2006): Does Culture Affect Economic Outcomes? *Journal of Economic Perspectives*, 20 (2), 23-48.

Harris, C. and Vickers, J. (1987): Racing with Uncertainty. *Review of Economic Studies*, 54 (1), pp. 1-21.

Hauswald, R. and Hege, U. (2003): Ownership and Control in Joint Ventures: Theory and Evidence. CEPR Discussion Paper No. 4056.

Henrich, J. (2000): Does Culture Matter in Economic Behavior? Ultimatum Game Bargaining Among the Machiguenga of the Peruvian Amazon. *American Economic Review*, 90 (4), pp. 973-979.

Henrich, J., Boyd, R., Bowles, S., Camerer, C., Fehr, E., Gintis, H. and McElreath, R. (2001): In Search of Homo Economicus: Behavioral Experiments in 15 Small-Scale Societies. *American Economic Review*, 91 (2), pp. 73-78.

Hinloopen, J. (2000): Subsidizing Cooperative and Noncooperative R&D: An Equivalence Result. *Economics of Innovation and Technology*, 9 (4), pp. 317-329.

Hinloopen, J. (2001): Subsidizing R&D Cooperatives. *De Economist*, 149 (3), pp. 313-345.

Isaac, R. M. and Reynolds, S. S. (1986): Innovation and Property Rights in Information: An Experimental Approach to Testing Hypotheses about Private R&D Behavior. In: Libecap, G. (Ed.), Advances in the Study of

Entrepreneurship, Innovation, and Economic Growth, JAI Press, Greenwich, pp. 129-156.

Isaac, R. M. and Reynolds, S. S. (1988): Appropriability and Market Structure in a Stochastic Invention Model. *Quarterly Journal of Economics*, 103 (4), pp. 647-671.

Isaac, R. M. and Reynolds, S. S. (1992): Schumpeterian Competition in Experimental Markets. *Journal of Economic Behavior and Organization*, 17 (1), pp. 59-100.

Jehiel, P. and Moldovanu, B. (2001): Efficient Design with Interdependent Valuations. *Econometrica*, 69 (5), pp. 1237-1259.

Jehiel, P. and Pauzner, A. (2006): Partnership Dissolution with Interdependent Values. *RAND Journal of Economics*, 37 (1), pp. 1-22.

Jones, C. I. and Williams, J. C. (1998): Measuring the Social Rate of Return to R&D. *Quarterly Journal of Economics*, 113 (4), pp. 1119-1135.

Jones, C. I. and Williams, J. C. (2000): Too Much of a Good Thing? The Economics of Investment in R&D. *Journal of Economic Growth*, 5 (1), pp. 65-85.

Jullien, C. and Ruffieux, B. (2001): Innovation, Avantages Concurrentiels et Concurrence. *Revue d'Economie Politique*, 111 (1), pp. 121-149.

Kachelmeier, S. J. and Shehata, M. (1992): Culture and Competition – A Laboratory Market Comparison between China and the West. *Journal of Economic Behavior and Organization*, 19 (2), 145-168.

Kähkönen, A. (2005): Patent Race Experiment Revisited: Are Differences between Experiments just Random Variation? Working Paper, Keskustelualoitteita No 25, University of Joensuu, Finland.

Kagel, J. H. and Levin, D. (1986): The Winner's Curse and Public Information in Common Value Auctions. *American Economic Review*, 76 (5), pp. 894-920.

Kagel, J. H. and Levin, D. (1999): Common Value Auctions with Insider Information, *Econometrica*, 67 (5), 1219-1238.

Kagel, J. H. and Levin, D. (2001): Bidding in Common Value Auctions: A Survey of Experimental Research. In: Kagel, J. H. and Lewin, D.: Common Value Auctions and the Winner's Curse, Princeton University Press.

Kagel, J. H., Levin, D., Battalio, R. and Meyer, D. (1989): First-Price Common Value Auctions: Bidder Behavior and the "Winner's Curse". *Economic Inquiry*, 27 (2), pp. 241-258.

Kagel, J. H. and Richard, J.-F. (2001): Super-Experienced Bidders in First-Price Common-Value Auctions: Rules of Thumb, Nash Equilibrium Bidding, and the Winner's Curse. *The Review of Economics and Statistics*, 83 (3), pp. 408-419.

Kamien, M. I., Muller, E. and Zang, I. (1992): Research Joint Ventures and R&D Cartels. *American Economic Review*, 82 (5), pp. 1293-1306.

Kamien, M. I. and Schwartz, N. L. (1975): Market Structure and Innovation: A Survey. *Journal of Economic Literature*, 13 (1), pp. 1-37.

Keser, C. and Vogt, B. (2000): Why Do Experimental Subjects Choose an Equilibrium which is neither Payoff nor Risk Dominant? CIRANO Working Paper 2000, pp. 1-34.

Kirchkamp, O. and Moldovanu, B. (2004): An Experimental Analysis of Auctions with Interdependent Valuations. *Games and Economic Behavior*, 48 (1), pp. 54-85.

Kittsteiner, T. (2003): Partnerships and Double Auctions with Interdependent Valuations. *Games and Economic Behavior*, 44 (1), pp. 54-76.

Kittsteiner, T. and Ockenfels, A. (2006): Market Design: A Selective Review. *Zeitschrift für Betriebswirtschaft*, Special Issue 5/2006, pp. 121-143.

Kittsteiner, T., Ockenfels, A. and Trhal, N. (2009): An Experimental Investigation of Partnership Dissolution Mechanisms. Working Paper.

Klemperer, P. (1990): How Broad Should the Scope of Patent Protection Be? *RAND Journal of Economics*, 21 (1), pp. 113-130.

Krishna, V. (2002): Auction Theory. Academic Press, San Diego.

Laffont, J.-J. (1997): Game Theory and Empirical Economics: The Case of Auction Data. *European Economic Review*, 41 (1), pp. 1-35.

Lind, E. A. and Tyler, T. R. (1988): The Social Psychology of Procedural Justice. Series Critical Issues in Social Justice. New York: Plenum Press.

Loury, G. C. (1979): Market Structure and Innovation. *Quarterly Journal of Economics*, 93 (3), pp. 395-410.

Mann, L., Radford, M., Burnett, P., Ford, S., Bond, M., Leung, K., Nakamura, H., Vaughan, G. and Yang, K.-S. (1998): Cross-Cultural Differences in Self-Reported Decision-Making Style and Confidence. *International Journal of Psychology*, 33(5), pp. 325-335.

McAfee, R. P. (1992): Amicable Divorce: Dissolving a Partnership with Simple Mechanisms. *Journal of Economic Theory*, 56 (2), pp. 266-293.

Meyer, J. and Mulherin, A. (1980): From Attribution to Helping: An Analysis of the Mediating Effects of Affect and Expectancy. *Journal of Personality and Social Psychology*, 39 (2), 201-210.

Moldovanu, B. (2002): How to Dissolve a Partnership. *Journal of Institutional and Theoretical Economics*, 158 (1), pp. 66-80.

Moldovanu, B. and Sela, A. (2006): Contest Architecture. *Journal of Economic Theory*, 126 (1), pp. 70-96.

Morgan, J. (2001): Efficiency in Auctions: Theory and Practice. *Journal of International Money and Finance*, 20 (6), pp. 809-838.

Morgan, J. (2004): Dissolving a Partnership (Un)fairly. *Economic Theory*, 23 (4), pp. 909-923.

Morasch, K. (1995): Moral Hazard and Optimal Contract Form for R&D Cooperation. *Journal of Economic Behavior and Organization*, 28 (1), pp. 63-78.

Motta, M. (2004): Competition Policy: Theory and Practice, Cambridge University Press, Cambridge.

Myerson, R. and Satterthwaite, M. (1983): Efficient Mechanisms for Bilateral Trading. *Journal of Economic Theory*, 29 (2), pp. 265-281.

Nadiri, M. I. (1993): Innovations and Technological Spillovers. NBER Working Paper Series, No. 4423.

National Science Foundation, Division of Science Resources Statistics (2008): InfoBrief - New Estimates of National Research and Development Expenditures Show 5.8% Growth in 2007. NSF 08-317, Arlington, VA.

Neugebauer, T. and Selten, R. (2006): Individual Behavior of First-Price Auctions: The Importance of Information Feedback in Computerized Experimental Markets. *Games and Economic Behavior*, 54 (1), pp. 183-204.

Nordhaus, W. D. (1969): Invention, Growth and Welfare, MIT Press, Cambridge, MA.

Ockenfels, A. and Selten, R. (2005): Impulse Balance Equilibrium and Feedback in First Price Auctions. *Games and Economic Behavior*, 51 (2), pp. 155-170.

Ockenfels, A. and Weimann, J. (1999): Types and Patterns: an Experimental East-West-German Comparison of Cooperation and Solidarity. *Journal of Public Economics*, 71 (2), pp. 275-287.

OECD (2004): Science, Technology and Innovation for the 21st Century. Meeting of the OECD Committee for Scientific and Technological Policy at Ministerial Level, 29-30 January 2004 - Final Communique, http://www.oecd.org/document/0,2340,en_2649_34487_25998799_1_1_1_1,00.html (January, 7th 2009).

Rabin, M. (1993): Incorporating Fairness into Game Theory and Economics. *American Economic Review*, 83 (5), pp. 1281-1302.

Radermacher, R. and Trhal, N. (work in progress): A Cross-Cultural Study of Procedural Fairness in Germany and India.

Reinganum, J. F. (1983): Uncertain Innovation and the Persistence of Monopoly. *American Economic Review*, 73 (4), pp. 741-748.

Roth, A., Prasnikar, V., Okuno-Fujiwara, M. and Zamir, S. (1991): Bargaining and Market Behavior in Jerusalem, Ljubljana, Pittsburgh and Tokyo: An Experimental Study. *American Economic Review*, 81(5), pp. 1068-1095.

Sacco, D. and Schmutzler, A. (2008): Competition and Innovation: An Experimental Investigation, Socioeconomic Institute, University of Zurich, Working Paper No. 0807.

Sahlman, W. A. (1990), Parenting Magazine. Harvard Business School Case 291-015.

Sakakibara, M. and Branstetter, L. (2001): Do Stronger Patents Induce More Innovation? Evidence from the 1988 Japanese Patent Law Reforms. *RAND Journal of Economics*, 32 (1), pp. 77-100.

Schmutzler, A. (2007): The Relation between Competition and Innovation – Why Is It Such a Mess?, Socioeconomic Institute, University of Zurich, Working Paper No. 0716.

Schokkaert, E. and Devooght, K. (2003): Responsibility-Sensitive Fair Compensation in Different Cultures. *Social Choice and Welfare*, 21 (2), pp. 207-242.

Schopler, J. and Matthews, M. W. (1965): The Influence of the Perceived Causal Locus of Partner's Dependence on the Use of Interpersonal Power. *Journal of Personality and Social Psychology*, 2, 609-612.

Scotchmer, S. (1991): Standing on the Shoulders of Giants: Cumulative Research and the Patent Law. *Journal of Economic Perspectives*, 5 (1), pp. 29-41.

Scotchmer, S. (2005): Innovation and Incentives. MIT Press, Cambridge, MA.

Selten, R. and Ockenfels, A. (1998): An Experimental Solidarity Game. *Journal of Economic Behavior and Organization*, 34 (4), pp. 517-539.

Sen, A. (1995): Rationality and Social Choice. *American Economic Review*, 85 (1), pp. 1-24.

Spencer, B. J. and Brander J. A. (1983): International R&D Rivalry and Industrial Strategy. *Review of Economic Studies*, 50 (4), pp. 707-722.

Steger, T. M. (2005): Welfare Implications of Non-Scale R&D-Based Growth Model. *Scandinavian Journal of Economics*, 107 (4), pp. 737-757.

Suetens, S. (2005): Cooperative and Noncooperative R&D in Experimental Duopoly Markets. *International Journal of Industrial Organization*, 23 (1-2), pp. 63-82.

Suetens, S. (2008): Does R&D Cooperation Facilitate Price Collusion? An Experiment. *Journal of Economic Behavior and Organization*, 66 (3-4), pp. 822-836.

Suzumura, K. (1992): Cooperative and Noncooperative R&D in an Oligopoly with Spillovers. *American Economic Review*, 82 (5), pp. 1307-1320.

Tajfel, H., Billig, M.G., Bundy, R.P. and Flament, C. (1970): Social Categorization and Intergroup Behavior. *European Journal of Social Psychology*, 1, pp. 149-178.

Thibaut, J. and Walker, L. (1975): Procedural Justice: A Psychological Analysis. Hillsdale, NJ: Erlbaum.

Trhal, N. (2009): Partnership Dissolution Mechanisms with Interdependent Valuations – An Experimental Investigation. Working Paper.

Trhal, N. and Radermacher, R. (2008): Bad Luck vs. Self-Inflicted Neediness – An Experimental Investigation of Gift Giving in a Solidarity Game. Cologne Working Paper Series, No. 28.

United States Patent and Trademark Office (2008): Performance and Accountability Report, Fiscal Year 2008.

Veugelers, R. and Kastelroot, K. (1996): Bargained Shares in Joint Ventures among Asymmetric Partners: Is the Matthew Effect Catalyzing? *Journal of Economics*, 64 (1), pp. 23-51.

Vives, X. (2006): Innovation and Competitive Pressure. IESE Research Papers D/634, IESE Business School.

Weiner, B. (1980): A Cognitive (Attribution) – Emotion – Action Model of Motivated Behavior: An Analysis of Judgments of Help-Giving. *Journal of Personality and Social Psychology*, 39 (2), 186-200.

Weiner, B. (1993): On Sin versus Sickness – A Theory of Perceived Responsibility and Social Motivation. *American Psychologist*, 48 (9), 957-965.

Wolfstetter, E. (2002): How to Dissolve a Partnership – Comment. *Journal of Institutional and Theoretical Economics*, 158 (1), pp. 86-90.

Worldbank (2007): World Development Indicators 2007.

Yaari, M.E. and Bar-Hillel, M. (1984): On Dividing Justly. *Social Choice and Welfare*, 1, pp. 1-24.

Young, H.P. (1994): Equity in Theory and Practice. Princeton University Press, Princeton.

Zizzo, D. J. (2002): Racing with Uncertainty: A Patent Race Experiment. *International Journal of Industrial Organization*, 20 (6), pp. 877-902.

The manufacturer's authorised representative in the EU is Springer Nature Customer Service Centre GmbH, Europaplatz 3, 69115 Heidelberg, Germany. If you have any concerns regarding our products, please contact ProductSafety@springernature.com

Printed and bound by CPI Group (UK) Ltd, Croydon, CR0 4YY

25/03/2026

02078186-0015